MW01253938

THE TRAVELS OF A JOURNEY-MAN TEACHER

Henry Pluckrose is one of those fortunate people who have managed to marry their profession with their hobbies – the profession, teaching, the hobbies writing and travel. His first book was published in 1960 since when he has written in excess of 250 titles, the majority of which were directed at children under 11. Some were activity books linked to art and craft, others featured the built environment or explored ideas in mathematics, science, history and geography.

These were supported by books for teachers and parents which explained the methodology employed in nursery, infant and junior schools. Many of these titles were bought by foreign publishers which resulted in him being invited to give lectures in places as distant as Calgary and Hong Kong.

Schools and some form of schooling are to be found in almost every country in the world. Governments build schools, train and employ teachers in the hope that tomorrow's workforce will be able to cope with demands as yet unknown. Because these institutions we call schools are universal, they have much in common. There are eccentric headteachers in Singapore, indifferent administrators in New York brilliant Maths teachers in Sofia, politicians in Montreal or Paris who pretend an interest in education in order to advance their careers – just as there are in the United Kingdom.

In "The Travels of a Journey-Man Teacher" the author tells of schools and the cultural, historical and political strands which shape them. But schools are only part of his story. Unlikely moments are recorded too… of being detained at Gothenburg Airport by two unsmiling Swedish policemen, of confronting leaping rabbits and a hamster who was a surrogate husband, of the moving blessing given by a richly-robed Russian Orthodox priest to a group of Bulgarian children in their parish church.

This is a travel book with a difference which will appeal to teachers, parents and all who like seeing the world from an unusual angle.

Two views of the child-centred approach to the education of primary children advocated by Henry Pluckrose, sometime headteacher of Prior Weston School, London.

Dr Christina Banfi, Teacher-trainer and Lecturer at the University of Buenos Aires comments on her experience as a pupil at the school

"Joining the school when I spoke so little English, had a profound impact on me. Firstly there were great differences between my school back home and this new school in the methods employed for learning and teaching. Also, there was the lasting influence I derived from experience. Apart from the wealth of resources, the atmosphere was different. We didn't sit at desks in rows. We had tables and chairs which were arranged according to what we were doing. There were different areas in each classroom, each one featuring displays of our Maths, Language, Science and Art work. We were immersed in books. My overall impression was one of personal fulfilment."

Dr Georges Kalushev, Professor at the Department of National & World Economics, University of Sofia, Bulgaria.

Henry Pluckrose first appeared in front of a group of Bulgarian educators in 1981 when the educational system had stagnated. This was a time when independent thinking in teachers and pupils was unwelcome and often punished. His audience, isolated from the world and starved of models of educational excellence, were surprised by his simple yet powerful ideas which advocated child-centred education. Having been introduced to his methods by visiting the innovative Prior Weston School in London, I regarded it as an obligation to myself to accompany Henry on each of his six visits through 1995. Although the country had formally turned its back on the communist regime, many minds continued in their old ways and Henry's words of wisdom were as necessary as ever.

In addition to the ideas which people from all levels in the education service took from Henry's lectures and demonstrations, he made a real difference to the lives of teachers, children, their parents and the community of one particular school (No 98) on the outskirts of Sofia. With the help of his colleague and companion Hilary Devonshire, herself a gifted and devoted teacher, they transformed the gloomy atmosphere of the school and provided precious moments of revelation, introducing children and staff to materials they had not used before: coloured papers, paints crayons and other aids. This was learning which I am sure none of them will ever forget.

By regarding schooling simply as preparation for life we ignore the fact that children are alive now. It is in the present that children live. It is in the present that their potential should be recognised and allowed to flower...

Henry used to walk his talk wherever he went.

THE TRAVELS OF A JOURNEY-MAN TEACHER

About the author

After completing National Service Henry Pluckrose trained as a primary school teacher. He worked in Inner London from 1954 – 1986, his final 18 years as head of Prior Weston School, an open plan building, which served the City of London's Barbican Estate and estates run by the London Borough of Islington and the Peabody Trust. The curriculum of the school centred around the arts – spoken word, poetry, pottery, music dance drama and picture making in a wide range of media.

From 1969 onwards he served on a number of educational committees – the National Trust, The Civic Trust, The Royal Opera House, The Book league. He also was a member of the advisory panel for BBC Radio London and was a committee member of The Publishers Association Enquiry which reported on 'Books in School'.

He was awarded an Hon. FCP for services to education and a worked M.Phil. by London University in 1987. Between 1977-1981 he was a council member of the Council for Academic Awards (which accredited all Polytechnic courses in England and Wales).

His first book was published in 1960 since when he was written (and edited) over 300 titles, of which 30 were prepared especially for teachers. His work has been published in France, Italy, Spain, Germany, Sweden, Norway, Canada and the United States.

Henry Pluckrose

THE TRAVELS OF A JOURNEY-MAN TEACHER

Olympia Publishers
London

www.olympiapublishers.com

OLYMPIA PAPERBACK EDITION

A CIP catalogue record for this title is available from the British Library

ISBN: 978-1-905513-31-4

First Published in 2007

Olympia Publishers
60 Cannon Street
London
EC4N 6NQ

Printed in Great Britain

Author's Notes

This manuscript has been prepared for my three children – Patrick, Elspeth and Hilary – and my two grandchildren – Rosaline and Poppy.

I would like to record my thanks to all the people who provided the material for the events I describe. Some of the people I include might be embarrassed to find themselves the main subject of an amusing story. To conceal their identity I have provided each with an invented name.

My particular thanks go to – Jan Källberg for designing a programme of seminars in Sweden and his help in advising me on the Swedish chapter – George Kalushev for his help on my writing about Bulgaria – Hilary Devonshire for reading my m/s during its initial draft and, in the process, improving my prose and finally to Anne Clark for her perceptive interpretation of my handwriting and the hours before a computer screen which this entailed.

HP
London 2007

Contents

Personal View, Roger Tingle 19
Prologue 21

1. Scandinavia 25
2. New York 1966 62
3. New York 1976 The Urban Challenge 78
4. A Divided Europe 1972 Berlin 89
5. Beyond the Wall 1979 Serbia 98
6. Canada 1973–74 115
7. Paris, France 1989 126
8. Bulgaria 1981–1992 136
9. The Far East 173
10. Around the Mediterranean 193

Epilogue 219

Personal View

Roger Tingle, sometime Director of the Urban Studies Centre, East London, taught with Henry Pluckrose at Evelyn Lowe School, Bermondsey, London and at Prior Weston School, Barbican, London. He writes this appreciation of the child-centred model of Education described in the pages which follow.

The John Ruskin School still stands today, as do many London Board schools which were built towards the end of the nineteenth century. It is a permanent reminder of those early socialists who, like the first Labour MP Thomas Burt, believed that: 'we educate a man not simply because he has got political power or simply to make him a good workman; we educate him because he is a man.' It is a dignified, red brick building close to the Walworth Road and within reasonable walking distance of Kennington Oval or the Elephant and Castle. Charlie Chaplin was born nearby, somewhere down East Lane market. Nobody is sure exactly where.

In the spring term of 1965, Henry was teaching on the very top floor of the John Ruskin School and I joined him there as a student, a humble Apprentice to a Master Sorcerer. His classroom was quite unlike any I had ever visited before and his teaching methods unlike anything I had previously experienced. The teaching space itself resembled an artist's studio and was buzzing with a level of activity that only 42 lively ten and eleven year olds can generate. Whilst practical art and craft work was most clearly in evidence, it was the Arts in the broadest sense that formed the basis of the curriculum: drama, music, poetry and dance. Particular importance was given to direct, personal experience. In practice this meant that much of the children's learning took place in a variety of settings outside the school: in museums, art galleries, churches and other historic buildings as well as the natural environment.

The impact of this approach was soon felt well beyond the Walworth Road. In 1968, Henry was appointed to headship in central London and his school became a Mecca for anyone committed to a more open educational model from which others could learn, but Henry himself was a remarkable communicator who, as 'The Travels of a Journey-Man Teacher' attests, was able to share his ideas with parents, teachers and politicians across the world from Sweden to Sophia and from New York to Hong Kong. For a brief moment in time, probably from about the mid-sixties to the late seventies, it seemed that the vision generated by Henry and by other creative teachers and administrators would change the focus of educational policy for good. It was not to be. Margaret Thatcher and a succession of weak or inept ministers in the Department of Education and Science turned their backs on human progress. Pavlov replaced Piaget, the local education authorities were emasculated and a unique opportunity to enrich the lives of millions of children was lost.

The only argument I have is with the title of this book. Having had the rare privilege of working alongside Henry for so many years, I believe that this teacher will be remembered not as a journey-man but as a genius.

Roger Tingle
Sautern, France, January 2007

Prologue

Like Geoffrey Chaucer, I believe that every storybook deserves a Prologue. And like 'The Canterbury Tales' this is a collection of anecdotes related to journeys.

Chaucer created a variety of personalities and voices to tell his stories. My narrative is singular, a personal account of the people and places that have intrigued me on the many journeys I have made.

The roots of my travels began with my gaining a teaching qualification at St. Mark and St. John College, Chelsea. On leaving college, in July 1954, I was offered a permanent post with the London County Council (LCC) which eventually became The Inner London Education Authority (ILEA)

When in September 1954, aged 23, I stood for the first time in front of "my class" in a drab, brown-brick, four-decker school I'm sure I did not give much thought to my professional future – of 40 years working in primary schools or dream of retirement in distant 1995 and the pension that beckoned beyond. Nor did I dream that I might write a book or present papers in colleges in Oxford, Cambridge or Durham. The proposition that sometime in my professional future I would find myself sitting in the private office of a Minister for Education in a foreign capital city discussing the Diary of Samuel Pepys, was too ludicrous to imagine.

Yet all of these improbable things came to pass.

My early years as a teacher were uneventful. Like many a young person I somehow managed to live on a comparatively small salary (£43 per month in 1954–55). Then, in 1961, without realising the opportunities he would indirectly bring me, I met Frank Waters. (We were introduced during a coffee break at a lecture I was attending at the Institute of Education in London).

Frank, a benign fifty-something was interested in three things – books, Roman Catholicism and choral music. He was editor in chief at Oldbourne Press, a long-dead publishing house belonging to the Express group of newspapers. Having learned of my interest in children's creative work and there being a 'hole in my list', he surprised me by suggesting that I write a book to fill it. My simple book on picture making appeared in Oldbourne's 1962 spring list, a list heavy with the archaic, academic outpourings of celebrated and respected professors of education. My first book was the first of many

(300+). Much of my subsequent output was for children, some 30 for adults. I have found myself published in German, French, Italian, Bulgarian, Swedish and even Welsh.

My writings resulted in invitations to lecture. As many of my initial publications were about the importance of practical creative activities for young children (i.e. the children as participators and experimenters rather than as passive receivers), I was invited to lead practical workshops for teachers. During this period (1962–66) I continued to work as a full-time classroom teacher, passing through the post of Deputy-Head (1966–68) to Headship (1968–86).

It was immediately before becoming Deputy-Head of the 'experimental' Eveline Lowe School in Bermondsey in May 1966 that my writing caused me to be invited to the United States. In the years which followed (1968–98) I spent many days working in Sweden and a number of two week secondments to places as far apart as Calgary, Singapore, Rome and Belgrade. I was invited to state schools, privately funded schools, schools run by religious and secular foundations, schools provided by the Service Children's Schools Education Authority (SCSEA) for the children of our military families living overseas and for children attending school supported by the Canadian Diplomatic Service.

No two schools were the same. Some, recently built, were barren, barn-like wildernesses; some in slum-like buildings on decaying estates were rich in displays of children's work; some were run like factories, all targets and gold stars; others saw individual growth as the centre piece of their activities. Some schools were squeezed onto the top floor of a tower block in an area of intense urbanisation and ran part-time; some enjoyed green fields and acres of woodland. Each school was unique. Trapped in time, teachers and children performed their daily rituals, each set of rituals and the expectations flowing from them as unique and individual as the teachers and children who composed this tiny 'body pedagogic.'

In the process of visiting I met eccentric headteachers, dreamy assistants, overweening secretaries, teachers with a cause to proclaim, teachers for whom one Friday was identical to the last (and not dissimilar to Monday) and teachers whose final year would be a replica of their very first. There were teachers with charisma (leaders and innovators) and teachers whose dull conformity encouraged yawns from all who met them.

To all of these schools and teachers I offered such experience as I had gleaned from watching children. My comments sharpened by

22

hours of shaping words on paper. I supported these workshops, talks and seminars with displays of children's paintings, writings and notebooks and with photo transparencies, video, film and tape. Wherever I went I found I learned new things. These new ideas proved welcome additions to my own personal miscellany of approaches to learning and teaching.

Through the years I am describing I was little more than a wandering journey-man, a peddler of things academic, a medieval tinker in a time warp, offering educational recipes in place of pots, pans and ribbons. In the medieval world a journeyman rarely became a master. And so it was with me. I never felt I had the right to tell a fellow professional "Do it my way, I know!" All effective learning requires time for the learner to make new ideas his/her own. There must always be time for reflection and the thought "What if…"

Hence the title for these short dips into my past, 'The Travels of a Journey-man Teacher'. Some of the episodes I have described read more like fiction than fact – how could a Swedish policeman end up carrying a false leg on a blanket? Other episodes touch upon the great issues of our time – should schools be manipulated by the State?

Hard to believe it may be, but all the stories are true. There really was a monkey who lived with a lady in a hotel room in Gothenburg. There really was a bouncing Norwegian.

And finally a note of explanation. I have used first names when a person, though central to my narrative, does not need individual identification. When organisations or people are key to an event, I have recorded their name in full.

1. Scandinavia 1976–1998
Sweden, Denmark, Norway, Finland

Writing a book for publication is a strange and solitary process. Before putting pen to paper (or finger on keyboard) the aspiring author must be convinced that his/her thoughts are worth sharing... and that there are sufficient potential readers who wish to do so. The problem facing an author is very similar to that facing an actor. What is the point of words written or spoken if there is no audience to appreciate them?

In 1968 I was appointed headteacher of a new primary school, Prior Weston, situated on the edge of the Corporation of London's Barbican development. With a team of gifted teachers and supported by parents, we managed to create a school which was more community orientated than most of the schools in the area. So many visitors came to study our approach that after 5 years I felt a book would help clarify my thoughts as well as record something of the achievements of the teaching and support staff. I shared my thoughts with Audrey White, an editor I knew well. Audrey had approved the publication of several of my books. But a book on 'Open Education'? Did the title mean anything? Would such a book attract readers? (i.e. buyers). After some discussion it was agreed that I would prepare a ms. Evan's Brothers (the publishers) would take it 'in house' and enjoy the privilege of first rejection.

Towards the end of 1974 I handed my ms. now entitled 'Open School, Open Society' to Audrey who immediately gave it to her assistant to read. I forget the junior's name so I'll call him Bob.

Bob travelled to and from work using the Central Line between Tottenham Court Road and Leytonstone. Bob decided to dip into my text on the way home. He phoned me next day to say that he felt certain the book would sell when he discovered himself at Epping – the end of the line and 8 stations beyond Leytonstone.

True to their promise, in the spring of 1975 Evans Brothers published the book, a slim volume in hardback. Its theme was uncomplicated, reflecting how schools could become more open to the society they served. It looked at openness through a series of interrelated topics – a freer curriculum, child-centred learning, the role of the parent and teacher, the school as an important focal point in the life of the community. Its tenor was educationally left of centre, but it was liberal in tone and far from revolutionary. There was no reason –

25

in my opinion then, nor in my opinion now – for it to make more than a small ripple in the educational pond. Instead, and to my astonishment, it created a whirlpool.

At much the same time a request came from TV2 (a Swedish television station) for permission to film in the school. This was granted by the Education Authority. Leading the Swedish team was Inger Sandberg, an internationally acclaimed writer of children's books. Inger seemed delighted with the resulting 45-minute documentary and decided that my book should be published in Sweden to support it. This duly happened, the Swedish translation being handled by Ràben och Sjögren.

In the 1970s there were many links between Swedish and Italian educationalists – from university academics to nursery school teachers. This co-operation resulted in 'Open School' appearing in Italian, from the publishing house Emme Edizioni.

The impact on my life of the exposure of my thoughts on the education of young children to a wider public was far reaching. To support the launch of the book and the TV programme in Sweden I was invited to Stockholm and Uppsala. For a week I suffered from being treated like a celebrity, giving TV, radio and press interviews and discussing the 'issues' raised by my book with Swedish teachers and academics at the two universities.

Of course my views were challenged by the traditionally-minded who saw my writing as a threat to coventional methods. I did not realise that at this time there was already a feeling of insecurity and self-questioning within the Swedish educational establishment. It was a period of radical reform, a completely new system of school organisation having been set up in 1962 and a revised curriculum in 1968. Was it wise, I wonder now, to throw more petrol on the fire, petrol manufactured by Pluckrose?

I returned to London a wiser person than I went. For I had embarked on an important learning process – how to present ideas without sounding dogmatic; how to answer questions so that the questioner felt hopeful that they, too, could become agents of change; how to employ humour to lighten but at the same time illustrate lectures; how to bridge the gap between cultures so that the audience could grasp the ways in which my suggestions could fit into their schools.

It was on returning from Sweden that I had a letter from Jan Kälberg a psychologist and psychotherapist who lived in Västerås, a city 90 km north of Stockholm. He invited me to meet him in London, in the hope that he could persuade me to return to Sweden for one weekend to run a course for him. The title of the course? 'Open School, Open Society'.

We met. I accepted his invitation. The course, of 12 hours duration, would broadly follow the themes explored in the book. It would be illustrated by video, film and slide and an exhibition of children's work. Little did we realise that this formula, adapted down the years, would still be in demand in 1998!

Jan is tall, his impressive dome-shaped head sports a thinning coat of black hair. Now (2007) in his late 50s, he looks the same as he did 20 years ago. Always informally (one might say waywardly) dressed, bearded and with heavy spectacles, Jan was at ease with himself – wherever he went and whoever he met. We soon became close friends – perhaps because conceitedly, we both felt we understood each other…

Following upon my weekend lectures in Västerås, Jan became my agent setting up all manner of courses in a wide range of venues – schools, day homes, hotels, universities, church halls, even churches. Whatever the course, however unlikely the place, Jan was a model of efficiency and logistical brilliance.

The key to working with Jan was to appreciate his predictability. He has a fierce pride in work well done and far from complimentary when faced with laziness or inefficiency. He was incensed when teachers did not give fully to the children in their care for, he argued, "children live as children only once. During their childhood they deserve the love, support, understanding and help of all the adults in their lives".

This – obsession (?) – with quality can possibly be attributed to Jan's first job on leaving school. He was apprenticed to a master carpenter. "The worker in wood cherishes his materials and his tools in order to create fine furniture. Children deserve to be cherished too!"

Jan's humour is divergent and very un-Swedish. (I don't think Swedish folk are happy laughing at themselves). Let me illustrate this with a story.

Jan and I had been invited to the home of an editor, Britta, who was preparing some writing of mine for a publishing house in Uppsala. We arrived at her house and after exchanging brief greetings were shown to the dining room.

The table was neatly set for Britta, her daughter, Jan and me *and one other.*

'The other' needed special feeding, for it was housed in a cage. *'The other' was a hamster.*

Being polite and experienced enough to accept the unexpected, we sat down to eat… Britta, her daughter, Jan, the Hamster and me. Perhaps it's here that I should point out that the hamster was off his food. All he would do was drive his wheel round at great speed, making human conversation somewhat difficult. After some minutes had passed, Jan enquired whether the hamster ate here often. Britta sighed and replied, utterly serious in voice and manner. "Ever since my husband left me Hunky the Hamster sits in his place and helps me realise what little I've lost".

We finished the meal and the hamster was hurried off to bed, but not before we'd said 'Sov gott' (sleep well). "Where do you think he sleeps?" said Jan, sotto voce. "Who ever would want to go to bed with a wheel?"

On leaving the house, we both wondered about the nature of 'husband replacement with animal'. Why a hamster? What if she saw her husband as a lion or boa constrictor? Coming to a meal then would carry a certain bite!

It was a story with a message which grew with the telling. "Mend your emotional hang-ups. Buy a hamster."

Jan, like me a person with working-class roots, is a democrat with very strong views on creating a society which protects the vulnerable and gives social equality to all. Let me illustrate this with another story centred on an evening meal.

We were in Stockholm. The headteacher of the school in which I was teaching invited us to supper. We found the house and knocked on the door. It was opened by an elderly woman. She wore the dress of a house servant… black with a short white apron, dark stockings, white lace headband, collar and cuffs, black shoes and a pair of black silk gloves.

She greeted us meekly, took our coats and led us to a room whose walls were heavy with bookcases, rich-red mahogany furniture and deep luxurious armchairs. Almost hidden away in a corner of this room was a grand piano. Beneath two large velvet curtained windows there was a heavy, but elegant desk. At it, shuffling papers, sat the headteacher's husband, a physician. Around the walls hung family portraits in gilt frames. As was the custom, we had left our outdoor shoes by the front door. Our feet sank into the carpet, itself protected by rugs from Afghanistan.

The black-gloved maid returned with drinks. Eventually we moved to a dining room, furnished expensively, but with immaculate taste, in the style of a 'man of property' of the 1890s. Everything about the room, the furniture, the cutlery, the wine glasses indicated a family comfortable in its wealth. The setting was Anthony Trollope rather than Jane Austin. The only elements which jarred were the two visitors – both wearing open necked shirts and corduroy trousers (appropriately aged but far from valuable).

We took our places at the table and at a signal from the 'Master' the maid reappeared and served each course – as though we were eating in an exclusive restaurant. Her evening, through five courses, followed a strict routine:

Enter dining room
Serve
Retreat from dining room
Return to clear
Retreat
Enter dining room
Serve...

All the while she wore black gloves... and never spoke a word.

At the end of the meal we returned to the room of grand desk and grand piano. The 'Master' dismissed the maid for the rest of the evening – to the washing up and her bedroom below the roof?

Driving back to our hotel it was obvious that Jan was incensed at the way the silent, black-gloved servant had been treated. I think he was even more vexed by the fact that I had witnessed what could happen behind the window, blinds and shutters of Social Democratic Sweden.

Whenever we recalled the experience Jan would mutter. "How can this be! In 1980! In Sweden!"

Jan is also a person of great generosity. He provided cottages for 'breaks' following upon an August of courses. Some were by the sea, others in the countryside behind Göteborg, one on 'Sun Mountain' in Dalarna, a 'land' (c.f. English county) rich in folk art and country customs. On one occasion he had led us on an expedition to the far north. Arriving at Kiruna by air, we took a hired car and drove north-west on the road to Narvik. In Kiruna in early June the sun shone at midnight. But it was quite cold. Rock faces still carried the icicles of winter past. The lakes were frozen, the distant hills snow-covered.

As we travelled north, the season changed from winter into spring. The small twisted trees carried a hint of green; on the lakes the ice was melting. The shards of broken ice, touching each other in the wind, made unearthly fairy music that would have delighted the ears of Titania or Pan.

On the third day we reached the port of Narvik. Warmed by the Gulf Stream, it was high summer... green trees, lawns and flower beds.

World War II touched Narvik. Control of the Norwegian coast and the valuable iron ore deposits in its hinterland made this region one of strategic importance. In April 1940 an advance party of the German army captured the harbour. A small allied naval force attempted to eject the invaders, but without success. In early June the remnants of the Allied force was evacuated.

Whilst in Narvik we visited the town's War Museum – in an underwater wreck nearby lies a war grave. I recalled Wilfred Owen's reflection on such things... the 'old lie'...

"Dulce et Decorum est
Pro Patria
Mori"

I have described Jan at some length because of the work we did together over 20 years. Perhaps it is appropriate to add to my thoughts a comment of Mike Pegg an English psychotherapist who knew Jan well. "Jan", he said, "is the most honest man I have ever met, honest in every way."

The initial 'open school' course was repeated. It sought to answer the 'What?' and 'Why?' questions underlying education. What do we teach? Why do we teach it? What sort of school?

There followed requests that we also answer the equally important questions which begin with 'How?' How do you introduce a more creative approach to Maths or Language? How do you use story or music to illuminate a Science topic? The 'How?' questions inspired Jan to organise a range of practical courses, each course lasting a minimum of three and a maximum of five days. To present such courses required an additional lecturer and my close colleague Hilary Devonshire agreed to fill the role. The practical courses included Picture Making (2, one basic and one follow-up). Mathematics (2), Science and Story Telling (which included Music and Movement). Hilary planned and watched over the Maths and Science courses (on which I played a supporting role). We also accepted invitations to teach in Swedish schools and Kindergartens, running a demonstration class for a week in parallel with an in-service programme for the teaching staff of the school.

It would serve little purpose to include the minutiae of these courses here. The observations which follow offer a view of Sweden through the eyes of an itinerant, immigrant worker. Because my trips were so regular I became aware of the nuances in the social fabric which would not be apparent to the casual tourist.

Here I must insert a very personal comment. My visits to Sweden did not break into my work at Prior Weston School. Courses were only arranged over weekends, (it is as quick to fly to Göteborg as it is to Inverness), during half-term breaks and during the 3 longer, between-term holidays. On average I suppose I stayed in Sweden 100 days each year (1977–1998).

Everything we did involved travel – usually in Jan's VW bus, tightly packed with the materials required for a course. Journeys of 450 km in an evening from Stockholm or Göteborg were not uncommon. It must be remembered that Sweden is a very large country with a small population (8,800,000). Imagine, if one could swing Sweden through an arc using the southern port of Malmö as the fixed point of the swing, its northern coastline would touch Rome.

In the 20 years I worked with Jan we covered much of the country... from Ystad and Vaxjö in the south, to Stockholm and Göteborg, to Umcå and Skellefteå on the Baltic. Some towns and cities we visited many times, some small settlements but once. By the end of 1988 over 7000 people employed in education had attended Jan's courses. By 1998 the number probably exceeded 14,000.

There were moments when travelling occupied my thoughts rather more than did course leading. I'll never forget the bitterly cold winter's night, snow falling steadily on the road through the northern woods, when the car's engine coughed, let out one final burst of exhaust fumes and expired. The nearest town being about 8 km away and with little hope of finding a house with a telephone (this all happened before the age of mobiles) Jan decided to seek assistance. Looking a bit like Captain Oates in 'Scott of the Antarctic' he bid me farewell with the immortal observation that "he wouldn't be long". So I sat in the front seat covered with blankets and my food ration, a large bar of chocolate. I also had a torch and some reserve batteries. It was 8.30 p.m.

Three hours later Jan returned in a hire car, which we loaded with the numerous boxes that were in the dead one. Jan noticed I had exhausted all the batteries. I explained that I had quietened my anxieties by finishing my book, 'The Mill on the Floss,' quietened them, that is, until I reached the last line, which reads 'In death they were not divided'. A local garage removed the broken car from the road when the conditions had improved.

Most journeys by road were uneventful. One remains in my memory for it illustrates the generosity and efficiency which I found almost everywhere in Sweden.

We were driving in early September from Leksand to Göteborg, a journey of about 450 km. It was mid-morning and I hoped to be in Göteborg in the early evening. Our boat left at 9.00 a.m. next day for Newcastle.

Just before we reached Borlange the car, a 1600cc Ford Orion with a 16-valve engine, stopped without warning. No bang, no judder, no whimper. Just silence. I tried to restart the engine. I looked at it knowingly. No effect. No joy. No movement.

I stopped a passing pedestrian to ask where I might find a convenient garage. I was lucky to find anybody at all – there were usually no pedestrians to be seen away from the towns and larger villages. He came over and peered at the open bonnet. "Electronics", he muttered. Then he turned to me and said. "If it was a proper old-fashioned engine I could possibly have helped you... but this". (long pause) "Garage? There are two. That way" (he pointed in the direction we were travelling) "is not too good. Walk the way you've come. After ½ km there's a little road and a small garage. Ask for Gören. He's a friend of mine. Say Sven sent you." With that, and a doubting shake of the head as he looked once again at my silent engine, he went on his way. Meeting Sven was our first piece of luck.

I did as he suggested. Gören looked at, then prodded our recalcitrant engine. His diagnosis was bad. A broken cam belt fitted only a month earlier – had caused the cylinders to mistime, tearing the valves from their mountings. He could not get parts and rebuild the engine within three weeks (at the earliest). But he would allow his mechanic, who was in the process of servicing a car, to tow us to the Ford garage in Börlange, some 15 km away. Meeting Gören was our second piece of luck.

Börlange Ford was a franchised garage with a large workshop and busy mechanics. We met the manager, Fillip. Fillip looked at the engine, tut-tutted, confirmed that broken cam belts destroyed car engines, said he was certain he hadn't got the parts but would look – and – IF a mechanic would agree to stay late, he might be able to effect a repair by midnight. "Come back at lunchtime (12.30) I'll be able to tell you then if we can help." Meeting Fillip was our third piece of luck.

Hilary and I left the car and disconsolately walked back towards Börlange town centre. On the way we saw a petrol station which also sold drinks and refreshments. We went in.

There was a pay-phone on the counter and I rang Jan to tell him of my problem. Sitting at a nearby table, close by the phone, was a comfortably-large, middle aged man. He listened while I spoke to Jan and continued to listen as I explained to the café/petrol station manager our predicament. Had he a car, I enquired, that I could hire and deposit at a similar franchise in Göteborg? He had cars he said, but "hire in Börlange return to Börlange." I should here explain my idea. We could catch the ferry in Göteborg if only we could get there – my car, when repaired could be collected by Jan.

The comfortably large gentleman, who had until this moment been silent, said "I've rudely followed your conversation. Until recently I owned a Citroen dealership in Falun. They also rent for Hertz (cars you can leave almost anywhere) I'll phone them for you if you wish and reserve a car. I thought this generous and accepted his offer.

He made the call and followed it immediately by suggesting that as he was about to go to Falun – some 20 km away – he would be pleased to take us to his 'old' garage. Here we could hire a car to take us back to the Ford Garage should my own car be repaired. "But we'll go to the Ford Garage first", said the rubicund gentleman (whose name I discovered was Erik). "We'll find out whether they can repair it in time." So to Börlange Ford we went. The manager was a little happier. He had the necessary parts *and* a mechanic. "Come back about 11.00 tonight we'll try to help you". Meeting Erik was our fourth piece of luck.

Erik was chatty. His English was not quite as haphazard as our Swedish and we talked fairly freely. "Now", said Erik, "I can't take you straight to Falun to get a car. I've arranged to pick up a friend, Nils, from my stuga in the woods. We'll take a little tour". We drove along dirt roads and unmade tracks for 20 km in search of Nils. It occurred to me later that we could have been taken anywhere. Such was our trust!

Nils was an odd character. The first impression I had of him was that he was very similar to Erik. They were a pair, like Tweedledum and Tweedledee. Both were in late middle age, both moustached, both wore sports jackets and bow ties (unusual in Sweden), both had loud voices and seemed to enjoy talking over each other. Both had retired and both enjoyed fishing in Scotland "because of the malt whisky tours you could do instead". When we entered the woodland clearing to pick up Nils, we found him sprawling in a chair clutching a beer bottle and a glass "He's doing that to tease me" said Erik. "He's as sober as you and me". And he was!

We descended the hilly woodland along dusty and pitted roads and eventually arrived at Falun Citroen. Erik and Nils departed, waving like a pair demented, and wishing us well. It was now 4.00 p.m. Göteborg and the boat were 450 km or 16 hours away. We now had the means to reach Göteborg, but in which car? Only time would tell.

The next seven hours crawled by. We had a slow meal. We sat and waited... looking out over woodland and river. It grew dark. There was nothing to look at and nowhere to go.

At 11.00 p.m. we returned to Börlange Ford and were greeted by Fillip, the manager. "Listen to the music", he said.

The 'music' was my car engine purring happily. I settled the bill (4000sk = £400+, in cash) thanked Peter, the mechanic for his efficiency and skill and drove once more to Falun – Hilary in the Ford me in the Citroen. At Falun I deposited the Citroen and, thirteen hours late, set off for Göteborg.

The drive to Göteborg along virtually empty roads through forest and woodland and deserted town and village was one of the most difficult I have ever attempted. Fighting drowsiness, taking care not to drive fast in order to be able to avoid any wandering elk or deer, handicapped by the limitations of my headlamps, which were masked for driving on the right, I followed a regime of stopping every hour, drinking juice, driving with an open window and playing tapes loudly.

At 5.00 a.m. we found a roadside café, open for lorry drivers. We stopped for a coffee drenched meal. Two and a half hours later we had reached the English ferry in Göteborg, poorer in pocket and richer in experience. I found the cabin and slept for the entire journey.

On returning to England I wrote to Börlange Ford, thanking them for their exceptional service and efficiency. A thought remains. Could I expect similar help in England from such a range of people – a pedestrian, two garage owners, two mechanics and a retired, bow-tied Tweedledum? I wonder!

I was set a more demanding challenge when travelling from Heathrow to Göteborg. It was the spring of 1980... I had passed through all controls and checks and was in the waiting area when I noticed my passport was missing. I reported its loss and, no sooner had I done so, my flight was called. When I reached the gate I had boarding pass but no passport. No passport, no flight!

The British Airways staff were helpful, but decided that they could only wait 15 minutes. Still no passport. "The captain will take you if you feel you can explain your problem in Göteborg", said the stewardess, as she prepared to close the cabin door. "But I'm sure Drake would have come". The historical analogy encouraged me to risk all. There was a course and Jan was waiting for me in Göteborg.

On landing at Landvetter passportless, I was taken by the immigration officer into a small grey walled room to be interviewed. Two blue uniformed policemen followed me. They were tall, broad, blond and carried firearms. They seem to have been selected for this work because of their size and their piercing unblinking blue eyes.

They examined the contents of my overnight bag – boxes of transparencies for my lectures, 2 books, my cheque book, a toilet bag… then they emptied my wallet and my pockets. All that I possessed at that moment was scattered before us on a low table.

"Sit down". It was an instruction said with such firmness, I obeyed instantly.

A torrent of questions followed. Name? Address? Occupation – then those which at first hearing seem easy to answer.

Why have you no money?

No Swedish money at all?

No English notes?

Do you often visit a foreign country without money?

Why have you come for just the weekend?

When were you last in Sweden?

Why do you have so little luggage?

Who do you say is meeting you?

What do you say he does?

Not entirely satisfied with my answers, the two inquisitors whispered to each other. Then one left the room to put a call out over the tannoy for Jan. There was no response.

The remaining policeman browsed through my belongings and picked up one of the books.

"Titta," (look) he said, "the person who wrote this book has the same name as you!"

"Yes", I replied, "that's to be expected, I wrote it. Inside the back flyleaf is my photograph."

"Forfattare?" (author) he muttered… his amazing detective work seemed to have drained him. He stood shaking his head. The second policeman returned. They spoke together before telling me of the solution to my problem. Immigration would grant me a special entry/exit visa of 48 hours duration. The cost would be 25 Swedish kroner.

"But I have no money"

You have some English cheques and a driving licence. We will take you to the airport bank to draw money."

I was escorted to the bank like a violent criminal, a police officer on my left and on my right.

My difficulties were explained to a thin, worried, very smartly dressed bank clerk. He thought before he replied.

"Yes, of course we will help. But I must have a passport for documentation. The bank's rules..." The taller of the two tall policemen looked down at him sternly. "We'll be responsible. Take the cheque and give him the money. Now!"

Without a word, the worried clerk looked even more worried, but took my cheque and gave me money for the visa. Collecting my belongings en route, I was taken through customs to the exit.

The policemen smiled.

"Have a nice day", said the first.

"Welcome to Sweden, author," said the second.

And there beyond the exit stood Jan, smiling too.

That episode took place behind closed airport doors, but just as odd things are open to public view.

Returning home from Arlanda Airport, Stockholm, I wandered to the gate to await the incoming flight which would take me to Heathrow. Although I was rather early, the area around the gate was a scene of great activity. There were policemen with dogs, suited gentlemen with clipboards, airport staff with industrial floor cleaners, and in the background a TV crew.

Then, quite suddenly, the concourse emptied. Policemen, suited officials, airport staff melted away and to 'our' gate came a young lady bearing a large bouquet. A disembodied voice announced that the flight from London would arrive in 15 minutes.

There was a noisy bustle at the gate next to 'ours'. An aircraft had landed and began disembarking passengers. They hurried across the space which had so recently been cleaned and checked. A man of about 40, bearded and wearing shorts stopped, looked around, took a small backpack from his shoulders and sat down on the floor.

Without as much as a glance at his surroundings he opened his bag and delved into it, satisfied himself that he had what he needed – and took off his shoes and socks.

His fellow travellers flowed around him as though it was the most natural thing in the world – to encounter a sockless passenger on the floor of an airport. The dog handlers watched, the suited gentlemen watched, the bouquet lady watched, Hilary watched, I watched. Nobody moved except the stripper.

Slowly he undid his belt, unbuttoned his shorts and wiggled them down his legs and over his feet... to expose a highly coloured pair of Y-fronts. The shorts and the discarded socks he stuffed into his bag, pulling from it his replacement clothing – a pair of old jeans and some fresher socks. He proceeded to dress with care and with difficulty, for he was still sitting on the floor.

By now the last of the passengers had left the plane... the next people to pass around him, again giving no indication that they were confronting anything unexpected... were the airline crew and cabin staff, smartly dressed in their SAS uniforms.

The bearded man slowly rose to his feet, picked up his bag and wandered off.

Nobody took any action, nobody seemed surprised.

There the story ends. I had retreated to the sanity of the toilet so I've no idea who the important visitors were!

It's comparatively easy to caricature a nation or race applying the characteristics of one to the many. So I must dismiss all those adjectives which I have heard used to describe the Swedes... words like dour, conformist, remote, humourless, self-satisfied, robot-like, self-contained, cold. They are certainly people who are comfortable with themselves, and their way of life. Compared with many Europeans they live in a model democracy, a state which cares and provides for them from birth to the grave.

Sweden has not been engaged in a war since the age of Napoleon. In recent times its Governments (mainly left of centre) have followed a policy of thoughtful and politically astute neutrality. This accounts for members of the Swedish armed forces being used to ease tensions in many of the world's trouble spots. So let me try to escape from generalisations and use the little snippets of life that I have observed to illustrate 'Swedishness'.

All that I record here must be set within a historical context. Sweden is a country whose industrial revolution began over a hundred years later than it did in the UK. There were industrial complexes in

18th Century Sweden (e.g. the copper mines at Falun) but compared to the factories of Manchester, Leeds, Bradford, Glasgow and Birmingham industrial units were small. In the last 125 years Sweden has moved from an agricultural economy, to one based on industry and technology.

This said, Theresa, a ten year old living in a tower block in Stockholm in September 2004 is only separated from her great grandfather by 3 generations – a man who was employed as a forest worker in remote Dalarna and whose wife was a 'piga' (general servant) in the house of a member of the gentry.

The feeling that "we are a nation of people rooted in the countryside", is expressed by almost every Swede. Both sexes enjoy boating, swimming, hunting, shooting (elk and deer), skiing, ice skating, walking and camping. Many town and city families own or rent a 'stuga' or country cottage to which they retreat on as many weekends as they possibly can. Even in central Stockholm there are neatly kept allotment patches alongside a section of the main railway line, each with its own tiny house-like shed.

The most obvious sign of the pull of the great outdoors comes in late August. At weekends the woods and forests are dotted with Swedish couples on a special quest. Each couple is dressed for protection against brambles and thick undergrowth and weighed down with pails and buckets. They are hunting the Kantarell.

The Kantarell is a singularly particular mushroom with an unspectacular flavour which appeals to Swedish taste buds

Kantarell obviously dislike being hunted and being eaten. So they continue to hide. This means that when a patch of Kantarell is uncovered the hunters use all their guile to attract the attention of other members of their family and at the same time to divert the attention of others from the newly discovered treasure.

Most roadside, lakeside and woodland halts have dedicated resting places where families may sit and eat their meals in comfort. The benches and tables, toilets and provision for waste collection are of very high standard and invariably immaculately maintained. When travelling with Jan, we usually dined on his homemade 'rinny sandwiches'. These were made with part-fried eggs – hence the 'rinny', which always coagulated in Jan's beard (and was difficult to remove).

Hilary and I quickly adopted this policy of outdoor eating. During a series of courses we were running in Göteborg we decided that our classroom, hot, airless and smelling of paint, was no place to

While Annika encouraged a none too happy rabbit to leave the cage, her sister was preparing the jumping course. This was a green cloth about 3 metres long and 40 cm wide. On the green cloth, at suitable intervals, little wooden walls and gates were placed, each about 15 cm high. The course looked like those to be seen at a gymkhana.

The rabbit was fitted with a collar, placed at one end of the course and encouraged to clear the gates. It did an indifferent hop and lost interest. The rabbit being returned to his hutch and the course cleared, we were taken up to a first floor bedroom to meet a retired jumping rabbit, the walls of his room covered with championship rosettes, and certificates. This rabbit had no cage, ran freely throughout the house and enjoyed all those little luxuries that a retired champion deserves – central heating, quality bedding, regular exercise and home grown carrots. It appears that regular *kanin hoppning* meetings are held throughout the year.

Rabbit gymkhanas. Was this particularly odd? Is it more civilised to have dwarf throwing competitions (recently banned in Finland) or devise culturally more sophisticated ways to endanger life and limb like chasing a round cheese downhill, as practised every spring by the inhabitants of a Warwickshire village?

Fascination with things natural is revealed in a variety of ways. *The* animal of the Swedish landscape is the elk, a great beast characterised by its bulk, its antlers, its long, thin legs and its invariably sad expression. It is important to limit the number of elk running free in Sweden. When involved in a road accident they cause considerable damage to the car, and more significantly, to its occupants. The legs of the elk being long and thin and its torso so heavy the injured elk on impact tends to be thrown onto the windscreen or roof of the car. I saw a VW Beetle on the Uppsala–Stockholm motorway with the passenger cabin crushed to the level of the door handles.

On one course in autumn, a demure lady teacher (the jean and T-shirt model) told me she was leaving the course early. I mention the T-shirt because over the previous days it had shouted 'Green Peace' or proclaimed a need to 'Save a Whale'. Apologising, she explained that she was to join the elk hunt overnight and had to be at the hide by 4.00 p.m. Did she enjoy killing the elk, I asked. "Love it", she exclaimed, blood lust in her eyes.

The successful lecturer is always looking for ways to use the immediate locality to colour his/her presentation. So when nature in the form of a hedgehog (*iglelkot*) fortuitously arrived at the classroom door I decided to incorporate him into my opening talk to a group of teachers I had not yet met. Foolishly I decided to show that I had learned some words of Swedish. But foreign words change as they are spoken. Instead of *igelkot* I described the *pendeltåg* curled up behind the door.

The expression on the faces of my students were pictures of polite restraint. A *pendeltåg*? Curled up behind the door? Was he drugged, this Englishman or drunk? Or mad?

Perhaps I should now explain. A *pendeltåg* is a commuter train.

Hamster husbands, jumping rabbits, culled elk and trains disguised as hedgehogs may seem unlikely stories. But, then, devoting hours to train a horse to trot instead of move naturally might, by some, also seem eccentric.

Trotting is the Swedish equivalent to flat racing. In trotting races, however, the jockey – wearing racing silks and perhaps blessed with a name like Olly Goop – sits behind the horse in a light, two wheeled chariot.

The race track, of which there are many in Sweden, is oval. Along one side stands the state controlled Tote where bets are placed. On the more important courses (e.g. Stockholm, Göteborg) there is a stepped, glass fronted restaurant in which racegoers can eat a meal and watch the proceedings in comfort.

The surface of the track is made up of a mixture of grit, fine gravel and sand. Before each race this surface is smoothed with a motorised rake. Race lengths vary, but most involve at least one and three quarter circuits of the track. There are no starting gates. Two other methods are favoured. In one a car, fitted with a wide fence-like frame across its boot, slowly drives around the track. The horses and chariots nestle as closely to the frame as they can. When the start is reached the car accelerates away and the race begins.

A more traditional start sees the competitors divide into three groups of 4. Slowly they rotate behind the starting line. When all three lines are straight and facing in the right direction, the starter gives a signal and the race begins.

'Trotting', the motion of the horse, gives the name to the sport. Trotters have an unusual movement, lifting their legs so high that the trot is exaggerated. Should a horse gallop during a race, it is slowed down until the trotting pattern is re-established. If this is not done quickly, the horse is disqualified.

Jan took us trotting 5 or 6 times in 20 years… "To better understand Swedish culture." At least this was his justification for our

41

going. However a more likely reason was that he enjoyed 'a little flutter' and the atmosphere of the racecourse. 'All human life' was certainly there, from the ostentatiously rich to the inadequate poor. (Swedish 'poor' in no way equates to English 'poor'. The great majority of the Swedish 'poor' drive their cars to the meeting, pay for parking, entry to the track, race cards, back a loser in every race and buy refreshments.)

Jan advised us never to confess we knew anything about trotting. It was very 'working-class' and rather frowned upon by teachers. This is an indication, perhaps, that although Sweden is a very tolerant and socially integrated society, tensions of class and race simmer below its surface. 'Right' and 'Left' exist in politics, but the right is to the left of Tony Blair's 'New Labour'… and the economics and social policies of Thatcherism were never appreciated or understood.

One is never far from water in Sweden – the lakes, rivers and sea make all forms of water sport accessible. Jan in his early years with us spent much of his free time teaching us the art of 'fishing for jack' (i.e. fresh water pike, a predatory fish which can grow to a metre in length and weigh up to 25 kilos.) Jan was, I am certain, an excellent theorist in the black arts of ledger-fishing, but in 22 years of demonstration we only saw him catch one rather small specimen. To be fair to Jan he did have photographs which showed him holding fish of prestigious size… but as I told him, I have photographs showing me standing beside Queen Margaretha of Denmark. Being in the photograph didn't mean I was Crown Prince.

Perhaps the strangest animal story of all concerns an old lady dressed entirely in black. We had booked into the OK Hotel in Partille, Göteborg. It was an evening in late spring. We were sitting in Jan's van, about to drive to the city centre. A taxi, a large Volvo, stopped across the junction of the hotel entrance and the slipway on which we were waiting, making it impossible for us to drive away.

A lady in her late sixties eased herself from the taxi. She had a lead in her hand and on the end of the lead was a large black and white monkey. Reassuring the animal, she gently pulled it into the rose bed which ran along the edge of the road to the hotel entrance. Choosing a particularly thick bush she encouraged the monkey to squat beneath it, looping the lead around the bush to prevent the animal from following her. The monkey kept very still.

Meanwhile the lady in black returned to the car, took a case from the boot and hurried to the hotel to confirm her room. By now we were too interested to think of moving. Astonished, we watched as people walked past the rose bed. Nobody saw the monkey. Monkeys are not expected to be sitting under rose bushes in April outside hotels in Göteborg!

The lady returned and helped the taxi driver lift a supermarket trolley from the boot. He then struggled with a large bundle of hay which he balanced in its basket. While this was happening the monkey was untied. In a flash it leapt on the platform below the basket and its hay load.

The taxi driver paid off, lady, trolley, hay and monkey disappeared across a parking lot to a side entrance to the hotel.

I suggested to Jan that it was unhygienic for a monkey to live in a bedroom which some unknowing traveller might use later in the week. "There must be rules" said Jan. "There are rules for everything we do in Sweden. I am certain there are rules about monkeys living in hotels".

On returning to the hotel Jan innocently enquired whether the staff knew about the lady and the monkey (living we discovered in Room 103). "Yes" replied the receptionist, discussions are in progress".

With all the seriousness I could muster I took my room key and said. "Could you please tell the housekeeper not to let the water out of my bath for the duration of my stay".

"And could I ask why?"

"Yes, of course. You see, I brought my pet alligator with me and he hates the dry atmosphere in the hotels we stay in…"

For a brief moment I think she believed me.

We met so many Swedish folk that choosing who to write about poses a dilemma. Everyday occurrences and unexceptional behaviour of lifestyle are easily forgotten. What makes travel interesting – at home or abroad – is the range of accomplishment, social awareness and achievement in the people one meets. The little episodes which follow are a pot-pourri, an assortment of Scandinavian characters.

For example I must have met several hundred headteachers during my time in Sweden. Only one is fixed in my memory. His school was in Uppsala, his large school hall prepared for the 300+ audience which was expected. When I arrived at the school, half an hour or so before my talk was to begin, his secretary emerged from his office and informed me that the head would meet us "when he was dressed". This meant that on a hot, summer day he only appeared in public in waistcoat, jacket, trousers with razor sharp creases, the whole image completed with matching tie and pocket handkerchief.

"We must be dignified" seemed to be his motto. I remember him also for one other quirk of character. He seemed to love locks. He told me that when everybody had come he would "secure the hall doors" – which he duly did. It was as if an immaculately dressed prison warder having 'counted his customers' into their cells, locked them in to prevent escape... or was he locking out those who sought to rescue my captive audience from becoming bewitched by my siren words?

Similarly I've met many thousands of excellent teachers. Would my reader want to know how competent they all were – or prefer to learn of the secondary school teacher in Västerås who told the course how much his class "loved him". To prove his point he took me to his room. He stood still and watchful like Peter Sellers playing Inspector Clouseau. Suddenly from all parts of the room (from underneath desks, behind cupboards and bookcases) his class emerged. They leapt on him, throwing him to the floor. "See how they love me", he said as he disappeared from sight beneath a tornado of flailing arms and legs.

And so to my collection of vignettes, gentle, one-off pictures of people I met in Scandinavia.

There were politicians. Claus X had been instrumental in helping Jan set up a course. The local TV station wanted to feature the course as a news item. Claus was desperate to use TV to win votes at a forthcoming election. He needed publicity but the TV producer did not want political overtones to colour his 'general interest' story. So Claus was banned. On being told he would not take part in the discussion which ended the news item, Claus was distraught... until he discovered that this part of the TV feature would be filmed beneath a tree in parkland, the participants sitting on rugs and low stools. So what did Claus do? He ran from tree to tree, a little distance in front of the camera, jumping up and down and waving his arms like a demented clown. I think he was re-elected!

It was wise to avoid politicians. One, Krister, did cause us a little worry. He was found, after an official audit, to have been careless in his use of his entertainment allowance (which was drawn on public funds). Our worry – he had twice taken us to a rather expensive restaurant where we had been generously wined and dined. Thankfully it wasn't conventional entertaining that proved his undoing. He took a group from the Temperance Society on a day trip. Inadvertently he provided wine for their midday refreshment.

Swedes are rather trusting. Jan and I were having a meal with the British Council representative – whom I'll call Tom. We were having lunch in a very well known cellar restaurant in Gamla Stad (the old town Stockholm). It is a restaurant with an ambiance of elegance. On every table each place setting centred around a large, decorated, finely crafted brass dish. These dishes were used to 'hold' the china plates on which meals were served.

When we entered the cellar, a group of six tourists – not Swedish but adequate in the language – were just finishing their meal. There were four men and two women. Apart from this group and us there were no other customers.

The tourists prepared to leave. They paid the bill and, judging by the response from the waiter as he took the 1000sk note, the tip was generous. Then one of the women took out a camera. She moved towards the watching waiter – a little slinkily I later thought. She spoke to him quickly, the import of the conversation being to ask if they could "have a photograph of all four waiters as a reminiscence of a happy occasion". The waiter spoke to his colleagues. Flattered, they agreed to have a group photograph taken. One of the male tourists took the camera and ushered the waiters to an alcove at the end of the cellar. This alcove was at the opposite end of the cellar to the stairway which led to the street above.

The waiters conveniently corralled, the lady tourist sidled up to the table she had just vacated. The table was out of sight of the posing waiters. We watched dumbfounded as she opened a large bag and quickly and quietly placed all six brass dishes inside it – and fled silently upstairs.

The tourists contrived through much banter and chat to give their colleague time to escape. Then they quickly followed disappearing into the crowded pavements of the old town.

All this happened in a flash. In the time it took Jan to reach the nearest waiter, the thieves had fled. Tom and Jan, talking over the incident, agreed that Swedes were too naïve and trusting to cope with the more outrageous aspects of modern living. Perhaps the murder of Prime Minister Olaf Palme, shot in a Stockholm street in 1986 will in retrospect, mark the moment that Sweden entered the 20th Century.

The episode which follows also involves a law breaker but it also illustrates something of the respect which Swedes show for each other, their attitude to authority and their sense of humour.

Hilary and I had just had supper in the Chinese Restaurant in Drottning-gaten in central Göteborg. Close by the restaurant, his back against a high brick wall stood a man aged about 36. He was the sort of man who would be invisible in a crowd. Small (91.5 cm/4 ft 8 in), undistinguished, he wore a scruffy T-shirt, loose baggy trousers and blue and white trainers. He stood motionless, as if glued to the wall.

Then we noticed the police officers, two men and one woman. They faced the man, forming a half circle around him. The police trio moved a little closer, hands by their belts, close to revolver and truncheon. Nobody spoke. The antagonists eyed each other. Surely he was not going to attempt to escape. The female officer took the initiative. She whispered to her colleagues and a plan of action was agreed. Call for reinforcements.

While this was happening the man remained by the wall, but he adjusted his position. He put his right hand into his trouser pocket and began to fidget, just a little.

A second police Volvo drew up and parked behind the first. By now the developing drama had attracted a small crowd of onlookers. We joined it. The behaviour of this crowd is worthy of analysis. The Swedes are a private people. They wanted to see the situation resolved but felt guilty at staying to stare. Those who felt particularly embarrassed noticed that their shoelaces needed tightening or that a sudden pain in knee or hip forced them to stop.

There were now five police officers in the half circle. All were tall, all looked fit, all looked strong. All were armed.

Slowly they inched towards the small man, who seemingly oblivious of his plight, continued to fidget – his hand remaining in his trouser pocket. Then with a sudden rush, the police seized him. The effect on the captive was dramatic. He seemed to have a fit, his body went rigid, his legs straight and unbending, his arms tight against his sides.

The police were disturbed by this turn of events. Their attitude changed from one of outright aggression to one of bemused concern.

The crowd, now numbering about sixty, played the role of Chorus – as in a Greek tragedy.

A collective sigh, long and sustained.

A collective snigger, begun quietly but increasing in volume
Developing into
A collective laugh.

The reason for this response? As the police lifted the man (who in their arms looked smaller than he was) a leg fell from his trousers and an empty trouser leg flapped in the wind.

There, in the road, lay one false leg. Complete with strapping at one end and sock and blue and white trainer at the other.

The crowd, smilingly happy, stayed to watch the final denouement. The now one-legged man was gently escorted, hopping to the first police car. One of the female officers went to the support car and returned. She moved like an actor. Her upper arms close to her body, her forearms, parallel to the ground with hands palm upwards, she moved towards the lonely leg. Across her outstretched arms lay a heavy, light blue blanket.

With due solemnity the second female officer bowed before the leg as if genuflecting to a religious image. The blanket bearer approached, the leg was reverently placed across the blanket and taken in sombre procession to the second police car and laid on a back seat. The two police cars sped away. The crowd melted into the night. Hopefully man and leg were eventually reunited!

The ability of most Swedish people to remain 'private' has certain advantages. It helped me, for example, not to feel too great a fool when I committed an inexcusable social gaff.

Anna-Mai, a lady I have known for many years, enjoys opera. Before the modern Opera House was opened in the mid 1990s, Göteborg Opera performed in a charming 19th century theatre (Stora Teater) close to the parks and canal. It was to this old theatre we went with Anna-Mai. We were comfortably seated in the upper circle (and very upper it was!) Hilary and Anna-Mai were sitting together, some distance from Jan and me. The house lights dimmed. The audience stilled. The conductor raised his baton… there was a long roll of drums. The significance of a drum roll must be hidden deep within my soul.

I stood up. Jan, being supportive, stood up too… the only standing people in a packed opera house.

The drum roll led into the overture and I sank red-faced into my seat. The orchestra weren't playing 'The Queen's tune,' after all!

"Henry" said Jan much later in the evening. "Why should we play 'God Save the Queen' in Göteborg in August?"

A second example of this Scandinavian acceptance of human difference (a paradox in such an egalitarian society) and the sharpness of North European dry humour comes from Oslo.

The first week in June. A Sunday morning, early. The air heavy with the scent of lilac. We decided to walk from our hotel to the Vigelund sculpture park, a distance of about 4 km. After about 45 minutes of gentle walking I realised we were lost.

In the distance, at the far end of the street I saw an elderly man with an aged dog. I hurried towards him and said in that loud, slow,

47

distinctly pronounced fashion we use when addressing elderly foreigners "Do you speak English?"

The grey haired Norwegian looked down at his equally grey haired dog. Then turning to me and speaking in that loud, distinctly pronounced fashion the Norwegians use when speaking to the English, "Yes. – But – only – when – I – have – to." Then, in perfect English, he directed me to the sculpture park. "And now excuse me. I speak to my dog in Norwegian."

I have already hinted that Swedish people find comfort in the security which the state provides. But this has a downside – conformity can stifle initiative and independent thinking.

At Hudiksvall on the Baltic Coast there was a teacher training college. I was invited to give a two hour evening talk. In it I stressed the importance of using the environment to inspire talking, writing and the visual arts. At the end of my talk a lady lecturer in education, senior and long time in her post, approached me. "I've got a problem with your thesis. You must understand we have no environment here."

I was speechless. There was the beauty of the coastline, its granite rocks washed by the sea in summer, and wrapped in ice in winter; there were the traditional wooden cottages used by the fishermen; the rich variety of architectural styles in the town itself; the old railway station; the church; there were forests, hills, mountains, lakes and rivers in the countryside beyond the town… "What do you mean?" I said.

"Well" she replied. "You've got St. Paul's Cathedral, Buckingham Palace, Westminster Abbey. All we've got is Hudiksvall."

If lecturers are so restricted in their thinking, what hope is there for their students?

I left the college wondering whether the whole experience had been simply a bad dream. One of the key elements of my talk had been to stress the place of all the arts in the education of young children. When I referred to music, the Principal of the college stood up, raised his hand to silence me, and said,

"We are enjoying a most interesting time with Henry. I think he deserves a little break. Music is an art form we cannot ignore. Anticipating what our visitor might say, I've brought my violin to play to you. Living sound, living music."

And serenade the audience he did. I must record his bravery and his foolhardiness. A Bach partita written for the Clavier and transposed for unaccompanied violin, indifferently played on an

48

ill-tuned instrument, arbitrarily inserted into a lecture, was not the most effective way of endearing the Principal to the students or providing them a good example of effective teaching.

Had this happened in the UK. I think many students would have walked out of the lecture hall. Being Swedish they stayed, showing a sense of tolerant respect for their Principal and politeness to me.

Colleges and Departments of Education are unique in the way they operate. To work successfully in a teacher training institution for any length of time one needs to expect the unexpected and meet unplanned demands with good humour and flexibility. What happened to me in Stockholm illustrates my jaundiced observation.

I was contracted to take a 2-day course on 'the young learner' and present it to a group of 90 students. The sessions would be a mixture of talk, video, film and slides. Each training unit was related to the one preceding it – and the starting point for units yet to come.

At 9.00 a.m. on the first day I met my 90 students and delivered my first paper. The session was scheduled to end at 10.30 am. At 10.00 a.m. a message was brought to me by a secretary. It read "Mr. Pluckrose. Please release all English language students now and send them to their usual Monday lecture room. Thank you." 25 embarrassed students stood up and left. They were 'replaced' some 5 minutes later by 25 'new' students who had been sent to me 'to make up my numbers'. This happened twice during the first morning of my course.

To use a basketball term, I decided to 'take a time out' to try to unravel the mystery of the migrating students. (At the end of the first morning I had 35 of those with whom I began the day).

The Head of Language Studies explained why the situation had arisen. "The students who left you had to attend a lecture on English Language. It's so important, English!" He looked amazed when I asked him whether he thought I was lecturing in Swahili. Was it possible, I gently enquired, that migrating students might hear more idiomatic constructions from me, a native English speaker than from a lecturer for whom English was a second language? Peace declared and further migration prohibited.

When I left, next day, I vowed never to return... although I was thanked for drawing the Academic Faculty's attention to their 'little error' and in handling the situation with tact. Another example of Swedish skill in resolving difficulties through negotiation!

Not far from the college is the 'Vasa Museum'. On August 10th, 1628 the Swedish Navy's newest acquisition 'The Vasa', made her maiden voyage across Stockholm harbour. She never reached the other side, heeling over and sinking under a sudden gust of wind. The wreck of this great warship (she carried 64 canon) remained virtually untouched until 1956 when its resting place was discovered. Salvage operations to recover as much of the ship as possible were begun in 1961. Because the water in Stockholm harbour is salt-free, the worms which destroy wood cannot live in it. So when 'The Vasa' was raised her woodwork could be salvaged. After years of treatment the wooden beams were exposed to air and the ship reconstructed.

'The Vasa' now sits in a dry dock, a gloriously impressive baroque warship... 62 m (204 ft) in length, a maximum beam of 11.7 m (39 ft) and a displacement of 1400 tons. The hull is richly decorated with over 700 sculptures, the gun ports and cabin surrounds carefully carved. Now, her restoration complete, she sits in a dry dock inside her own museum supported by displays of the many artefacts recovered from the wreck and the sea bed in which she rested. 'The Vasa Museum' now enjoys the status of a World Heritage site.

Jan organised an unusual 5 day course centred upon 'The Vasa.' Two of these days were devoted to the theory and practice of education, the events of 1628 and 1961 providing the thematic element. The three days which followed were practical and held on the top floor of the children's' centre. This group based all their activities around 'The Vasa', visiting her at will.

On the last evening the senior curator of the Maritime Museum, Tomas, arranged a nautical party on board a vessel which was used as a floating information centre/classroom for visiting groups. On arriving at the centre we met members of the Museum staff – but no Tomas. We were told he had been 'missing' for three days. He arrived just before we left at the end of the party. We later discovered that his 'missing days' had been spent as a reserve officer in the Swedish navy, hunting a Soviet U-boat which was said to have illegally entered Swedish territorial waters.

Some time later a Soviet U-boat was apprehended. But Sweden's military, naval and air forces played little part in the operation. A fisherman going home one evening saw a U-boat beached on an outcrop of rock like a stranded whale. When the fisherman phoned the authorities nobody would believe his story. It took many hours for his phone calls to be taken seriously. Fortunately the U-boat remained beached... something which the Swedish forces could not depend upon in the event of real hostilities.

Incidentally, in the little port of Vastervik we met the Swedish navy... in the shape of an armed coastal patrol boat. All grey paint and with a rapid fire gun on the foredeck she looked quite out of place in such an idyllic setting. The ambiguity was confirmed by the white logo on her funnel – a dove and olive branch above the word 'Peace'.

Before and after courses it was possible to visit places of interest in the locality. We spent a little time in Öland, a long, thin island in the Baltic. Linked to the mainland at Kalmar by a magnificent bridge, Öland is a place of contrasts. There is rolling parkland and barren shrubby wilderness, quiet butterfly-rich meadows and petrified trees, isolated windmills and pretty hamlets, stugas, empty roads, sea birds and, circling high, eagles.

People have lived on Öland since prehistoric times. There are dolmen, standing stones and a restored walled settlement dating from the first millennium (when its inhabitants traded with Rome). There are numerous old churches, a mediaeval castle at Borgholm and a royal summer palace at Solliden. Above all Öland is an island of wooden post-mills. They stand singly, in small groups as if in conversation, and in long lines like soldiers dug in along a hilltop. In early times the mills were used both for pumping water and grinding corn.

For the nature lover there are acres of wild heathland, rare plants and many species of bird. In 'Island Song' the poet Sven Sjöholm wrote:

"Har ar fraga sommarlandet
Vindarnas och solns o
Hara r Karga vinterlandet
Stormarnas och fakens o"

Which roughly translated reads:
"Here is a fair summer land
A wind and sunshine island
Here is a barren winter land
A stormy and hard (to live in) island"

I have only visited Öland in August when it is indeed fair. I don't need to be a poet to imagine how bleak and unsparing the winters could be.

The indigenous Swedes delight in their past. Museums and historic sites are well presented. Many of the larger villages boast a *Gammelgård* a collection of traditional houses and farm buildings

51

built of wood in the local vernacular style. The *Gammelgård* is often the setting for folk festivals e.g. those for Midsummer's Day.

Sweden is dotted with the remains of settlements and sites linked to the Viking period. One doesn't have to travel far to discover a 'hällristning' or standing stone. On it, carved in the old Germanic 'futhork' alphabet of 16 letters, will be a dedication to a local chieftain. It might tell of his bravery, of an event in his life or record of his death. These 'rune' stones are often decorated with snakes or dragons, their bodies intertwined (similar to the patterns we associate with Viking jewellery).

We visited one particularly impressive Viking site at Birka on Lake Mälaren. It is reached by boat from Västerås, Jan's home town. Birka, with an excellent natural harbour, was one of two Viking trading centres in this part of Scandinavia.

The boat docked at the end of a causeway. The causeway passed through a great defensive wall (estimated by archaeologists to have been 30 m high when the settlement was at its peak). This wall ran all around the 'town'. As I stood in the shadow of the wall I felt quite moved – as though I had come back to a place I once knew.

We took the opportunity to visit the island's church. It is dedicated to the French saint, Anskar, a Christian teacher who 'carried the gospels to the Viking folk' c830AD. He was received by the chieftain Bjorn, and given permission to preach.

A number of attacks on the British Isles were launched from Birka and site excavations have uncovered a multitude of treasures (including the spoils of Viking raids along the coastlines of Western Europe).

By contriving, over the space of several years, to link the experience gained from visits to historical sites with the more detailed academic information gleaned from museums, I gained considerable insight into human settlement in Scandinavia.

I stood in the centre of a stone, ship-shaped grave of a Viking chief, near by a lake, with calling water birds. Listening to the wind caressing the grasses and gazing at the grey white moss coloured stones which mark the shape of the longboat… I wonder… what was this chief, Ales, like?… Perhaps he was involved in the great Battle of Maldon in Essex (991) a town in which Hilary, my daughter, now lives… Such speculation is at the root of history! (Ales' grave, a longboat, is in Skåne).

The stone ship-graves, though impressive, are insignificant when compared to the longboat in the museum at Roskilda in Denmark or the Gostad ship in Oslo. The Gostad ship was designed to carry a warrior on his last journey. It's humbling to think that in touching the wooden hull we forge a link with the craftsmen who centuries ago designed the ship and shaped the wood.

Developing this thought further, there are few things more certain to cause us to reflect on our own mortality than when gazing into the face of a human being whose body has been preserved by an accident of nature.

Tollundsmannen lived in Scandinavia around 200BC. His body was completely mummified by the soft, wet, peaty earth into which it was thrown. The twisted and contorted remains of Tollundsmannen now lies in an open grave in an exhibition case in Copenhagen's Historical Museum.

Look closely at his rigid face, blacky-brown from centuries of immersion in peat, racked with pain. His lips are pressed tightly together as if suppressing a scream; his eyes closed beneath full eyelids; his forehead deeply lined... around his thin, twisted neck a thick rope is tied. Was he murdered, and if he was, why? Or did he die contented, a willing participant in a sacrificial ceremony to propitiate some long forgotten God? Could Tollundsmannen be a distant relative of yours – or mine?

Perhaps people like Tollundsmannen carved the detailed drawings on rock faces which are to be found in several areas of Sweden. Near the town of Tonumshede (north of Göteborg on the way to Oslo) are a large number of these decorated stones. The carvings, overdrawn in red to make them more clearly visible, are as open to the elements as they were when they were first etched. They record the lifestyle and beliefs of early Scandinavians... the sun God crosses the sky in his two wheeled chariot, human figures journey in boats, hunt for elk and deer, fight, grow crops, make love. Watching over these scenes is Thor, God of Gods. The pictures flow from rock to rock and cover many square metres.

Sweden is also rich in Medieval treasures. These include the 'Slott' (castles). Often these 'Slott' have 4 or more narrow, round towers along the sides of the keep and the walls of the inner bailey. Each tower is topped with a cone shaped roof. To me they look more romantic than their English equivalents, perhaps because in my childhood storybooks round towers always housed an imprisoned princess waiting for the brave knight who would undoubtedly rescue her.

Gripsholm Slott, south of Stockholm, is one of my favourite castles. It contains the royal portrait gallery (2500 portraits of the court, kings, queens, princes and princesses) and, on the top floor a collection of contemporary Swedish art. There is also a quaint little theatre, complete with proscenium arch, where the court was entertained when the king was in residence.

The most famous early theatre, perhaps in the whole of Europe, is to be found in Drottningsholm Slott. (Drottning means Queen). Built in the 1680s it was once used as the principal royal palace in Stockholm.

It was in Drottningsholm theatre that Ingmar Bergman produced his 18th Century period-style 'The Magic Flute'. The film showed Mozart's opera in its entirety, the production being enriched by the back of house scenes. These showed the stage hands, in 18th Century costume, changing the stage sets using the original wooden machinery.

The Slott at Helsingör in Denmark (Elsinor in English) provided the backdrop for an outdoor production in English of 'Hamlet'. On entering the Slott we passed into the inner bailey. The stage was set against the side of the keep; facing the stage were steps of temporary tiered seating. We found our seats with some difficulty as it was getting dark and we were hampered by an unexpected item, given free, to each member of the audience… a large black plastic sack with 'Den Danska Bank' printed in gold on one side. These were to be used as raincoats in the event of wet weather. I noticed that my sack had a hole cut for my head, but there were no holes for my arms.

The moment the lights flooded the stage it began to rain. In unison, each member of the audience (about 500 people) rose, fumbled with their bags and struggled to get them over their heads. The head hole found, the rustle of the plastic increased in volume. The crescendo was caused by the collective desire to find armholes. A whisper 'no arms' spoken in many different tongues echoed around the arena. Then silent expectation.

The rain fell more heavily and the play began. Hamlet learns of the appearance of a figure on the castle ramparts – a figure which, spot-lit but very ghost-like, moved quietly behind our seats. For a brief moment I forgot I was watching a staged drama! When some moments later the ghost revealed himself to Hamlet with the words

"My hour is almost come…
I am thy father's spirit

54

Revenge his foul and most unnatural murder"

My spine tingled even more.

The rain continued to fall, a gentle rain that thoroughly dampens and seeps into the most waterproof of clothing. But the weather did not discourage either the players, led by Derek Jacobi (Hamlet, director and producer) or the audience.

At the final curtain the players were generously applauded and Jacobi congratulated the audience on braving the weather; whereupon the players clapped the audience.

Unthinkingly we stood up to leave. What had we, as an audience forgotten? Simply this. To take care when moving from a sitting position to a standing one when wearing plastic sacks as protection against the rain. A pool of water had collected in my lap. As I stood up it flowed over my feet and onto the stockinged legs of the lady in the seat in front of mine. Simultaneously the person behind me drenched the one part of my clothing which was still dry – the seat of my trousers.

To a drama of an altogether different kind – which began at the castle of the royal portraits – Gripsholm Slott.

At 3.00 p.m. on August 17th (I forget the year – 1991/2 – but I remember the date because it marks the beginning of the Swedish autumn). Hilary and I were walking by the shore of the lake. Two women were hurrying towards us. They were both in late middle age. Both seemed confused and anxious. They greeted us with the universal phrase, "Do you speak English?" We replied that when the necessity arose, we did.

Together, in duet, they told their story. They were on a Baltic cruise. Today they should have been in Gdansk (Poland) but the port was closed through industrial action by the dock workers. Their tour ship had docked in Stockholm instead and the tour members dispatched by coach to Gripsholm Slott. The tour party were meant to return to Stockholm by private launch. Everybody on the trip had caught the launch – except our two unfortunates.

Their problem was clear: they were in Gripsholm, their ship was in Stockholm 80 km away. It was departing for St. Petersburg in about 5 hours. There was no public transport to Stockholm harbour. All their documents and most of their money were on the ship.

The solution was obvious. I must drive them to Stockholm.

"Where is your ship docked?" I asked.

"We can't remember," replied Mary, a primary school teacher from Litchfield. "We didn't notice. Anyway you can't miss it. It's white with two blue funnels. You're certain to see it. It's such a big ship."

To appreciate the banality of this remark you must appreciate that the waterfront of Stockholm harbour is very extensive indeed.

And I knew nothing about passenger liners and their docking points... and to Stockholm come many 'big ships'.

After some miles, the ladies relaxed a little. Two blue funnels would be easy to find. (In a harbour of 1000 ships and boats of all sizes and shapes?) Mary remarked that she'd only agreed to go on holiday with Jill to make sure she didn't get lost – which apparently she had managed to do every previous time she had been abroad.

When from time to time I asked them to try to solve my problem. Could they try to remember the name of the dock where the ship was waiting, the name of the cruise line... perhaps the ship's name...? There was silence. Then their response. "You can't miss it, it's white with two blue funnels.

I drove into the Stockholm harbour district. It was now 6.00 p.m. and the traffic was heavy. The longer we sat in the slow moving queue the more restless our passengers became...

"Do you think...?"

"What will happen...?"

"I'll never try this sort of holiday again..."

"Are we nearly there?"

The only comments we could make to these observations and questions implied that we believed in miracles.

Then I noticed two police motor cyclists. I signalled to them that I required help. They came to the car. I explained that we had found two English ladies wandering through Gripsholm and that they had 'lost' their ship. The policeman smiled and asked.

"What's the ship called?"

"What is the name of the tour company?"

From the back of the car, as though delivering choral speech at a Welsh Eisteddfod came the response. "The ship is white with two blue funnels."

Perplexed, but obviously having dealt with the English before, one of the policemen sighed sympathetically and said to me. "You have a little problem. There are lots of white ships in Stockholm harbour. Drive straight ahead and follow the signs to the Finnish Ferry. Ask there." Wishing us well, the police departed.

I followed their directions and took the road to the Finnish Ferry. There was a doomed silence from the two ladies. For the first time that afternoon they had come to appreciate the enormity of the quest.

Then a squeal, followed by a scream "There it is. There it is. Stop. Let us get out!"

And there indeed it was, bathed in arc lights, the white ship with two blue funnels. The ladies leapt out and ran at speed towards the gang plank. They paused, shouted their thanks, and disappeared from view.

We later found two 50 dollar notes on the back seat of the car. An unnecessary gesture. They had already paid me – with this story.

If being an English lady caused the police in Sweden to smile, being an English man in Norway produced quite a different effect on shopkeepers.

At the end of a series of August courses we drove on a Jan-designed route across Norway to Trondheim. It took us past a living glacier and a stave church. The church was made completely of wood, each beam highly decorated with Viking motifs and symbols (dragons, twisting snakes). The roof and walls were tiled with wooden shingles.

It was on this journey that a difficult moment almost soured my memories of Norway. I went into the only shop I had seen for 100 km in a little village high in the mountains. I needed some fruit juice, biscuits and chocolate. There were several people waiting to be served and three others followed me in. There was one old, rather frail lady serving and she greeted each new customer warmly and completely ignored me. When I was the only person left in the shop, she glanced at me and said in Norwegian "I don't serve Germans."

I was taken aback because in all my trips to Scandinavia I had never met such blatant discrimination.

"That's fine by me," I said in English. "I'm from London. England." The lady's face broke into a warm smile. Apologising for her thoughtlessness she served me with the goods I asked for and packed them neatly in a bag. She then wished me well, apologised a second time and refused to accept payment. Although it is sad that bitter memories of World War II continue to bedevil Europe, it is all too easy to be judgemental. What did I know of the horrors that this elderly lady might have suffered during the occupation?

A castle in Bergen, Norway provided me with the rare opportunity to behave unconventionally.

57

Bergen is one of Northern Europe's prettiest towns, snuggling between hills at the end of a fiord. Its many picturesque wooden-frame houses painted in shades of red and yellow date from the time when the town was a member of the Hanseatic League. The Hanse were mainly German merchants who established an organisation in the 13th and early 14th centuries to control trade in the Baltic (a very early example of an European Trading Community).

A feature of the harbour was the fish market which was busy throughout the day selling all manner of freshly caught fish. To the right of the fish market was the castle, its curtain wall brightly decorated with banners advertising a music festival featuring the works of Edward Grieg. His villa, just outside the town has become a national shrine.

We entered the castle through a gateway in the bannered wall. In front of the solid keep on the far side of the courtyard was the ticket office. In front of the ticket office was a smallish man (about 1.5 m) dressed in a black track suit with white trainers. His skin was rather darker than that of most Norwegians. His head carried a thick mop of black hair.

It was not his appearance that intrigued me. It was his behaviour. His hands were close by his sides, his legs tight together and he was bouncing up and down without pausing or changing his speed. His bounce had the regularity and precision of a metronome.

Feeling extravagant. I decided to try to learn for myself the secret of the 'Bergen Bounce'. Putting down my camera I walked to where the Bergen Bounce was in progress. I stood facing the Bounce. After a few moments, having studied his bouncing mode, I bounced too.

He bounced.

I bounced.

Our initial bounces did not quite synchronise, but gradually, as my sense of rhythm improved, our joint bounce became as one.

He bounced on.

I bounced on.

All that could be heard in the castle courtyard was the sound of feet on stone…

I decided the time had come to ask why he behaved like this. But before I could ask such a provocative question, I began with my usual query:

"Do you speak English?"

"I avoid even *thinking* in English" he replied.

"And why should that be."

"You see I work in the castle. If I as much as think in English, I bounce."

And to prove that English caused him to behave oddly he bounced with greater intensity than before.

"How do bouncing, the castle and English relate to each other?" I was bouncing breathless and puzzled.

"It's easily explained. The passageways in the castle are very low. If I think in English I bounce, and hit my head. It can be very painful."

A small group of tourists looked at us bemused. What could cause two grown men to bounce face-to-face and talk as they did so? I thanked the Bergen Bouncer for his explanation and bounced myself into the castle, followed by a non-bouncing, tolerant and very dignified Hilary.

We toured the castle. I took some photographs with my camera (which Hilary had retrieved from the courtyard) and made our way to the exit.

He was there bouncing.

Confessing to a battered head caused by English-thinking in confined spaces, I bouncingly bade him farewell.

When I looked back from the castle entrance, he was bouncing.

I'm prepared to believe he is bouncing still!

Not all of our short escapes between courses fell within Jan's description of tourist attractions: "honey pots." We visited European/Scandinavian Book Fairs in Göteborg (at one of which I delivered a paper) watched over Jan's trade stands at Stockholm and Göteborg and at a 'Maths Fair' at Gävle, met Finnish educators in Helsinki (where we also ran courses) and enjoyed a private tour of the Lego headquarters at Billund in Denmark.

The journey to Billund on the western side of the Danish peninsular was hair-raising. It began after a course in the south of Sweden. We caught a ferry from Helsingborg to Helsingör (Denmark) – the busiest ferry crossing in Europe and particularly busy on the evening we used it. We eventually boarded the ferry at 6.00 p.m. It was raining. We had to drive without break to catch a second ferry on the far side of the very large island on which Helsingör stands. Every other motorist on the road seemed to want to catch it too! Rain continued to fall, at first gently, later like a monsoon. We finally reached the Lego Company's private hotel at 1.00 a.m. to be greeted by a nightwatchman and his unfriendly Alsatian guard dog.

The only good thing about the evening was our accommodation – bedrooms of great comfort and elegance. At breakfast we were overwhelmed with food – there was enough to sustain a small army. At 9.00 a.m. we were escorted to the main offices. At the entrance were three flag poles – at one flew the flag of Denmark, the second flew the flag of Sweden and the third flew the flag of the United Kingdom. Jan thought this a proud moment for "his little company."

We were visiting Billund as a consequence of a competition I was helping to organise for U.K. schoolchildren… Lego were in the process of introducing power units to their range and as the competition was based upon the theme of energy, it seemed appropriate to the sponsors that I visit Billund.

Alongside the design and 'new products' workshops were studios where giant models were created – the type of models which are displayed in the windows of departmental stores.

We were also given tickets to use at the nearby Lego theme park, an area full of working models, water-rides and train trips. It wasn't my idea of a rewarding afternoon, but it was interesting to watch children's reactions to the activities on offer.

If I learned anything from my visits to Sweden over a period of 20 years, it is this. Never comment with authority about a country not your own until you have met a range of its people from a variety of social backgrounds employed in different parts of the country; all this across a long period of time and in different seasons of the year.

As the British Council representative told me, "Meet a Swede that you vaguely know in the street on a cold winter's day and he'll walk by without acknowledging your presence. Pass him in the street in midsummer and he'll ask you to join him for coffee." The diplomat's observation carries more than a grain of truth: but it is still a generalisation. My stories should be read with a similar caveat. Don't expect every Norwegian to bounce or every estranged Swedish wife to keep a hamster.

Hopefully they also have a wider purpose, a purpose beyond a record of strange happenings. They also illustrate the way in which Scandinavian peoples view the world – balanced as they are between East and West on the very edge of Europe. The articulate presentation of a Scandinavian view of the world helps redress the entrenched attitudes so often adopted by their more powerful neighbours – France, Germany and Great Britain.

The polarisation of small states around the Great Powers has, over centuries, failed to bring lasting peace in Europe. Perhaps the world would be a safer place if its major powers took the ideals and social-consciousness of the Nordic fringe a little more seriously.

The Negotiators have something to teach us...

If only we could find the time to listen.

2. New York, 1966

May 1966. The Pan-Am jet in which I was travelling was coasting through low cloud. The air stewardess ran through her usual catalogue of pre-landing procedures. We would be on the ground, she assured us, in ten minutes.

I felt like a secret agent in a poorly written adventure story. To enable my host, Tad Girdler (a young and aspiring executive in the Binney and Smith Corporation) to identify me, I had in my cabin luggage a singularly large 'B&S' carrier bag. After passing through US immigration and customs, I was to make for the exit, my bag clearly visible. Hopefully Tad, clutching an identical green and yellow bag, would, as in some TV soap, sidle up and 'make himself known.'

The plan was simple. But what if something went wrong? Perhaps Tad wouldn't be there. What then? I had some dollars and a contact address in Connecticut but no experience of coping alone in a foreign land, even if the foreigners spoke a kind of bastard English! My imagination took over. What if the two plastic bags did meet – and what if the meeting, by its unconventional nature, attracted the attention of the airport police?

The plane landed, its passengers shepherded through immigration. My passport and visa were examined and stamped, my bags collected from the carousel and customs negotiated. And so I emerged, a little tired after my journey, into the scrum of the arrivals concourse. Far in the distance, on a balcony above 'the meeters and greeters' (to use an American idiom), I saw a diminutive figure waving a 'B&S' bag.

I responded enthusiastically and with relief, holding my bag above my head with both hands, my suitcase propped between my legs. Other travellers milled around me, equally self absorbed, many of them, like me, trying to identify a person they had never met before. Some carried rough boards bearing unlikely names, handwritten in crude capitals. One 'greeter' held a somewhat battered bunch of pink roses. A romance, I wondered, or a plea for forgiveness? A fellow traveller from London paused to take a small teddy bear from his hand luggage. I looked round briefly but I could see no bear-holders looking for a match. Some people scanned every passing face with a manic intensity, hoping that Aunt Mavis or

'Young Bobby' looked much the same now as they did when they last met 15 years ago. Over the hubbub of hurrying feet and cries of recognition and greeting, the tannoy droned on and on, providing a demented verbal overture to many an individual drama. After some minutes I found myself by the exit doors of the terminal building. There was a tap on my arm. Our bags met. "Hello Henry", said Tad.

We made our way to Tad's car which he had left in the short-stay car park. As we walked we explored common ground by exchanging those little intimacies that strangers make to each other on first meeting, intimacies which might serve to ease the hours and days ahead.

Tad found the car. Found is a significant verb, for Tad's red, two seater M.G. was hidden, dwarfed by the station wagons which were parked around it. These wagons, like most things American, were enormous, their heavy bull-bars, double exhaust pipes, giant tyres and mounted spots boasting of power and speed.

Tad told me that he lived in a 'condominium', an estate of expensive and exclusive houses just outside the town of Hartford, Connecticut. A condominium was a private estate with a perimeter wall and entered through a road watched over by a porter's lodge which was the security base for the whole estate.

The journey was not a long one. After a brief pause for coffee in a road-side diner on the outskirts of New York we took the freeway bound for Hartford. Tad had been fully briefed on the reason for my visit. Earlier in the year I had been commissioned to write a book for B.T. Batsford on ways in which wax crayons can be used for a wide range of art processes. I had been exploring the use of crayons with my class (and the after-school art club) at the school in which I was then teaching – John Ruskin Primary, in Southwark, South London. I wrote about my findings in 'The Teachers' World', at that time a flourishing magazine.

My writings and the commercial implications they had for crayon manufacturers attracted the attention of the Managing Director of a large company, (then known as 'Cosmic', now Binney and Smith), based in Bedford. Eric Clayton, its MD, was a shrewd businessman whose ways of working were far too complex and calculating for me, a simple teacher, to follow. He realised the value of my column to his company, and invited me to meet him for dinner in the Savoy Hotel, London. At this and subsequent dinner dates he arranged for me to receive, free of charge, as much material as I needed – for my classroom, for the photographs which supported my writing, and for the lectures which I was regularly giving to teachers at the London Institute of Education and at Teachers' Centres across the country. The literature and packets of crayons which I gave to the teachers who came to my talks made me very popular!

I should perhaps add here that at this time (1963–66) I was also preparing teaching material for all the principal school arts suppliers – Arnolds, Dryad, Harbutts, Reeves, Rowney, Windsor and Newton and Eagle Pencils. My relationship with these firms was limited to single commissions, whereas my involvement with 'Cosmic' was on a much more regular basis. For example, I was sufficiently trusted to be given samples of as yet unreleased materials and invited to 'test' them at school. Sometimes I was shown new techniques discovered by one of the 'Cosmic' reps on their visits to schools. As 'Cosmic' marketed chalks, crayons, paint and acrylic colours, my store of ideas was continually growing.

Eric Clayton and his Sales Manager (a swarthy rotund gentleman with the unlikely name of Parsee) had one big idea they wished to develop, mould-breaking in its time – practical 'hands-on' courses for small groups of infant and junior school teachers. These 'workshops' (a new term) were arranged in the early evenings or at weekends, and were at first confined to schools in and around Bedford. They were modelled on a scheme pioneered by Binney and Smith in the United States.

Just before Christmas 1965 I was invited to join Eric Clayton, his wife and members of his management team for dinner at 'The Kensington Park Hotel'. Incidentally, and quite gently, Eric "wondered out loud" (as he later put it) whether I would consider joining 'Cosmic' as an art consultant. The advantages of such a move were stressed – personal autonomy within a new 'company team', a much higher salary, expenses, private health cover, a company car… I have had no subsequent doubts that the decision I took was the correct one – to stay in mainstream teaching and to write and lecture as an 'extra'. Some months later an art consultant, Guy Scott, was appointed. He stayed with the company until reorganisation caused his section to close (and Guy to become redundant).

Eric Clayton was perceptive enough to realise that I was very unsure at the prospect of committing myself to the commercial world. However he appreciated that the Crayon book I was preparing for Batsford was of interest to his company. He suggested that I might pick up even more ideas in the United States. There was to be an Art and Craft Consultants' seminar "near Riverhead, Long Island from late May thru early June" (1966). Would I care to go?

There were no conditions attached to the offer – a programme of school visits arranged through Binney and Smith, free accommodation, air and travel expenses and a 'dollar grant' so that I would not be out of pocket. It was too good an opportunity to miss. I applied for, and was granted, eight days' leave from my teaching post which together with the week-long half-term holiday which ran on from my official absence, gave me a 16 days study trip to New York and the New England States (and I had two extra days to cover the flights.)

Tad Girdler was aware of my background, the reasons for Eric Clayton arranging the visit and meeting the costs. He also knew that I had rejected the offer of a full-time position with the company. I tried to explain to Tad the doubts I had about my ability to cope in the world of big business. My excuses must have sounded very lame to an American whose culture was dominated by the doctrine of upward mobility fuelled by an ever-rising income. I hoped that Eric had not encouraged Tad to lean on me to try to make me change my mind.

The MG attracted considerable attention as it sped along the freeways. The drivers of trucks, buses and even cars, smiled down at us. It took me some time to adjust to being in the smallest vehicle on the road. The seat held me in an almost prone position, my body parallel to the road – and only a few inches above it. I've never managed to feel comfortable in low slung sports cars. On returning to England I 'experienced' a Ferrari. It was just like the MG… a heart churning and bottom throbbing experience.

This was to be the first of a number of trips to the United States. My initial impression, repeatedly confirmed, is that the beauty of the natural world is less valued than the tasteless neon advertisements which flash and shine along freeway, road and street. To my knowledge there is no State or Federal authority that controls the height and position of bill boards. On our journey every burger bar, motel and restaurant seemed to proclaim the superior quality of its fare for several miles before it was reached… and then a new series of bill boards took over to try to tempt us into the bar immediately ahead. Add to these eating and rest room signs the advertisements for drinks, cosmetics, cigarettes, lingerie, cars, chocolates and petrol which sprung up around them visual squalor becomes the backcloth to everyday life.

We reached Tad's house late in the evening. It was situated on a private, wooded estate, each house in an unfenced spot, invisible to its neighbour. In fact there were two parts to 'The Girdler Residence', one where the family lived (Tad, his wife and young son) the second consisted of a nursery and a spacious guest apartment. I was impressed by the quality of the two buildings and the sensitive way all the properties on the condominium had been set within the woodland. Despite the incursions made by humankind, their cars, their portable radios, their very presence, wild life was thriving – insects, butterflies, small amphibians, mammals, birds. Most of the species were new to me… but I quickly came to recognise the American Robin. Like all things American he was at least three times bigger than his English namesake.

Tad's task was to orientate me, to explain the thinking behind the programme which had been prepared, and to answer any questions I might have on the administration and delivery of the education service in the United States. He explained how Federal Laws affected school autonomy at State level, the expectations parents had of Kindergarten, Elementary and Junior and Senior High School and of University programmes for teacher training. It was Tad that introduced me to the phrase "He did well in all his grades". The trust which parents and teachers had in the yearly academic 'weighing' of each student ('thru 1st grade to grade 12') was simplistic and naïve.

A spring interjection. The grading model came to England with the 1988 Education Reform Act. It currently operates in England – though not in Scotland, the Scots being far too canny to allow their schools or their pupils to be crippled by such a system.

To return to Tad. He explained that during my first week I would visit a number of schools in contrasting school districts and one university campus. These institutions were spread across the Eastern Seaboard , many miles apart. I would be collected on Sunday night – it was now Thursday – by a Binney and Smith Sales rep accommodated overnight in a motel in preparation for my visit to two schools on Monday. At the end of each day the pattern was repeated… driven to a motel (on one occasion 400 miles from the school I was visiting), and deposited – to be collected next day by another rep who would repeat the manoeuvre – school visits, drive, motel, drop. The whole week was so organised and it is therefore appropriate that I summarise my impressions.

Firstly I found the great majority of the schools to be too large and physically overwhelming. (See 'New York, the urban challenge').

There were buildings which reflected a creative architect's response by providing a visually stimulating environment in which children could learn and teachers could teach *effectively*. Most school buildings were characterised by wide, echoing, brick-faced, pictureless corridors. The doors which ran along each side gave entry to sterile 'boxes' in which students would spend their timetabled days; doors and corridors periodically came to life when at the staccato of an electric bell pupils and teachers swept through them, en masse and very noisily to their next subject lesson. At these moments of corporate movement a disembodied voice over the school tannoy system would invite Simon Ludvinski of Class 10 to the office, or urge Ms. Paddock "to repair to the faculty room immediately."

When empty of students, the majority of corridors I explored encapsulated the feeling of a nineteenth century institution (workhouse, infirmary, barrack block or detention centre). This impression was supported by the stale smell of passing humanity, the subtle odour of wet clothes and unwashed games kit and the hint of decaying food, which seemed to ooze from the cold, battered, unpainted student lockers which stood alongside each classroom door.

There was little student/pupil movement during lesson time. The teachers I had been invited to meet and to watch had been selected because they were knowledgeable and interesting and had the ability to control extrovert adolescents or bubbly first graders.

A second image stays with me. The Art-Cart Teacher.

To reduce expenditure on art materials and to obviate the need for a room specifically designated to the visual arts, a number of schools (Elementary and Junior High) had introduced the Art-Cart.

The Art-Cart was a large wooden four-wheeled trolley designed to carry all that might be needed to give a regulation 40 minute art lesson to a class of 30... brushes, paintblocks, water pots, crayons, chalks and mixing trays together with a supply of paper of a particular size. It had to be small enough to fit on a single desk top and large enough to occupy an 11 year old for 30 minutes. (At least five minutes at the beginning of every lesson I observed was spent looking for last week's painting... 'to finish'... It was rarely found.)

The cameo which follows was repeated in every lesson in every school I visited where the Art-Cart was in use.

Child, gently critical:

"This is the third time my painting has been lost this semester"

Teacher, guiltily:

"I'm sorry, Natalie. It's very difficult to look after so many paintings from so many students"

Child:

"Shall I start again then?"

Teacher, buying Child's co-operation:

"Choose the paper and materials you would like to use…"

Child:

"If she loses this one I'll…"

Five minutes before the lesson ends I notice that Natalie, unhappy with her latest efforts, is slyly depositing it in a bin marked 'garbage'.

Natalie's actions are well concealed. The room is a hive of neurotic activity. Paintings are being collected, damp, dry or dripping and laid one upon another in a folder; the desks are wiped; pots emptied; brushes, many paint-laden, are dropped into the Art-Cart jug. The bell rings and the students pour into the corridor followed by the Art-Cart teacher pushing the cart somewhat irregularly to her next class – and to the several Natalies it will doubtless contain.

The Art-Cart also carried with it the power of transformation. At the beginning of each day it was impossible to distinguish an Art-Cart teacher from her colleagues. All the lady members of the 'teaching faculty' were smartly dressed with carefully styled hair and make up that would "do a Revlon girl proud".

At the end of each period the specialist teachers (at both elementary and junior high grades) looked as cool and self possessed as they had been when they first entered school. But there was a change in the appearance of the Art-Cart teacher. Somehow she was degenerating. After five lessons hair had escaped from bow, clips and comb, the make up had decayed, the dress awry, hands paint-spattered, voice intense, eyes wandering and wild.

After the final lesson the Art-Cart teacher would be seen zig-zagging back to base. Were the path taken repeated on a freeway in a car the driver would be charged with 'driving without due care'.

So the Art-Cart did not impress me – either as a means of carrying paint from one place to another, as a means of encouraging young people to enjoy art or as a means of preserving the sanity of teachers!

One Kindergarten deserves mention. It was in the centre of a small settlement some 6 miles from Springfield, Massachusetts. The class occupied the ground floor of 'The Old School House', a historic

Colonial style building with wooden 'Essex' cladding, a stepped veranda and shuttered windows. Nestling in a clearing and surrounded by mature oaks, the school site was atmospheric and appealing. A brass plaque by the door recorded its first use as a school – some 100 years ago.

I went into the school, through a lobby where hats and coats were hung and entered a large room, each wall broken by two enormous Georgian-style windows. The walls, floor and ceiling were all of wood.

Sitting in a corner of the room on low benches was the Kindergarten. Twenty under-sevens. An elderly lady was talking to them in that strange stilted way that serves only to alienate and patronise. "And then if we are *very*, very good…" There was a second adult in the room, equally worn by the passage of time. Both wore black dresses made to look less funereal by the addition of white cuffs and collars. It was the sort of dress worn by waitresses employed by the Lyon's Corner Houses in London's West End in the 1930s.

"Mary had a little lamb…" Edith began, conducting the children with her right hand. They were about to open their mouths when Edith caught sight of me. "Oh I forgot to tell you. Silly me! We have a visitor today, all the way from London. We know a rhyme about a pussy cat who went to London to see the Queen, don't we?" There was a nodded mix of agreement and ignorance of both Queen and London. The children looked like every group of six year olds I'd previously met – bright eyed, curious, itching to be active. But under the grey hair and pale blue eyes of Edith and Martha (her assistant) the class were wary and watchful.

A sudden change of activity. "As we have a visitor I think you could play outside. Martha will look after you…" there was an audible sigh of relief as the children escaped to temporary freedom.

"I can't guess why they have sent you to me", said Edith. She surveyed the room . But I'll miss all this when I retire next year." I glanced around the room looking for 'all this'. In one corner stood an elderly, scratched upright piano, in another the 'Stars and Stripes', on one wall a dusty, curling drawing of President Washington; close by it and almost overlapping, a Mercator projection of the world. There were a few picture books in a home made bookcase, some battered and well used toys, a brick box… on the floor beneath Washington, was a pile of tired paintings. The furniture was scruffy, the room clean but lacking human warmth.

eat lunch. So we bought food daily at the delicatessen and went to the nearest open space to eat. The nearest open space which had seats was the city cemetery. We were respectful, only sitting in those parts which were the preserve of the long-dead, and we always avoided funeral parties. As a course member observed. "The English have strange eating habits".

So for every Swede the word 'naturen' (nature) has a special resonance. To me it also carries a certain frissance. On one of our earliest courses a young lady teacher approached me. Could she paint 'in the nature' she asked. Seeing my confusion, but not knowing the cause, she explained 'out of doors', (not as I thought 'Eve-like'). But then my misunderstanding could be excused, for many an Adam and Eve are to be found by lake, sea and river.

I naturen can be carried to extremes. Hilary and I chanced to find two elderly pensioners deep in a wood, far from a made up road. As happy as the local nymphs and fairies, they were enthusiastically washing their equally elderly Volvo (all the necessary materials and the water having been carried from their home). We crept by, ashamed of our intrusion on so magical a moment!

The short summers and the long winters, encourage the Swedes, especially the women-folk, to worship the sun. To drink in its rays, she will find a place to sit, shut her eyes and – motionless – gaze upwards at the sun. Should you find groups of tourists behaving like this, you can assume they come from Scandinavia.

Most of the Swedes I met were professed animal lovers. This love was manifest in many ways. Replacement of husband with hamster (see above) is not very common, but *kanin hoppning* (rabbit jumping) is more widely practised. (I suppose *kanin hoppning* is the sport you follow if you enjoy show jumping but can't afford a horse).

We were in Stockholm, employed by a deputy headteacher to run an art course. We had run several courses in the school and knew Inger well. We had also worked with her husband, Bo, a headmaster in another district. As often happened, we were invited to their house for supper. It was mid-February.

Inger and Bo had two daughters – eighteen year old Elizabet and Annika, eleven. They lived in a small house set in a tiny garden. During the evening Annika asked whether we were interested in rabbits as she had some to show us – "there's one" she said, "that jumps".

We put on our coats and went outside. In a corner of the patio was the cage and somewhere in the cage was the jumping rabbit.

"You see", Edith continued, "I've spent most of my life here. I came to the Elementary (grades) in this very room. Sat over on that side with the other girls." She waved her hand to the left in a vague way and paused. I realised she was reminiscing and waited for her to continue. "Then I went through the High Schools and into Teacher Training. That was in New York. Only time I've been away from Springfield. Never been back to New York or visited places like Washington... Sometimes I wish I'd been more venturesome. It's too late to change now."

"Oh yes. When I came back from getting my teacher qualification – the Fall of 1928 by my reckoning – there was a job here, in the Kindergarten, in this room. Been here ever since. You must think it strange – but I lived with my parents. When they passed on I took over the house. So you can see I'm a Springfield girl through and through."

"I listen to all these new educational ideas. But I say Springfield and its children haven't changed much since I was at school. So in here," she surveyed the room proudly, "things are much as they always were." She turned and summoned Martha and the children back into the room.

They sat meekly waiting for the recitations to recommence under the even bluer eyes and whiter hair of Martha. My final memories of the visit remain. As Martha bid me goodbye, the pussy cat was telling of London, the mouse, the chair and the Queen... even at a distance the children's voices evoked boredom born of repetition. Or was I hearing a ghostly chorus of all the children who had experienced decades of Edith's 'traditional' care?

I hope I left Edith with the feeling that the visit had proved of use to me. It had. There are probably a number of Ediths and Marthas (or Franks and Johns) in the teaching force of every developed nation in the world. Edith was proud – and rightly so – of her devotion to Springfield's five-year olds. She would soon be retiring after 40 years service. A question remains with me. Should she claim 40 years teaching experience or 1 year of experience repeated 40 times?

I left Springfield, its 'Old School House', Martha, Edith and 20 children cocooned in an educational time warp. The experience presented me with a philosophical challenge. Was I wrong to feel so discomforted by the visit? I felt the age of the children made them vulnerable within a regime which, though not particularly repressive or cruel, was extremely depressing and devaluing of childhood.

A memory of quite a different kind, unconnected with schools and schooling, also stays with me, a memory of life 'in the raw'.

A neighbour of Tad – I'll call her Mary – was to be married in her own home on the first Saturday of my visit. A local priest had been booked to conduct the ceremony. As a house guest of Tad I was invited to attend.

At 3 o'clock the wedding party assembled. The priest arrived and then the groom. But where was Mary? She had gone to the local Mall (Shopping Centre) to buy some additional flowers just after twelve noon and nobody had seen her since. Her station wagon was not in the garage, so she had not returned home.

At 3.30 the police were phoned. Tom, her husband-to-be, was given the briefest of information... she was safe and well, in no trouble of any kind and was simply "helping the police with their enquiries". (Remember this happened in 1966 when there were no mobile phones and all calls were made via fixed phone points.)

An hour later, Mary, visibly shaken and far from bride-like, returned home in a police car, aided by a lady police officer, and slowly recounted her story.

She had collected the flowers, as arranged. Driving home, she decided to 'fill up with gas' at the local petrol station, a filling station whose owner knew her well. She filled the tank and walked into the forecourt shop to pay. The proprietor took the proffered 50 dollar bill, held it to the sunlight, fingered it enquiringly and said. "Mary you've a problem. As you were walking in here to pay I saw a man climb into the back of your car. I'll phone 112 immediately (the police). In the meantime I suggest you look along the magazine shelf... you'll need to go to the car eventually, but go very slowly..."

A disbelieving Mary did as she was told. Fortunately the police arrived and surrounded her car before Mary had left the shop. From the back of the station wagon they pulled a scruffily dressed man whom they promptly arrested. He was later found to be armed with a 12 inch knife. Mary and would-be attacker were then taken to the neighbourhood police station. After making a statement, Mary learned that her car would be required for forensic tests and that she would be 'driven to her marriage' by the police!

She was duly married, as one guest put it "a little behind schedule". When asked why she didn't 'call' to tell her family of her predicament her response was womanly. "Isn't it obvious? I didn't want to upset Tom on his wedding day!"

My final school visit over, I was taken to New York and booked into an expensive hotel on Madison Avenue. Like most first time visitors to New York I was stunned by the height of the buildings, the noise of the traffic, the constant wail of police sirens, the throngs of people who filled the sidewalks and overflowed onto the road. I took in the usual sights – the Statue of Liberty, the United Nations Building, Times Square, Central Park (in daylight), Staten Island.

I attended several meetings with Binney and Smith art consultants and paid a courtesy call to my American publishers, Watson-Gupthill, who had agreed to take my yet-to-be-written crayon book.

I joined the art consultants for their 3 day 'teach-in' on Sunday morning. At the 'teach-in' each consultant was given time to present new processes and techniques using Binney and Smith products. The venue was a pleasant river-front hotel. The weather being fine, we spent most of our discussion time on a large outdoor terrace.

The workshop ended with a theatrical-supper. Both were dramatic! The play, I forget both the title and the writer, was well performed by the local repertory company. Its plot centred upon events following upon the assassination of Lincoln. I much admired the acting of the eponymous hero who said nothing and acted 'dead'. He spent the whole of Act 1 spread-eagled and motionless, draped over the front apron of the stage. I came to the conclusion that his final resting position was the consequence of an untimely trip as he fell rather than bizarre directing.

The supper party was equally theatrical. We assembled in the foyer of a fish restaurant – the eastern seaboard of the United States enjoys a rich and varied stock of fish. All along the wall of the dining area were large aquariums – in all containing some 50–60 Maine Lobsters. They moved sparingly, their feelers twitching, their bodies reflecting a myriad of colours and tones under the spotlights which played upon them.

The principle on which the restaurant operated was straightforward. Before taking a place at table each guest chose the lobster they wished to eat. Taken from the aquarium the unfortunate creature was dropped into boiling water, cooked and prepared for the table. While this was happening, the guest consumed a generous portion of prawn, squid and shrimp. I could not bring myself to be a lobster killer. I excused myself like the coward I sometimes feel I am by developing an instant allergy to lobster and crab. A fish dish was prepared for me instead. So I wasn't responsible for the death of a lobster, only for that of a hake. It was clear I had avoided making a moral choice… no lobster, no supper! My lobster lived only to be consumed by some later guest.

"Some evening" I remarked to Tad. "The deaths of Lincoln and Lobsters." Thirty years later I realise that the union of Lincoln and Lobster would make an intriguing title for this chapter.

A senior executive of the company, Mr. McChesney, a relative of Tad Girdler, had visited the workshop. When he learned in detail of the somewhat hectic programme I had followed, he suggested a change of plans might be appropriate. With a smile he asked whether I would like to visit a real colony rather than remain in a 'rebel state'. His secretary would be happy to change my hotel reservations and re-route my return home via Bermuda. I happily agreed to this change of plan.

On Tuesday evening I was once more in New York. Next morning a taxi took me from my hotel to the Pan-Am building in Manhattan. The Pan-Am building was a high tower block, on the top of which was a heliport. From here passengers were conveyed by helicopter to the international airport. Travel by bus or taxi to the airport had become increasingly difficult. New York roads enjoyed a rush hour which lasted all day and well into the night. The helicopter guaranteed that connections would be made.

I booked my bags through the Pan-Am desk on the ground floor and took the lift to the roof. My passport and tickets checked, I found myself in a 'departure lounge in the sky'. Far below lay New York with its ant-sized inhabitants and its traffic choked streets. My horizon was bounded by the tops of neighbouring skyscrapers. Like unnatural plants, they stretched upwards from the concrete ground in which they were rooted.

An announcement over the tannoy to six passengers making the next flight:

"Good morning and welcome. Before embarking on this flight I would like to advise passengers – on behalf of Captain Kirk and his crew – that one aspect of take-off is unusual. When taking off from a high building such as this in an urban complex, the helicopter has to cope with many small eddies of wind. The helicopter will take off vertically, move to the right over the concourse below and hover. It may, in certain wind conditions drop a little before it stabilises. Do not worry if this should happen. When in the aircraft all baggage must be firmly secured and seat belts worn throughout your flight. Thank you for using the 'quick route' to the terminal. Have a good day."

To encourage passengers to take the idea of 'wind conditions' and 'dropping' seriously, a leaflet was distributed repeating the information with 'dropping' printed in red.

With much screaming of high pitched engines and flurry of rotor blades the inward coming helicopter landed on the roof above us. The passengers, chatting and obviously contented with their flight passed through the lounge and disappeared into the lift.

Our turn. We were ushered onto the roof. The helicopter sat easily on its pad, a man-made dragonfly. Into the cabin. Our hand luggage was taken by the stewardess and stowed away. Then we were stowed away just as securely, the full harness binding us to our seats.

"Good morning and welcome aboard this short flight to New York International Airport." The welcome was followed by flight time, weather condition and that catalogue of instructions on what action to take "in the unlikely event of putting down on water." Somewhere in this passenger briefing, the phrases 'eddies of wind' and 'drop a little' occurred, but so gently were they spoken, they offered no threat.

The engines purred, then roared before they screamed. The blades whirled and the whole machine was enveloped in a cloud of fine dust. The helicopter shuddered, the stewardess pulled the harness straps around her so hard that her knuckles whitened. An apprehensive smile crossed her lips and then she shut her eyes... tightly.

The helicopter rose a few feet. No feelings of anxiety. It rose a little more. I could just see the cross marking the landing pad below me. We gently slipped to the right and without warning fell some twenty floors in the air space between the Pan-Am building and its nearest neighbour.

I was struck with a gut-wrenching fear as people in offices and the windows through which they watched us flew upwards, passing me at incredible speed. The world went up as we went down.

Then a jolt and a judder. The eddies defeated, the helicopter paused as if to take breath. My stomach reunited itself with the rest of my body. At this moment I remember looking through a window into an office. A young secretary was touching up her make-up, an older man looked on amused. Then sanity returned. The pilot took the machine smoothly upwards over the forest of skyscrapers and on to the International Terminal. During the short time that this took, each passenger was invited to complete a questionnaire. Among the questions. 'Rate your enjoyment of the flight'. There were five boxes. A tick in box 1 meant 'very much'. I ticked box 5.

A diversion. This helicopter flight no longer operates. Some years after my 'experience' an outgoing flight from New York centre failed to stabilise. It crashed into the sidewalk, killing all on board. 'Have a good day', the American corporate 'Goodbye' proved to be an ironic farewell to the passengers and crew who took what was to be the last flight from the roof top.

And so to Bermuda where I had been sent to relax after my immersion into 'Education, USA style'. When I landed in Bermuda I knew nothing about the island... a George VI coronation stamp, owned as a child, marked the limit of my knowledge.

On landing I noted that it was hot. The clothes I had brought with me were unsuitable for the climate. Finance being limited I decided to manage with those I had. At the airport exit (the airport was a quaint little building, sporting the Union Flag and some colourful windsocks) I hailed a taxi. It was an open-backed Morris 1000 with a large parasol over the back seat. The driver, his skin almond-coloured from continuous exposure to the sun, greeted me like a long-lost brother and asked me where I wanted to go.

An aside is necessary here. The taxi driver was wearing a smart cotton shirt, khaki shorts with razor sharp creases, knee length socks and sandals. On his head his crowning glory... a wide brimmed straw hat. In contrast I looked as though I had slept in my sports jacket and trousers, my substantial walking shoes were dusty with travel, my shirt damp with perspiration.

"Where to?" the driver asked. My reply was not in keeping with my appearance. "The Elbow Beach Surf Club, please".

My request caused him to shuffle in the dust of the roadside. He looked very puzzled and ill at ease. "You do have a reservation, Sir?" I showed him the papers which Alice, Mr. McChesney's secretary, had given me. It was becoming obvious to me that my Bermudan taxi driver did not see the Surf Club and me (to use a contemporary phrase) 'as an item'.

"You are a guest there, then Sir" he said. "Not working there I mean... only there *are* two entrances..."

I must admit to feeling a little out of place when, bags deposited and thoughtful driver tipped, I approached reception. I gave my name and passed the travel documents given me by Binney and Smith to the desk clerk. The gentleman receptionist, dressed from head to toe in brilliant white (smooth white shirt, sharply creased white shorts, long white socks and white shoes) looked rather like the bullying sergeant-major I feared during the early days of my National Service in Wales.

75

"We do have a room for you, Sir" he said, eyeing me with a mixture of disgust and disbelief. "As you know we entertain many of your company's more important clients. We must honour the reservation made for you."

"However" – diplomatic pause – "I must stress that at the Elbow Beach Surf Club you can only enter the dining room" – he glanced at me – "when... when you are properly dressed. This means white, Bermuda Shorts and suitable socks and footwear. Of course" – he went on, humbling me further – "It's usually black jacket and tie for dinner." Silence.

He looked at me again, a look in which initial disgust slowly turned to pity. "If I can do anything to help...?" As he spoke his voice faded into a whisper. He never completed the sentence.

A diminutive bag-boy helped me to my room, which overlooked a wide sandy beach washed by small blue-green foam-topped breakers. There was no sign of human beings... just the odd seabird.

Back to reality. How best to cope with my problem... the worst dressed man in a luxurious hotel on an island paradise? I decided to explore the area immediately around the hotel, hoping that it may offer a solution to my dilemma.

I slipped past reception and retraced the road the taxi had taken. I came to a road junction around which was a small cluster of houses. One of these houses doubled as a working man's café. It was here that I took all my meals. The local inhabitants were amused that I "slept rich and ate rough." It's the nearest I've ever come to feeling like Hemingway!

I explored Bermuda by taxi and on foot. Car hire was impossible for anybody who had not lived for six unbroken months on the island.

My memories of Bermuda are positive. Forget the embarrassing hotel, my inappropriate dress and the gastronomic limitations of the working men's tearoom. What Bermuda gave me was the taste of an Empire on its death-bed... the expat Englishman county-class, with a stiff upper lip, strangely dressed with crystal-sharp accent and matching lady (debutante c1927); The Queen's Birthday Parade which necessitated the local guard to don uniforms of red and gold and march to patriotic melodies while the Governor, much decorated with military and civic awards, took the salute; the flying of the Union Flag from so many domestic flagpoles.

It intrigued me to discover how many American citizens, many of whom holiday in Bermuda, viewed these things. They were certainly impressed, expressing awe and admiration at our love of tradition.

"Must be great to have a Queen," one said to me as we stood watching the band march by. I think I observed that there was more to Britain than diplomats in fancy dress, old houses, castle ruins, knights and Harrods. "But you look after old things so well. Back home we'd want them all brought up to date."

The tradition of Empire provided a distinct contrast to the natural life of the island, the bits untouched by man. Moonlight, starlight, the copper colours of the sky at dawn and dusk were reflected in the spray of the Atlantic breakers. Shaped by the wind, they spilled and tumbled along the shore, something they had done for a million years. The ebb and flow of the sea provided a constant background, a gentle ground bass to the staccato 'clack-clack' of the cricket-like insects (which slept all day to be better able to chatter all night). The extravagance of the morning and evening skies, all yellowy-red, competed with the massed bougainvillea which flourished across the island... in my memory Bermuda is an island of reds and pinks, tones echoed in the feathers of the flamingo which strut proudly in the ornamental lake in its capital, Hamilton.

On Saturday I left Elbow Beach Surf Club and Bermuda. I doubt that I will ever again make such an unexpected trip. My few days in Bermuda were "such stuff as dreams are made on"... an appropriate quote from Shakespeare's 'The Tempest', said by some to be the legendary island in the play.

In conclusion, I *did* write the book on crayons. It *was* published simultaneously in London and New York and I do hope that Eric Clayton approved of it!

3. New York – the urban challenge 1976

Ten years on. 23rd October 1976. My 45th birthday. Once more I find myself in New York for a week long visit arranged by the New York Urban Coalition (NYUC).

The Coalition had been established in the 1960s with the support of 35 inner-city organisations – banks, business houses and corporate companies – to study middle school education in New York City. Its brief was to analyse problems, note and record successful practice and to offer suggestions for the future. Included within these broad plans was a wish to compare and contrast New York's attempts to find a solution to the rejection of schools by many of its young people with the methods employed in a similarly placed metropolis. London was chosen.

A week long project was designed to bring together educators from the Coalition and from London and the Home Counties to examine specific aspects of inner-city schooling – multi-ethnicity, school management, school-industry partnerships, the setting of social and educational goals and methods of measuring achievement.

A representative of NYUC had visited London a year earlier and following upon this visit, Louis McCagg, the Director of NYUC's education programme, began to make plans for a London delegation to visit New York.

Who were we? It may seem invidious to comment only on the principal personalities among our party. But I will do so.

Leading the London team was Peter Newsam, at this time Deputy Education Officer, Inner London Education Authority (ILEA). Peter subsequently became Education Officer, a post he filled with considerable skill and political dexterity. He brought to London education a freshness of vision and an infectious sense of humour. He was concerned about the quality of experience that schools offered young people. An excellent public speaker he was a true progressive, i.e. schools, whatever methods they employed, should enable each student to *progress* – quickly in subjects in which they were gifted; steadily through a network of support, in subjects which were proving more difficult.

Adam Hopkins, Education Correspondent of the 'Sunday Times' and with whom I had previously worked, represented the press. He kept a diary of each day's events which he later transcribed. It was published, supported by the photographs I took specifically for the purpose, in the ILEA journal 'Contact' (vol.5 issue 25). Adam also used his New York notes as the basis of a number of other press articles. Adam was also a poet. We shared a room at the Harvard Club (our New York base). On several mornings I woke only to find Adam in an impenetrable fog of sleep. Essentially a night person, he had a habit of disappearing at the end of the day's programme for a 'drink and a write'. He said that he composed his most expressive poetry after midnight. Indeed he woke me at 3.00 a.m. one morning and, fortified by the quantities of bourbon he had consumed, insisted that I read "his best poem so far" – a sonnet entitled 'Down and out in Manhattan's Midnight.'

(I think I've remembered the title correctly).

Anne Sofar represented the political dimension. Originally an elected Labour Party representative on ILEA, she later joined the Council for Social Democracy (the forerunner of the Social Democratic Party founded in January 1981 by David Owen and three senior Labour Party colleagues). Anne is possessed of an excellent brain. Quick thinking, her observations were always sharp and pertinent, often focussing upon the problems faced by economically or socially deprived parents when raising children in the inner city.

Michael Marland was a well known face in the world of education in the 1970s. An ebullient character, he was perhaps a member of too many 'committees of enquiry' for his own professional good. Headteacher of an inner-city comprehensive, Michael was convinced that young people should have the opportunity to become involved in the Arts: literature, music, painting, ballet and dance.

Our group had a further 10 members. There were 3 inspectors, 3 teacher-centre wardens, 2 headteachers, 1 housemaster of a residential school and 1 university lecturer.

The five days of the symposium were full, intense and varied. Most days began at 8.00 a.m. with a breakfast held at the office of a sponsor (e.g. the publisher, Harper Row) and were followed by a series of visits to schools. In the evenings there were receptions with a lecture input. Finally – to end the day – we attended a public function. For example, on Tuesday 26th October we were guests at an open session of the Board of Education for New York, a meeting which ended at 10.00 p.m.

The programme of the symposium is before me as I write. I notice that every moment of every day is accounted for – from the moment we appear at a working breakfast to the moment we are free to retire to our beds in the Harvard Club. The timings for Wednesday, October 27th looked like this:

8.00–9.30 a.m.	9.30–10.30 a.m.
10.30–12.30 a.m.	12.30–1.30 p.m. (working lunch)
1.30–2.30 p.m.	2.30–3.00 p.m.
3.00–4.40 p.m.	4.40–7.00 p.m. (working supper)
7.00–7.30 p.m.	7.30–10.00 p.m.

To illustrate this further, the following day (28th) began with an early call (5.30 a.m.) to catch the subway and the 7.00 a.m. ferry boat to Staten Island. On the island we breakfasted with a Parent-Teacher Association in a Junior High School. This particular day ended early, at 8.45 p.m., with a buffet supper provided by the United Federation of Teachers.

It would be too time consuming to list in detail the areas which were discussed. Time has moved on and many a central concern of 1976 has become a peripheral concern today. However some of the issues we confronted remain with us, issues which have not been resolved and which, unchecked, threaten educational progress in the US, the United Kingdom and mainland Europe.

A major concern I leave for Adam Hopkin to outline. Writing in 'Contact' his article, 'A problem city', he begins:

"If you arrived in South Bronx unprepared you might conclude that a civil war had ended within the last half an hour. Rubble and rubbish lie deep among buildings hollowed out by fire. The inhabitants pick their way warily along the streets as if hostilities might begin again at any moment. The poor prey on the poor and nobody is safe."

The consequence of living against a backdrop of squalor, poverty and violence caused – and continues to cause – white middle class and aspiring black and Haitian families to move away from New York, leaving a vacuum into which move the rootless immigrant, the socially and economically feckless, the drug taker, the hardened criminal, the prostitute. As the centres decay, large companies, their offices and administrative headquarters, their factory and workshop premises relocate. Greenfield sites and business parks offer security and pleasanter living and working conditions. Such a drift can quickly become a rush. It has already touched these shores. Many a UK high street is now little more than a pot pourri of charity shops which, like its US equivalent, provides a plentiful supply of shop doorways for dossers and tramps to peacefully spend their days and nights.

Flight from town and city causes the tax base to erode. This had happened to New York in the early 1970s. In 1976 the city was in virtual bankruptcy. The traditional route had been taken to rectify the situation. Of a teaching force of over 58,000 over a quarter had their contracts terminated. Teachers of Art subjects were targeted. Art and Music rooms were closed – in one school I visited the rooms used for the Arts were blocked off with a metal screen. Painting, printing, ceramics, music, sculpture, drama, needlecraft, homecraft, metal work, woodwork and dance were at a stroke removed from the curriculum.

The effect of staff cuts and an austere curriculum was disastrous. It served only to put additional pressure upon an already disenchanted teaching force. It had a similar effect upon the even more disenchanted students. By removing the creative elements of the programme, schools became even less enjoyable. Many students 'voted with their feet', finding the companionship of the streets more attractive than the ordered boredom of school.

A second aspect of New York and its schools which was studied at depth was that of cultural diversity. We examined a centuries old, world-wide 'problem' – could incoming cultures be assimilated into an already established institution (be the institution a nation, a state, a city, a street or a school)? The ethnic composition of New York schools in 1976 almost exactly replicated that of New York State. i.e.

37.4% Black American
1% American Indians
2.2% Oriental (Japanese/Chinese)
23.3% Puerto Rican
4.9% Spanish American
32.1% 'Others' (this included White Americans)

In my opinion it was not racial background or colour which lay at the root of the clash of cultures in New York and its schools. Ability in spoken and written *English* was often the key to earning a wage large enough to support a family. The mother tongue of many of the young people in New York's schools was Spanish.

The city schools taught and measured their students' success in English, the language of the nation state. It follows that if students are speaking English as a second language they are likely to perform less efficiently in tests in which English is a key component. I met children whose heritage was Cervantes (rather than Shakespeare), who could read and write Spanish fluently yet were graded as 'illiterate' on the results of their school tests. I appreciate that to live and work in any state, its citizens must be masters of its language. Nevertheless I am certain that the early devaluing of children was a contributory factor to the schools' very high truancy figures – 47% a day in one school we visited.

Lack of success in school, continual personal failure and the disenchantment with authority which followed, seemed inevitably to lead to petty crime, drug taking, alcoholism and the school malaise which follow in their wake. Away from school and with a private life on the street, young people spoke the 'patois' of their group (be this pure Spanish, Creole, or 'gang-speak'). English was never assimilated – and the impact of this was evident in the workplace. The non English speakers sunk to the bottom strata of the job market. This served to strengthen the feeling among ethnic minorities that their employment was poorly paid and of a low social order *because* of their cultural identity. Poverty of language was never accepted by them or their spokespeople as a factor for their economic isolation.

Beyond this disheartening viewpoint there is a ray of hope – for what I have described above is the cycle of despair (disenchanted children grow into disenchanted adults who produce disenchanted children…).

The ray of hope? Some new thinking. I met a professor of mathematics at Bank Street College who encouraged each of his students to work in their mother tongue. "We think in the language of our birth. You make all scientific study twice as hard if you are continually switching in your mind from one language to another".

A further element served to confuse the ethnic divisions in New York. Before the in-rush of Haitians and Puerto Ricans, black Americans had satisfied the demand for unsophisticated manual labour. The arrival, in growing numbers, of Haitians and Puerto Ricans who were prepared to undercut the wages paid to black Americans, challenged the status quo. There was resentment in the black American community, a resentment which found its way into schools.

So, for a variety of reasons, the streets of New York were threatening. When using the sidewalk or subway, the wise adult always carried two wallets, one with two twenty dollar bills, a few postage stamps, a family picture and a fictitious pocket diary, a second for his/her own money and credit cards. The first wallet was to hand over sweetly to the mugger, 40 dollars being enough to buy off a physical assault; the second wallet was thereby protected. The 'Sunday Times' New York correspondent, a friend of Adam Hopkins, told me he had been saved a beating by using this ploy. "Not one beating, Henry, but three. I've been mugged on average once every two months." He *did* live close to Central Park!

The threat did not stay on the sidewalks. It also came into school. Some months before our visit the teacher union (UTF) published a leaflet entitled 'Security in Schools'. I quote *"Elementary school youngsters are especially prone to kicking and biting. Teachers should also be wary of flying objects: light, movable furniture is a recent favourite... Don't resist the armed robber. Talk slowly, talk softly and avoid quick movements. Many robbers are prone to gratuitous assaults, particularly on teachers. Go down with the first blow and stay down."*

This potential for violence was met by a firm response from the New York School Board and the Police Department. It was not unusual to see two armed police officers pacing the school corridors, their squad car on standby in the yard below. I asked a police officer standing by a boys' 'restroom' why they needed to patrol in pairs. The officer's reply was interrupted by a spotty white adolescent. "Tell them the truth. If you were alone we'd knock you down and take your gear" (gun, telephone, baton etc.).

So teachers had every reason to be apprehensive. The treatment of a young woman teacher, raped in her classroom by two Junior High School boys when she was preparing her morning lesson served as a reminder of the consequences of not taking adequate precautions for one's own safety. The teacher who was sexually assaulted received no compensation, no sickness benefit, no help from her employers. In the view of the School Board she "facilitated the assault by entering an area of the school when police were not on duty."

The difficulties faced by teachers were compounded by the size of the schools – some 2,500 students in each Junior High and around 4,000 in a High School. Experiments in school design had not eased the logistical problems associated with having so many adolescent students sharing so large a campus.

In one school I visited an attempt had been made to reduce education 'repairs' by having every room and every corridor lit with artificial light. It was a school without a single window. No windows meant that the vandals, who entertained themselves by shattering windows in the twilight hours, had no windows to shatter. (In 1975 the New York School Board spent 1 million dollars on 'replacement glazing' i.e. repairing broken windows. The no-windows school certainly saved money, but I found living under strip lighting for half a day truly depressing).

Another Junior High School I visited had been recently built around a simple concept. The architect designed each teaching floor in the style of a large open-plan office. Each floor had its own colour – blue, red, yellow – and each unit of furniture, every door, window frame, carpet, notice board – took the same colour. The huge learning space was divided into teaching 'plots' by the mobile furniture. This was carefully arranged so that movement was possible between one 'plot' and its neighbour and from one side of the room to the other. I watched, transfixed, as over 250 students and their teachers attempted to cope with an architect's solution to the problems and needs of middle years schooling.

The students sat on the yellow chairs at yellow tables, within a space defined by yellow screens, yellow cupboards and yellow bookcases in a yellow hall (the size of an Egyptian Temple). A teacher struggling with her remedial language group sat on a yellow chair while her remedial students draped themselves on a yellow rug at her feet. Nearby her faculty colleague (yellow faculty) struggled to teach object drawing with inadequate materials and inappropriate equipment within a cramped, and far from creative, setting. Behind me I could hear a trainee teacher struggling to make a lesson on 'Our Motherland – Florida' appeal to a class of youngsters from Haiti.

The continuous mutter and buzz from students and teachers provided a background soundscape within which everyone worked. The sound was irritating, but the visual distractions were even more disturbing. What *was* happening in the distant corner of the hall near the yellow stairwell? Was that really Mr. Smith standing on a yellow, wheeled storage unit holding a paper kite in one hand and a balloon in the other?

Imagine this form of 'open learning' happening on all three teaching floors of the school simultaneously. Along one edge of each hall was a space which was used for lunch, with yellow garbage holes in the wall for rubbish, yellow beakers for drinking, yellow cloths for drying hands. On a second side of the hall were restrooms (toilets) for the students and a faculty room for teaching staff.

To me, the whole concept seemed bizarre, ill-conceived and unworkable. The Principal, a gentle, caring man, struggled to keep the project afloat with a team of teachers too battered by the experience to do anything but, zombie-like, follow his lead. Some 6 months after

84

our visit I learned that the Principal had collapsed under the strain and undergone heart surgery... the sad but inevitable consequence of being expected to manage the unmanageable.

In contrast, some projects flourished. The August Martin High School was situated close to Kennedy Airport. In 1971 the airline industry took the lead in an attempt to breathe new life into a failing school. After considerable detailed planning the fuselage of a DC10 passenger jet, fully equipped with seats, galley, wireless intercom, stewards' trolleys, emergency exits, passenger safety cards, seat belts... was erected on the school campus. With logistical, technical and staff support from the industry, the plane became the focus for a curriculum followed by all students – a curriculum to prepare them for employment in the ever-expanding travel industry.

The scheme proved to be a great success, with student applications far exceeding the places available. The school, which I found both professionally and intellectually challenging, followed an academic year of four, ten-week sessions. This was done to keep enthusiasm for learning alive – to have as continuous an input as possible. In its pre-plane existence attendance had often fallen below 50%.

We visited a similar but smaller project, a school within a refurbished Liberty ship, 'The SS John Brown'. Its address? Pier 42, The Hudson River. Here the curriculum was slewed towards training young people for a life at sea – as general ratings, stewards, cooks. The curriculum centred upon seagoing topics – navigation, technology, radio and electronics, stewarding, world trade, shipping law...

Institutions which centred on life and work (like the two featured above) acquired the name 'Magnet Schools'. i.e. schools with a 'key' theme would draw students to them. They were effective and popular in New York at the time of our visit. The problem they caused should not be ignored. Students who were unable to win a place tended to become even more disenchanted and rejected.

To try to resolve the discontent felt by many students and their parents by the sheer size and gargantuan complexity of the New York High Schools, 'schools-within-schools' were established. These were units of around 100 students housed with their own teaching staff within a conventional High School. They were autonomous, following their own curriculum and timetable. These 'mini-schools' gave young people with social and emotional problems the opportunity to re-establish social relationships within a more intimate setting than the giant school complex could provide.

The importance of this was highlighted for me, when, about to talk to a class of 14 year olds in a mini-school, I was told to be very sensitive to my approach. Two of their classmates had been murdered the previous evening in an arson attack upon the tenement block in which they lived – victims of a long running feud between two rival property 'developers'.

It must be apparent from what I have written that the symposium was a vehicle for sharing ideas and insights. It confirmed that there was no one solution to the social disintegration which followed upon inner city decay. Approaches which were effective in one part of the city lacked appeal in a similar community five blocks away. A coherent police and social-work programme seemed to reduce drug taking and alcoholism in some districts but have little impact in others. Ad-hoc parent organisations had turned some schools from ghettos into thriving communities, in others free-wheeling parent activists merely added to the daily problems teachers had to face.

We talk today (spring 2007) of 'joined-up Government', of a solution of problems by uniting a plethora of departments, organisations and agencies. My New York experience would suggest that each school is a unique social unit with its own particular and peculiar strengths and stresses. Its uniqueness means that no one centrally prepared programme can be applied, umbrella-like, to guarantee progress and to resolve problems. What makes a school attractive is its 'specialness' rather than the common features it shares with others.

The final official meeting of the Symposium was held at our 'home base' – the Harvard Club. The meeting ended at about 8.30 p.m. For me the most provoking incident of the visit began to unfold.

A black social worker we had met on one of our visits invited six of us to supper at his home in the South Bronx. We accepted, in the knowledge that his home was in an area of some notoriety and that we would be journeying through it after nightfall.

Ben arranged for us to be picked up by a black taxi driver who was 'known and respected' in the Bronx. The same driver would be available to (and I quote) "care for our return".

We safely navigated the Bronx and arrived at Ben's house at 9.30 p.m. We were introduced to Alice, Ben's wife and their children, all under 14. I was surprised to see the older children helping the younger members of the family to dress. We chatted, drank light beer and cola and waited for Ben to arrive – which he did at about 10.30 p.m. A substantial buffet was served.

The meal over, the children politely excused themselves and returned dressed in more workaday clothes to bid farewell before going out into the streets to play. It was now nearly midnight.

I enquired of Alice whether it was unusual for the children to be up and about at so late an hour. She sat me down, put her hand on my arm as if to reassure, and explained that Ben often worked until late evening. "It's the nature of his work. The streets come alive at night."

"Now", she said, "If our children went to bed at 8.o'clock when would Ben see them? Just at weekends? Is that good?"

"Of course not! So we always eat together as a family when Ben comes home, around 10.o'clock... though the younger ones sometimes have a nap in the early evening. Usually they are all in bed by midnight – and sleep over a little in the morning. I have difficulty in getting them up, serve breakfast and have them catch the school bus at 7.30."

She paused, tapping my arm to emphasise her next point.

"You see Henry, white rules still govern schools, even if most of the kids attending them in New York are black. If schools started at 10 in the morning and went on until later in the day, I'm sure students would attend more regularly."

Then came her most telling remark:

"To understand what makes a person tick, to understand people not your own, you must understand the pattern of mothering of that person, of that community."

"Understand mothering and you will begin to understand the children you are responsible for – as teachers and educators."

Her words were simple and humbling. I've never forgotten them.

My flight to Heathrow did not leave until late on Saturday evening. In the morning, I explored the streets around Times Square. In the afternoon I managed to acquire an excellent grand circle seat at The Metropolitan Opera House... a memorable production of Verdi's 'Il Trovatore.' (This opera should be advertised with a health warning. The 'Anvil Chorus' remained with me for the weeks which followed, its melody and infectious rhythm continually playing in my mind...)

It was a relief to return to the tranquil peace and quiet of a London primary school. In my thoughtful moments I wondered whether our English inner city secondary schools would follow those I had visited in New York...

Was it conceivable that violence, ethnic tension, drugs and truancy would blight our schools too?

In 1976 my questions were, in the main theoretical and academic. And today? I leave such comparisons to you, my reader.

4. A divided Europe – Berlin 1972

There was more than a tinge of apprehension on my part when the military car in which I was travelling finally entered 'Checkpoint Charlie', the gateway through the wall into East Berlin. It was odd that I should find myself here at all, a primary school teacher at an international hot-spot during the tense days of the cold war.

I had come to Berlin to run a practical art course for teachers employed by The Service children's Schools Education Authority (SCSEA). Presumably the invitation for my brief tour was a result of the lectures I had given throughout the 1960s at Teachers' Centres and on University extra-mural courses and my several books on primary school teaching.

Earlier in the day I had seen the wall from the safety of an observation platform in West Berlin. As I stood gazing into the East, my companion and guide, a lieutenant in the British army gave me background information of the kind beloved of tourists.

He told me that 1960 marked a flash point in the relationship between the Great Powers over Berlin. The number of refugees fleeing to the West to escape the repressive regime of the German Democratic Republic escalated to over 5000 over the Easter weekend. To stop this haemorrhaging, Walter Ulbricht, the East German leader decided to prevent further movement to the West. The frontier, where communist East met capitalist West, would be secured with high fences, barbed wire, mine fields, watch towers and guard posts on every possible crossing point into West Germany. In August 1961 the Berlin element of the plan was implemented. Bulldozers created a *cordon sanitaire* by demolishing every building and felling every tree that might obstruct the line of the wall.

An additional precaution was taken to discourage would-be escapees. In all the buildings in close proximity to the wall the windows and doors which faced the West were filled with brick. Viewed from the West the tenements, shops, offices and workshops in East Berlin looked blind, faceless and dead.

By August 13th 1961, East Berlin, occupied by Russia following upon the end of the 1939–45 war, was cut off from the rest of the city (the sectors occupied by Britain, France and USA).

I must have become very preoccupied during Bob's brief history lesson. Most of his words drifted over me. Only one of his remarks fixed in my mind. "It's been here for over ten years. How much longer I wonder?"

Like many another western visitor the wall was casting a strange spell over me. It seemed to exude evil, yet how can an object as inanimate as a wall embody feeling? "Something there is that doesn't love a wall, that wants it down". A knowledge of the poetry of Robert Frost was a comfort!

I realised later that I was experiencing 'the wall effect' – a phrase used to explain the impact the wall made upon western visitors. It stretched away to left and to right. I was transfixed.

The prefabricated concrete blocks from which the wall was fashioned, its barrel-like top, its height (about 4 metres), the mined and gravelled path beyond it, the second wall, a fence of concrete posts and razor wire. United, these simple elements created a landscape more brutal, bleak and threatening than anything I had ever seen. Yet the scene was not static, for as I watched the wall was being tended, fussed over even, by acolytes in green-grey uniforms.

East German border guards gazed at us through binoculars as we stared back at them, an army truck gently reversed into a narrow opening near a block house, a pair of dog handlers chatted by a watch tower, a dispatch rider appeared in a cloud of dust disturbing a flock of crows which flew off, protesting noisily. For a moment it seemed that I had become a bit player in a post-war action movie.

It was when we had left the observation post and walked along the canal path that followed the wall that I realised what Berliners – of both East and West – lived with through every moment of their lives. Tension; a tension emphasised by the crude, white wooden crosses along the canal bank, moving memorials to refugees who had conquered the wall only to be riddled with bullets fired by the guns of their eastern comrades as they swam to freedom.

I suppose my gut reaction to the wall was similar to that of the Archbishop of Canterbury, Rowan Williams who, over 40 years later found the fence which the Israelis have built across Palestine equally inhumane. "It is an horrific representation of fear and anxiety".

The feelings I had about the wall that afternoon in early May were heightened later in the day… but before I describe my journey into East Berlin a little background detail is necessary.

The three allied powers had been unable to prevent the erection of the wall. However they insisted that international treaties gave British, French and American citizens working for their respective governments in West Berlin, the right to enter the Eastern Sector. This "right of passage without let or hindrance" was reluctantly accepted by the Russians and gleefully acted upon by Britain, France and America.

So official visitors, like me, were taken to the only gateway which was open to them, 'Checkpoint Charlie' and driven through.

Dusk was falling when our car halted inside the wall. A border guard stepped forward to look at our papers. We were quickly motioned on, past the guard house and onto the dimly lit, cobbled streets of the Eastern Sector. My first impression was one of dereliction very similar to the blitzed urban landscape of my London childhood. Compared to West Berlin there were very few cars; indeed the East resembled an empty parking lot, housing an occasional Trabent and elderly Lada.

As we left the immediate vicinity of the wall East Berlin began to take shape. We passed hotels and enormous grey tenement buildings. There were few pedestrians, perhaps because there was little reason for anybody to stray out of doors. All the shops were closed, their windows darkened.

Our journey was not purposeless. Common to every overseas lecture tour I have undertaken (1966–2000), my hosts invariably insisted that one evening be given over to entertainment and relaxation. Before I left England I had been asked to list my leisure interests. I replied "Music and Heritage". (How pompous this looks when written down!) My request had unexpected and unwelcome results. I would be taken to a Wagner opera. When told of these plans, my face must have conveyed a mixture of disappointment and despair. The music of Wagner is not beauty to my ear, nor his opera easy on my eye. Tactfully Wagner was replaced with an orchestral concert.

We duly arrived at a concert hall. Leaving our army driver to care for the car, Bob and I went to look for our seats. We found them, in the front row of a narrow balcony at the back of the hall.

The hall, of indeterminate age was somewhat unusual. It was very long and very thin. There was no stage, simply a gently sloping platform. Sounding boards of polished wood patterned wall and ceiling. At the bottom of the apron stood a glistening grand piano and a small platform for the conductor. At first glance it seemed as though the orchestra were somewhat short of space, a supposition which later proved correct.

Just before 8 o'clock the ladies and gentlemen of the orchestra filed onto the stage, picking their way delicately between chairs and music stands. The grand piano trembled, the acoustic board hung over the apron and the musicians like a threatening storm cloud. One prayed that it was fixed securely. The leader appeared to polite applause, followed by the conductor and a diminutive Chinese girl.

It was at this moment that the audience were suddenly overcome with what I can only describe as "seat fatigue". Let me explain. Every member of the audience of some 500 was sitting on an individual chair of gold leafed wood, square backed and tapestry covered… chairs more appropriate to the salons of 18th century Paris, Vienna and St. Petersburg than a modern concert hall.

The conductor must have sensed this corporate discomfort. He waited for what seemed like minutes for the fidgeting audience to settle. Perhaps he realised that considerable personal discipline would be required on everybody's part if the concert was to follow its appointed course.

And its appointed course was unusual. The programme consisted of three piano concertos played by three different soloists. The young Chinese artiste would play Tchaikovsky's Piano Concerto No 1 (in B flat minor) to be followed by Rachmaninov's Piano Concerto No 1 (in F sharp minor) played by an even younger and smaller lad from East Germany. Rachmaninov's Concerto No 2 (in C minor) would conclude the concert, presented by a fifteen stone, barrel-chested and generously-moustached Czech.

The programme notes indicated that intervals of 26 minutes would separate the first and second concertos. Obviously the evening was to be a long one.

The audience arranged its collective bottom on the hard, padded seats, folded its collective spine into the upright embroidered chair backs, wiggled a little and fell silent.

The familiar crash of the opening chords and pianist, orchestra and conductor swept with imperious speed and dramatic action through the first movement.

A pause for polite coughs and general body adjustment?

No!

With a deep sigh and universal relief, the audience stood up as one being – and shook. Legs and arms gyrated; elderly ladies, immaculately dressed, kneaded their bottoms; respectable silver haired, suited gentlemen rubbed their thighs and publicly adjusted their belts and braces. I, too, participated in this unusual example of music and movement, a corporate attempt by each member of the audience to re-connect hips and legs with spine, hip and shoulders.

(Incidentally this pattern of behaviour occurred after every movement in each concerto.)

It was apparent from the very first entry of the piano that the orchestra was equally stressed. The reason was obvious... space, or rather the lack of it. Each member of the orchestra was seated so tightly against his or her neighbour that the slightest unexpected movement would inevitably result in an entanglement of bows or an intertwining of woodwind. Even the soloist was at risk, one leg of the piano resting perilously close to the edge of the apron. The whirling conductor added to the feeling of impending disaster, the sword like movements of his baton threatening the violinists on the front bench with decapitation.

Yet the orchestra performed gloriously: so successful were the musicians in avoiding each other that I concluded that the Philharmonic employed a choreographer as well as a musical director.

The evening over, we returned stiffer and wiser to our car for the return journey through the gloomy streets to the wall and 'Checkpoint Charlie'. The checkpoint lit with yellowy lights, looked like a bizarre stage set. The pervasiveness of the light meant that there were no shadows. I'm sure, like Peter Pan, a shadow is something you only miss when it's not there! The guards seemed ghost-like in smooth, creaseless uniforms, the light removing every fold and neutralising colour. The faces of the guards who looked at our papers and poked their long handled mirrors under our car were blanched, the light making them virtually featureless.

A cursory nod from the guard and our car moved slowly out of the threatening lights of East Berlin into the bright, hopeful lights of the West.

I had little spare time to explore Berlin. I made several journeys on the U-Barn – the underground – for no other reason than I could say I'd experienced public transport.

My driver, an incredibly smart corporal in the RASC, took me to the Brandenburg Gate, beyond which, running eastwards lay the 'Unter den Linden' perhaps the most famous street in Berlin. We also drove to the Kaiser Wilhelm Church. It stands heavily damaged by war, as a cry for reconciliation, a reminder like the ruins of Coventry Cathedral, that it is easy to make war and so much harder to win peace.

The wall, the church, the gate. Each a symbol of Berlin in the latter part of the 20th century. I experienced one other view of Europe past when I stood on a podium in the ruins of the Olympic Stadium.

Here, in 1936, Hitler's belief in the superiority of the Ayrian race was mocked by Jesse Owens. A black athlete, Owens won the 100 and 200 metre sprints, the long jump and a fourth gold medal in the victorious USA 400 m relay team.

During the six days I spent in Berlin, I attempted to establish a friendly relationship with my army driver. Sadly, he remained very distant and taciturn. Indeed he was one of those soldiers, so brainwashed by authority that his responses to his immediate environment could be described as "military". If something inanimate was placed in front of him he would eat it, drink it, polish it, iron it, sweep it or paint it. If the 'object' moved he shot to attention and saluted it. I attributed this to the fact that he had enrolled in the army as a boy soldier and was now nearing the time for his discharge.

In his late 30s he saw no point in wasting good words on a temporary civilian visitor to the Officers' Mess.

However he could not entirely ignore me. When I spoke, he was – out of politeness – forced to respond. His method was simple. Say "Sir" to everything. Some examples

Me."You're very early this morning, Corporal"

C. "Sir?" Said in a falling cadence indicating genuine pleasure at having his promptness acknowledged.

Me."That meeting ended early. You'll surprise everybody at home, being back before five".

C."Sir?" Said somewhat regretfully with a sucking in of breath. The meaning was clear. "That's the last thing I want to do."

Me."Could you please help me move these boxes?"

C."Sir!", spat out like an expletive, indicating that I will because I have to, but it isn't my job.

Me, on saying farewell at the railway station. "Thank you for all your help."

C. "Sir" (very short and sharp, accompanied by clicking heels).

Meaning. "Thank God that's the last I see of him. I hope next week's customer is more exciting."

The station to which I had been driven looked no different from those to be found in most capital cities. It was the train that was special. As I climbed aboard and found a seat I realised that I was about to encounter a further example of how quixotic solutions are used to resolve international problems.

What was the problem? The settlement agreed by the four victorious powers in occupied Germany stipulated that each country would have equal rights of access to Berlin, which lay deep in the

Russian sector. In the early days of the 'Cold War' (June 1947) the Russians attempted to force the three allied powers out of Berlin by denying the passage of people, equipment and food along the road and rail 'corridors' agreed by treaty. West Berlin survived the inconvenience the blockade caused. For nearly a year everything that the city needed was flown in as air freight.

When the corridors reopened (May 1949), the allies decided to emphasise their rights of access by running a train across East Germany to Hanover in the West.

The train on which I travelled consisted of a steam locomotive and three carriages. There were few passengers (apart from me there was an officer in the WRAF in the carriage in which I travelled).

Guarding us was an officer and a complement of armed infantry whose task it was to protect the train and its occupants. Their presence heightened, rather than lowered, tension. The soldiers in combat camouflage and helmets were extremely vigilant, their attention centred on the countryside through which we slowly passed.

At the frontier between West Berlin and the East German Democratic Republic (GDR) the train stopped. The West German locomotive and its crew were replaced by an engine and crew from the East. Whilst this was happening the underneath of each piece of rolling stock was examined by the border guards with great care. Standing nonchalantly by the track were the ubiquitous dog handlers and their far from friendly 'German Shepherds'.

Passengers were little affected by this procedure. I remember holding my passport up for inspection, coat of arms showing. It was not closely examined.

There was a whistle, a shuddering sensation and the train moved slowly westwards across the GDR, halting for some minutes on the outskirts of Magdeburg. Close by the track was a castle-like prison, surrounded by razor-wire barricades which were watched over by guards, high in their wooden towers. It was like a castle owned by a wicked magician, in a book of Victorian fairy stories, a castle whose remembered and re-created image colours nightmares and bad dreams.

At the West German border engine and crew were once more changed, the underneath of the carriages once more inspected. Our papers checked, we chugged slowly into the West.

When the train reached Helmstadt in the Federal Republic I suddenly felt relief. It was not that I had been in any danger in Berlin. It was a relief – a relief from an unspoken thought which had continually surfaced over the week that had just passed… if they decide to suddenly come across the wall. What then?

At Hannover I was met by an army captain dressed in civilian clothes. He clutched a board, somewhat self consciously, with the legend 'Pluckrose' printed large across it. He introduced himself and led me to his car.

Stephen's plan was to drive to Rheindalen, a large military headquarters, to find our quarters and to have dinner in the Officer's mess.

We reached the base, our rooms and eventually the dining room. The dining room was empty apart from two bored waiters and a six piece band. On seeing us the musicians played us to our table, accompanied by a bored waiter, to smoochy, nightclub music.

We ordered a meal. The band played, albeit without much enthusiasm. Silence for a moment. Then a polite cough close by the table. The band leader smiled, bowed low over our table and whispered "Excuse me Sir. Do you need us? You are not proposing to dance after the meal"… (awkward pause) "or are you Sir?"

In silence Stephen surveyed the thirty empty tables, the vacant dance floor, the deserted bar beyond. He paused before replying. The band leader shifted from one leg to the other, growing increasingly uneasy.

"Do you mind not joining me for the last Waltz, Henry? I twisted my ankle last week." On learning he would not be needed the band leader hurried from the table. Reaching the low stage, he snatched up his saxophone, nodded to the man on the drums and positively galloped through two verses of 'God Save the Queen'. During the anthem we stood, the band stood and the soup-carrying waiter stood. Such a strange collective obeisance to the Crown! "Thank God we avoided dancing" said Stephen. "I don't know what my wife would have thought!"

My last few days in West Germany passed uneventfully. I lectured in Geilenkirchen and Bielefeld and recall only one atmospheric incident.

I was invited by Stephen to spend an evening at an RAF station on the Dutch border. We drove in the dusk through swirling, white mist for several miles across marshy meadowland. The road was a good one – straight, smooth and completely lacking in traffic. Then, without warning, the road swung to the right, dipping sharply. As the car braked the mist thickened and beams from the headlights were sucked into the clinging whiteness. The car slowed to walking pace, which was fortunate. A gate blocked the road. From behind the gate and half lit by red warning lights a helmeted figure emerged – armed, in grey-green uniform. It was quite surreal. For a moment I felt as though I was on a time machine, transported into the early 1940s. The spell was broken by the guard commander, for we had just reached the perimeter road of the air base. "Welcome. You were both expected…"

Some years later I was approached by a stranger on Charing Cross Station forecourt. His face looked familiar…

"Hallo Henry, fancy a dance?" It was Stephen now working for the Ministry of Defence!

End piece

The collapse of communism throughout Eastern Europe in the 1980s meant that the German Democratic Republic could no longer function. The wall was breached on November 9th, 1989 and quickly demolished. The two Germanys became one state in 1990.

5. Beyond the Wall – Serbia 1979

In the autumn of 1978 I received an invitation from the British Council to visit Serbia. A programme was suggested. The centre point would be a talk on creativity, illustrated with examples of children's' painting and poetry, presented in a public hall in the centre of Beograd (Belgrade). The Serbian Ministry of Education had asked that I visit primary schools and kindergartens and share my impressions of the programmes they offered with their headteachers and administrators. An additional possibility was suggested by the British Council – to 'gently' enquire about the provisions made for young people who are educationally disadvantaged.

Preparations began with a visit to the British Council Offices in central London. An official outlined the background to my visit – political, social and economic. It was hoped that on my return I would be able to prepare a written report which would indicate ways in which the United Kingdom could offer specific help and assistance to Serbia in the field of 'education in the early years'.

My visit was deliberately focused on Serbia, the most powerful of the semi-autonomous republics which together made up Yugoslavia (i.e. Croatia, Bosnia Herzegovina, Macedonia, and Montenegro). The President of the Republic at this time was General Tito, the leader of the communist partisans who had waged a guerrilla war against the Axis forces (Germany and her allies) throughout the Second World War (1939–45). Tito whose family name was Josip Bronz, became Yugoslav Prime Minister in 1945 and President of the Federal Republic in 1953, a position he enjoyed until his death in 1980. In the early 1990s the republics upon which the Federal Republic was built sought independence. The result was intense ethnic warfare in which many thousands of people were driven from their homes and many more butchered because of their race and creed.

Of course when I went to Serbia all of this was in the future. Looking back, it seems that Yugoslavia could function under Tito. Without him there could only be disintegration.

To return to the main thread of my story!

On May 4th, 1979, just before I was to go to Serbia, Mrs Thatcher and her Conservative party were returned to power at Westminster. I had never been an admirer of the lady or of her educational policies. My feelings for her were coloured by the aggressive attitude she adopted towards me when we met at a reception at my publishers (Evans Bros) on Thursday, December 2nd, 1971; a memorable date, it being the 5th birthday of my younger daughter, Hilary.

Having asked me of my opinion of Middle Schools in England and Wales, she instantly rejected it. Her shrill screech, audible throughout the crowded room, dismissed me as "doctrinaire" and guilty of having all those educational ideas that she, as Secretary of State for Education was determined to root out.

Her impressive verbal assault was followed by a stunned and total silence. Her voice had cut across and terminated every conversation in the room. "Whatever had been said?" was the unspoken question on everybody's lips, to cause so great a tantrum? With a graceless spin she ignored me, bade goodbye to the Directors of Evans Bros (publishers) and swiftly disappeared, her embarrassed entourage trotting off like lambs behind her.

A memorable moment. It's not everyone who can boast of upsetting, in two or three short sentences the future Tory leader: a Tory leader who Mr Norman St.John-Stevas MP called "The Blessed Margaret". It is poignant to observe that St.John-Stevas, a truly gentle and thoughtful man, was appointed Secretary of State for Education in Mrs Thatcher's first cabinet. He, too, upset her and quickly found himself on the back benches. At least I kept my job.

Her outburst aroused the interest of the 7 members of Parliament who witnessed my handbagging. All (Labour and Tory) were sympathetic, observing that I was not to worry because she often behaved like this.

Imagine, then, my thoughts, when 8 days later I received my travel documents for my trip to Belgrade. "Henry Pluckrose, enclosed one single ticket, Heathrow–Belgrade." Had the 'Iron Lady' so good a memory?

A phone call to the British Council eased my fears. The British Embassy in Belgrade had already arranged a return flight.

And so to Beograd (Belgrade) where I was met by James, the British Council representative, an interpreter supplied by my Serbian hosts and a small group of Serbian officials. I shook hands, hoping desperately that I would be able to remember each person's name and function.

There was Vera, a pretty, slim dark-haired lady in her mid-twenties. She oozed elegance and sophistication. "Vera is your interpreter and problem solver. She will be with you for every minute of your (official) time here. This is the first time she has been responsible for a complete ten-day visit. Take comfort. Vera is probably as nervous as you."

Standing close to Vera, but towering above her was Boris. He was introduced as "my driver". Olive skinned, moustachioed with a head of meticulously combed black hair, he wore a neatly cut grey suit. He looked almost too impressive to be merely a driver. When we shook hands he smiled, said nothing and blew quietly through his front teeth.

The third person who was to accompany me throughout my stay was Ivan. Ivan must have been in his late fifties. He had survived the war and was employed by the Serbian Ministry of Education. Compared with Vera and Boris, Ivan looked somewhat down at heel, dressing more like an impoverished office clerk than a senior civil servant. He was thin and decidedly underfed, his thinness being emphasised by his dress. His elderly brown suit (every element of it being too big) was crumpled, his shirt was crumpled, his tie was crumpled. The wisps of grey hair which strayed along the edge of his battered and crumpled brown hat provoked in me a hitherto undiscovered maternal streak. I wanted to encourage him to stand tall, learn to use an iron, visit a hairdresser, employ a tailor to take in his trousers and buy a new cap.

Ivan's handshake was damp and weak, which was the last thing one could say about his voice. Whenever Vera's attentions were elsewhere he spoke to me as if I were a church congregation… in fluent French delivered without a pause at machine-gun speed. (I was later to discover that his one love was beekeeping, *not* children. When I left Serbia to return home he presented me, at the aircraft steps with a 2 kilo jar of runny honey. The stewardess allowed me to carry it aboard smiling at my discomfiture.)

I was surprised that after our brief airport meeting, James left us, promising to contact me about my talk in Belgrade. I was taken to my hotel which was to be my base throughout my stay. My bags deposited in my room, I bid goodnight to Vera, Ivan and Boris in the hotel lobby. Vera and Ivan responded but the quietly whistling Boris smiled quizzically. And remained silent.

Within minutes of returning to my room I faced my first crisis. I suppose the moral of this incident is that one should never trust a strange toilet, a caution not given me by the programme planners. Put simply, the toilet collapsed around me – to my considerable embarrassment. A frantic phone call to the Embassy resulted in a knock on my door and the appearance of a very amused hotel handyman. With extravagant body movements and sweeping hand gestures he indicated that my problem was familiar to him. 'Three', holding up three fingers: 'Two days', holding up two. 'Crash'. He bent his knees, waved his arms and laughed. His limited English added humour to his impromptu mime.

By now it was nearly midnight. The hotel night-manager decided that my problem was best resolved by my transferring to a nearby room, one which had more secure bathroom fitments.

There was no breakfast next morning. I had to leave the hotel to go by car to Câcak, some 55 km south of Belgrade. The dangers of travelling early on an empty stomach in Serbia I was yet to realise.

Waiting for me in the hotel lobby and looking as though they had never left, was the elegant Vera, the crumpled Ivan and the grey-suited, whistling Boris. I was warmly greeted and walked to the car. Boris opened and closed the car doors for each of us as we took our seats in the car. (an imposing black Moskovitch). Certainly Boris was well trained in the arts of the chauffeur.

My first impression of Belgrade was one of grey drabness. If cities have colours (I see Stockholm as yellow, Copenhagen as red, Helsinki as white, Paris as gold and green) then I see Belgrade as sooty-grey. Even the splendid government offices which hinted at past Imperial glory were depressingly dowdy. Every building we passed would have benefited from a coat of paint, almost every window a pane of glass.

The streets, litter rich, were cobbled. Noisy trams (of pre-war vintage) clanked and rattled along the broad boulevards, daring cars, cyclists or pedestrians to get in their way. There were few advertisements to brighten the scene. None were illuminated, all were political. An occasional painted slogan caught the eye, but the overall impression was a city of drab, crumbling, grey uniformity into which Ivan neatly fitted. But did Vera or Boris?

101

Boris drove smoothly and effortlessly. He switched on the car radio, very low, seemingly to accompany his now sibilant whistle; I noticed that we stopped very rarely as we crossed the city. The drivers of other cars invariably gave us space and right of way. Perhaps they were deliberately avoiding us. I did learn, sometime later, that our car had special number plates, indicating a Government car on official business. The plate informed the police – of which there are many – that we should be ignored.

I was anxious to discover as much as I could about the people and places that I was to visit. Many of my questions related to the organisation of Primary schools and Kindergartens. Each question was answered at length by Ivan – pausing periodically to give Vera, twisting round in the front seat, time to translate. Boris said nothing, whistling almost silently to accompany his almost silent radio. We reached Câcak just before 7.30 a.m. If I thought that we were a little early for our 9.00 a.m. appointment with the Mayor, I quickly discovered that we were really just in time.

Meeting the Mayor – or any person of significance in the community – followed a clear ritual. I was taken, accompanied by Vera and Ivan into a reception area in the Town Hall where we were received by the Mayor's senior secretary. There was a short pause, during which time I studied a portrait of President Tito. Young and fresh-faced, resplendent in military uniform, the portrait taken in the distant past became very familiar to me. It was hung in every public room I entered – classroom, dining hall, lobby, bank, café, hotel, garage and store.

A lady clerk entered, carrying a tray. On the tray were glasses, small ones filled to the brim with a clear white liquid which I quickly discovered was the local brandy ('Slivervitch') and larger glasses some containing water, some blackcurrant juice. We were each given three glasses – brandy, water, juice.

It seemed that our formal introductions could only be made after the traditional welcoming ceremony:

1. Raise glass of Brandy, say a word of Serbo-Croat greeting (which I have forgotten) and swallow brandy in one swig.

2. Cool burning throat with water.

3. Recover poise and rediscover neck, thorax and abdomen by repeatedly sipping blackcurrant juice.

Talk could now commence, the lady clerk circulating the while, topping up empty brandy glasses. Taking such a liquid breakfast would be unwise at the best of times. On an empty stomach it would be disastrous. But what could I do? I followed the custom smilingly declining re-fills.

After about half an hour the Senior Secretary indicated that it was time to move on. To meet the Mayor? No! His Deputy must have the honour of meeting us all first. Another lady clerk, another tray of drinks identical to the first, another Serbo-Croat greeting, another ritual swallow. My mind, encouraged by my throat and stomach, told me that I could not participate for much longer. By chance, I noticed that Vera sipped a little water before appearing to drink the brandy. I watched her technique and decided to copy her. The method was a simple one. Drink a little water leaving sufficient in the glass to conceal the brandy which by sleight of hand was quickly poured into the water. Like Vera, I drank from the empty glass, sipped some juice and so fulfilled my role as guest.

And so, promptly at 9 o'clock, to the Mayor. Our party had grown in number. The Senior Secretary and the Deputy Mayor and their immediate entourage followed in our wake.

Once more the drinks, once more the toast, once more my brandy vanished into my water. The time had come for the 'official' part of my visit. The Mayor, through Vera, explained his many responsibilities. Like every Mayor in Serbia he ran all social services and the educational programmes for all young people under 21... a considerable task. Câcak commune had a population of over 50,000 (living in the town and 52 outlying villages) .

After spending an hour with the Mayor and a few moments with the local newspaper and radio reporters (more slivervitch!), Boris returned. With surprising authority and poise Boris announced that the local elementary school was expecting us. We followed him out – somewhat precipitously I thought – and he drove us to the school.

Like many Serbian Elementary (i.e. Primary) Schools, the school that I was to visit worked a shift system, two 'schools' functioning in the same building, the first from 7 a.m. to noon, the second from 12.30 p.m. to 5.30 p.m. The children attending 'Primary School' (i.e. Elementary) were aged between 7–11, although a child not achieving the required level might be 'kept back' for a further year. Each class – age based – was taught wherever possible by the same teacher for 4 years. The training of this 'teacher grade' was very basic and unsophisticated, for their task was defined... the early steps in literacy and numeracy, the learners being led, page by page, through state approved texts. All the teachers I met were women. Mrs V. Lukio, a somewhat sour squat, suited and jewelled doyen of the Communist

Party Federal Government Office observed icily that I was unusual. "Men didn't concern themselves much with young children" (This was in part due to the low social standing which teachers enjoyed).

Quoting from my notes, this school was like all the others I visited. "All the schools were conventional. All training followed a predetermined programme, taught in year groups in box-like classrooms. Apart from potted plants and portraits of Tito, there was little colour in the classrooms – which even for the youngest children were reminiscent of tutorial rooms at college."

To return to my visit. I was once again impressed by Boris. We arrived at the school one minute early, walked past a set of sculptured heads on stone plinths, and into a large office. Boris smiled, gestured us into the centre of the room, blew through his teeth and disappeared.

The reception committee (the School's Deputy Administrator, an English-language teacher, a senior member of the local communist party greeted us) and the drinking ritual began once more.

At 10.30 a.m. we proceeded to the office. More imbibing. By this time my liking for blackcurrant juice had evaporated though my ability to turn brandy into water almost bears comparison with a similar, but reverse feat; the transformation of water into wine at a wedding in Cana in Galilee, two thousand years ago.

To the classrooms in procession. Much standing up of children behind chairs, much puzzlement on my part at the Gradgrind approach to learning and teaching, much translation by Vera. As a writer, I was aghast at the text books. Because the curriculum was so strictly controlled a text book had to be approved by the State Education Council before it could be used in class (clause 6346 of 28/10/60). In contrast, fiction, including that of radical western authors – like Orwell – were not controlled in any way.

My perception of the role of headteacher was also challenged as we moved through the classrooms. I quickly realised that 'headteacher' had little association with 'teaching'. He was essentially an administrator with the task of ensuring that national goals were achieved. (A passing comment here. I am writing this memoir in the spring of 2004. Over 15 years have passed since the Education Reform Act of 1988 which imposed a top-down target-assessed programme into UK schools. We must take care not to become too restrictive and totalitarian as the model beloved of Tito.)

The administrator was about half way through his two term 'mandate'. A mandate lasted 3 years and he could work a maximum of 2 mandates in the school. This 6 year restriction was to prevent the concentration of power in one person's hands ('the cult of the individual'). The principle of mandate applied to most senior posts in medical, education and social services – but not the Presidency of Marshal Tito.

Boris returned, a little flustered, to tell Ivan that the programme had been adjusted so that I could visit a secondary school near by. The Mayor had insisted that I "see innovation." Innovation indeed, for the school was also the base for a community health project.

Close by the school's main entrance were two surgeries and a large waiting room. One surgery, staffed by two doctors and several nurses, attended to the medical needs of parents and children. The second surgery was fully equipped for dentistry and was run by a dentist and two dental nurses.

Now, some 20 minutes behind schedule, we descended on the Kindergarten. Would we make up time by missing the drinks? Vera doubted whether this would happen. "Custom must be respected. In this we are showing courtesy to the staff… and they to us."

And so it was. Brandy, water and blackcurrant juice, talk and a disappearing Boris. The liquid refreshment over, we finally entered the newly-built, beautifully furnished kindergarten. Designed by a Danish architect, both the inside and the outside of the building had been carefully planned. A variety of colours and textures made the walls visually stimulating; the classrooms (or rather the internal spaces) were linked by wide, doorless corridors; the furniture sturdy but bright, light and comfortable. Access to the outside equipment – sand, climbing-frames and large toys – was straightforward. One end of the building catered for very young children (6–12 months), there was a central kitchen where meals were prepared throughout the day, and a number of withdrawal areas where the youngest children could sleep.

These withdrawal areas were very important, for many of the children arrived as early as 5.30 a.m. and stayed until they were collected by their parents between 17.30 p.m. and 18.00 p.m.

I met several parents. One explained that Kindergartens like the one I was visiting – and which cared for her baby son – catered for children aged between 6 months and 7 years, were an essential social provision. "My husband and I both work for about 11 hours a day. Our wages are not high. We could not live on one person's income."

An interesting observation. A Swedish mother, collecting her daughter from a similar Stockholm kindergarten (Dagham) said to me – some years after I had visited Câcak – "these places are essential. We live in a very high wage economy and shop prices are high. We enjoy a good standard of living. My man and I couldn't afford to live as we do if we didn't both work."

The economies of both their nations required labour to maintain them, so the state met provision for child care. Currently, in the UK with its medium wage economy, there is no political commitment to a radical pre-school programme.

During my visit to the Câcak Kindergarten, I obtained an insight into how political ideology and the slogans which underpin it are fed into the school programme.

A group of six year olds were brought together by a teacher. Each child was given a set of clothes and told to change into them. The children dressed in costumes they had been arbitrarily given – one was transformed into a miner, another a nurse. There were costumes for soldiers, a doctor, a patient, a dentist, a group of citizens (identified by the tools of their trade: a broom for street cleaning, garden equipment needed for work on a small holding, a bag a carpenter might carry.)

The children stood in a circle. The teacher recapitulated the role each would play in the 'motherland'.

"Now you are the doctor. To become a doctor you must work hard at school and get good grades. Doctors are important in our society because they help keep our people well and fit for work."

Or again. "Soldiers. We need strong soldiers to defend the country. Pretend we are being attacked by an enemy. Take cover. Fire your rifles."

Another example. "The policeman keeps the traffic moving. He makes sure everybody behaves as a good citizen."

The dressing up was quite unlike any 'free play' I had seen anywhere in the West. Indeed it was quite the reverse of 'free play'. The teacher projected a subtle, political message through the costume and tools. Every word she spoke and every action the children made at her suggestion was weighted to prompt the concept of Serbian nationhood that the state was anxious to emphasise. With hindsight, one might ask what contribution such teaching made to the cultural conflict and ethnic bloodbath which erupted in Yugoslavia in the 1990s.

At 2.00 p.m. my visit was over and it was time for lunch, the only meal I was to have all day. Boris emerged from a café, collected us, patted his stomach to indicate that he at least had been fed and watered, smiled, opened the door for us to climb in, slammed each one authoritively – and drove off. Minutes later we arrived at a smart restaurant where a set meal awaited us. Half of the dishes, which were presented in small individual portions, I was forced to reject. Being allergic to cheese, I had to be very careful over content.

But if questioning the content of a dish which might contain cheese proves problematic in England, in most foreign countries it proves impossible.

"No cheese?" I gently ask indicating a dish of food I think it best to avoid.

"No cheese?" Responds the waiter. "I go get you some. No problem!" Without waiting for my response, the waiter hurries away, returning in seconds with a bowl of powdery cheese. I manage to stop him before every bowl of food near me is cheese-dusted.

I try again. "No cheese in this food?" I ask, slower, firmer, louder.

"Oh, we don't usually put cheese in that dish, Sir. But I can ask cook if he can…"

A third attempt sometimes achieves understanding.

"I cannot, do not, must not eat cheese…"

A smile crosses the waiter's face, "Oh you want no cheese! No problem."

By the time the situation has reached a culinary impasse I notice that the people with whom I am lunching – Vera, Ivan the Kindergaten principal, the Town Mayor and his Deputy, a communist party official and a radio reporter – are not eating. They are watching the waiter and my response to him. Laughing silently they dry their tear-filled eyes on their paper napkins.

With female empathy Vera intervened to break the amused silence. "So you don't eat cheese, Henry? How many times have you had that conversation?"

Lunch over, it being about 3.30 p.m., I was asked to give a live radio interview to the reporter. We stood in the middle of the town square for 'reality' and talked against the noise of passing traffic. Such moments always bothered me, for there was no way of knowing how accurately my English was represented by my interpreter's Serbo-Croat. The foray into sound media was something James had advised me to avoid. But how does one refuse to comment on things 'just seen' when the hosts have been charming and open all day?

Farewells made, we began our drive back to Belgrade. When we reached the outskirts of the city, Boris made a broad detour to drop Ivan and Vera outside their respective blocks of flats. At the entrance to my hotel he smiled and whistled a goodnight. I climbed out of the car and watched the car as it slipped away into the darkening night.

As the hotel restaurant was closed I visited the bar to ask if sandwiches were available. A nod of the head (which means "No") was quickly followed by "but we could share some brandy." The English was immaculate. On hearing the word 'slivervitch' I quickly made my excuses and fled to my room.

The rest of my time in Serbia followed a similar pattern. Each of my days began early and ended late. Each day involved my going to an elementary school, a kindergarten, or a high school – and on one occasion to an adventure camp. Because the education system was organised on a top-down principle, decisions were made by state-run committees and delivered to schools to unquestioningly implement. Whether the recommendations were relevant to the individual children – the clients of these institutions – was rarely considered.

However, drawing upon my experiences from visiting schools in different parts of the Serbian Republic, a number of common strands emerged which I will explore briefly.

All children under 14 were *encouraged* (read 'told') to join the 'Young Pioneers', the young persons' wing of the Communist Party. Once a week 'The Young Pioneers' wore their 'uniform' to school, a bright red triangular scarf wrapped round the neck like an American cow-hand. Each class in every school had a 'Young Pioneer' Leader, who, with the help of the teacher, was expected to develop the social consciousness of the class group. These 'leaders' seemed to be the hidden eyes and ears of authority, watching for and reporting inappropriate behaviour inside and outside the classroom and encouraging a united communal response to any situation that may arise.

At 14+ 'The Young Pioneers' fed into the Youth Wing of the Communist Party where their understanding of Tito's particular brand of Marxism was further developed through lectures, seminars and discussions.

This concentration upon communism, social solidarity and nationhood had a distinctly Serbian flavour. Every school foyer had its own sculpture gallery. Polished grey stone plinths, some 1½ metres high, held the larger-than-life, bronze 'memorial heads' of local Partisans who had died fighting the Nazi troops and their sympathisers in World War II (1939–45).

These 'patriots' or 'heroes' were honoured each time a visitor came to the school. A class of children were assembled in the foyer and the brave deeds of a particular Partisan were recalled. The visitor was then encouraged to take a wreath from the headteacher and reverently place it over the head and shoulders of the chosen hero.

This simple act of wreath-laying gave validity to the message which the governing party, the communists, was seeking to promote. Even foreigners held the Partisans in high regard! And who had been the leader of the Partisans throughout the war and was leader still – none other than, Tito, President of Yugoslavia.

A second common strand was the emphasis on sport. The classroom desks may be falling apart, its windows in need of glazing, but the gymnasium would be spotless and splendid. Each school had a cabinet prominently positioned which held cups, shields, certificates and medals recording its athletic and gymnastic achievements. The Director of the Republican Institute, Mr. Milenovic, justified the excessive concentration upon physical culture by arguing that "Physical development, games of all sorts, encourages intellectual development". Was this, I wondered, the Yugoslav equivalent of saying that the Battle of Waterloo was won on the playing fields of Eton? And is there an iota of truth in either?

Politics – of a specific slant – were embedded in the educational programmes offered to young people growing up in Serbia. Compulsory membership of 'The Young Pioneers', the idealisation of the Partisans, the portrait of Tito in every room in every school were examples of this all pervasive ideology.

Political education was also an important feature of the Summer Camps which most children attended. In 1976, for example, 500 children from Câcak spent 3 weeks in a purpose-built camp on the Adriatic Coast. All 500 aged between 7 and 14 moved to and from the camp as one group… an operation requiring meticulous planning, particularly as similar sized groups were leaving other major towns at the same time to undertake a similar programme. I visited an 'outdoor adventure centre' in the mountainous area of Jelica. The accommodation was good, the facilities adequate, if Spartan.

My programme of visits to schools under the watchful eyes of Ivan, Vera and Boris were interrupted by the open talk I gave in Belgrade. A room seating about 70 people had been booked; the date, time, place and subject (Young people and the creative process) announced in the Belgrade newspapers. When I arrived at the door of the hall with James we were confronted by two well-built gentlemen wearing suits and a uniformed policeman.

James observed, sotto voce, that their presence was "par for the course". He explained that the door keepers were there to make sure "that nothing got out of control". Some 30 people came to the talk which James kindly pronounced a success. Few Serb nationals attended, the bulk of the audience consisting of diplomatic staff and Serbs employed at the Embassy.

I had never before spoken in a hall with 'watchers' in the entrance lobby. It was an experience I was to repeat some months later when I gave a talk to teachers in the Republic of Ireland. The room, in Dublin, was within the Parliament complex. It was a time of mounting tension in the North and so armed guards were posted on the doors, to dissuade unwelcome visitors. The provocative title of my Dublin talk was 'Developing 3-dimensional work with young children'… a subject hardly likely to excite a terrorist.

Back to Serbia. My last two days were spent trying to discover how the needs of disabled children were met. Before I could progress I had to overcome a reticence on the part of Ivan and Vera to discuss handicap of any sort: "There are so few." "We provide for them but…" "Our schools are not happy with visitors…"

I explained to them the reason for my interest. I was at the time engaged in a linking activity with children from The Richard Cloudesley School, a specialist school for the physically disabled. The primary school of which I was headteacher, Prior Weston, assimilated Cloudesley children (aged between 7–11) who were at ease with themselves and who had mastered the basic elements of number and written language. Most of the children were paraplegics… the experiment was progressing well. Were there no examples in Serbia through which I could extend my knowledge?

I think I mentioned to Ivan (in the hearing of Boris) that the British Foreign Secretary, in the previous Labour administration David Owen, had two children in Prior Weston School. My gently provocative remark was followed by an animated discussion between Ivan and Boris. Their conversation began quietly, but their voices quickly rose to a high pitch. Intemperate Serbo-Croat is a fascinating language – to watch. The flowing sentences took over their bodies whilst Vera turned away, seemingly upset at this unexpected outburst.

An hour after this Balkan confrontation, I was taken to a school for disabled children on the outskirts of Belgrade. Class groups were small, the staff caring, facilities well maintained and adequate. Those attending suffered from a range of physical disabilities, including spina bifida. Referring to a report I wrote at the time, I note that boarding schools were also provided for the severely disabled.

There was one other, rather unconventional, opportunity open to Serbian parents seeking placement for their handicapped child. First a school which catered for their child's disability had to be located (anywhere in Serbia) and visited. The parents' next task was to find suitable accommodation close to the selected school and arrange for the child to stay there during term time. Vera confided that the scheme was "on paper" and "difficult to use."

I noticed this denial of the less able, the disabled, the genetically damaged child by educational workers in other European countries. For example, in Bulgaria I occasionally ran a video which showed a speech therapist working alongside a nine-year old paraplegic. The video was well produced – but in parts a little painful to watch. My host, a prominent member of the Bulgarian educational establishment, invariably asked me not to show it. "Henry, the images hurt me. I do not want to think about this kind of child."

There seemed to me to be a denial that the communist world could ever breed disabled children. It's noteworthy that it is only after the Romanian Revolution of December 1989 and the overthrow of President Nicolae Ceausecu that much attention was paid by people living in Western Europe to the treatment of the less able, the retarded and the handicapped under communist rule. In Tito's Serbia and Zhivkov's Bulgaria the disabled may have been handled more lovingly than they were in Romania – but in neither of these countries did I feel that they were readily initiated into schooling.

My final evening in Belgrade revealed dramatically the political undercurrents which rippled around me throughout my stay. A 'thank and farewell' party had been programmed in the 'Artist's Club'. In my simplicity, I assumed this to be a place where men and women involved in the arts gathered for meetings on cultural topics, exhibitions, talks, folk music festivals and poetry reading. It had been explained to me that every specialisation had its own club – architects, engineers, university lecturers – and that each club met on premises provided by the state government for the sole purpose "of sharing expertise and furthering excellence." One thing about these clubs was made very clear to me. Only party members would be invited to join and that all members of a club would have ideas which could be easily accommodated by the ruling hierarchy.

And so to the club. Boris met me at my hotel. An over-dressed, over-jewelled and over-made up Vera and a slightly more pressed, ironed and combed Ivan were waiting in the car. We drove through evening light to an area of Belgrade to which I had not previously been taken. The streets narrowed, blocks of flats gave way to tall, dark warehouses. As we drove further into this complex, darkness turned to blackness. The car-lights created strange shadows on the cobbled roadway…

At last we stopped. Boris intimated that we had reached 'The Club'. We stood outside the door of a grim looking warehouse and wondered whether Boris had made a mistake or whether this was some kind of Serbian joke. There was no sound. No light. No movement. Simply silence.

Boris, smiling no doubt at our discomfiture, moved his fingers around the edge of the door. He found a bell push. We waited patiently. The cracks around the door were suddenly edged with yellow light.

Boris had left us before the door opened. A club doorman (if that's what he was) dressed in a blue suit opened the door and led us across a dreary hallway to an ancient lift – the kind with metal gates which make a diamond pattern when closed. When we were all in the lift and the doors shut, blue suit pulled a thick rope. A bell sounded above us and the lift slowly rose three floors. We were now in a brightly lit corridor. A lady in a black dress with white collar and cuffs directed us through a velvet-draped door, its fitments of gold leaf more in keeping with a ducal palace than a Belgrade warehouse.

Ivan led the way. I heard him gasp. The scene before us was so unreal and so out of keeping with everything we had seen during the previous ten days, that a loud indrawing of breath was a very modest response. Pushing away the curtain and opening the door we found ourselves transported into the imperial glory of the Austro-Hungarian Empire. Beautifully set tables, flower and flag decked, welcomed the fortunate ones who were to dine here. Bow-tied, black jacketed waiters stood by each table, waiting to wait. The wine glasses, crystal-cut, sparkled in the candlelight, the cutlery shone. We were escorted to a table where, when we had re-gathered our composure, we sat and chatted.

Ivan and Vera responded to what they saw in two ways. They were impressed by the ambience of the club while at the same time resenting its expensive trappings (and the hypocrisy of the political machine which created it).

The quality and range of food and wine, the service, the quiet efficiency of the whole operation bred admiration and resentment in equal quantities. When curtains parted at the end of the hall to reveal a string orchestra and the opening bars of 'The Blue Danube' flowed across the seated diners, I really *did* believe I was in Vienna in the 1890s.

For a moment I forgot my misgivings about Yugoslav Communism: was not this cultured and civilised? Diners, men and women, on the tables around us seemed equally relaxed. Many of the guests seemed to be undertaking visits similar to my own. There was the tricolour of France on one table, the triple bands of the GDR on a second, the blue and white cross of Greece on a third.

Music, light talk and very traditional ball-room dancing whiled away an evening at which everybody drank a little (but I avoided brandy). We talked – though Vera did dance once with Ivan. Vera seemed more discreet than usual in her translations of my questions and her presentation of Ivan's answers. The club seemed to be weighing down on them. They were both puzzled at the affluence (or was it decadence) that the club paraded, particularly when set within the context of poverty and lack of resources we had so recently seen in village, town and city. A bomb had exploded in their minds, a nagging question unresolved. "How can this place flourish and provide a base where the privileged consume the sophistications of life while the ordinary citizen exists on so little? How can such a contrast be explained and justified by a thinking Marxist?"

At eleven o'clock, each of us much wiser than we had been at seven, thanked our waiter and took the lift to the ground floor and the street. The romantic candlelight, the food, the wine, the music ebbed away like a fading dream. We wandered across the cobbled street to where Boris waited with the car. In his deep-voiced Serbo-Croat he remarked, "I'm glad they arranged for you to go there. It's one of the better places to eat in Belgrade." (Vera translated) I remember wondering how he could speak about the club with such authority.

Next day the silently whistling Boris drove me to the airport. Vera and Ivan came too. Boris handed over my bags, shook my hand and said in perfectly pronounced and modulated English "I'm glad I drove you around, Henry. I did enjoy your jokes. It was sometimes difficult not to laugh at the English version. I had to laugh only after Vera's translation!" Vera, suddenly aware that Boris was a placeman who had been watching all three of us in the interests of the party went so ashen I feared she might faint. The crumpled Ivan crumpled even more and appeared to implode within his battered suit.

113

Boris meanwhile had departed to the boot of the car, no doubt smiling at the impact his remark had made. He returned, carrying the 2kg of runny honey given to me by Ivan and my shoulder bag which contained my camera and undeveloped film. As he passed the bag to me he said, somewhat wryly "I hope all turns out as you would wish..."

And so to London. Three days later I collected my film from the local chemist. Excitedly I took the prints from their packets. It was then that I remembered the remark made by Boris as we parted.

All my photographs were blank.

6. Canada – In the New World and in Europe (1973–1974)

Mrs. Abercrombie, a parent, had entered the school office when I was deep in a telephone conversation. I nodded to her, telling her to stay. She looked astonished when she heard me say "I'll be happy to come, but you tell me – is there a railway station in Edmonton?"

"Edmonton" said Mrs. Abercrombie when the phone call was over. "That's Canada, isn't it? Long way to go to catch a train!"

My question does not seem so odd when put into context. A senior administrator from Alberta – I'll call him Mr. Robin Smith – specialised in the creative arts. He was visiting the UK to extend his experience. One of his visits was to Prior Weston School where the teaching staff had developed an Arts programme which linked subjects across a curriculum – from Mathematics to Environmental Studies – which was enriched and illuminated by picture and model making, poetry, prose, music, dance and drama.

A key part of this programme involved taking the children (aged from 5 to 11+ to museums, art galleries and sites of historical and environmental significance and expose them to the creative work of men and women of different cultures and epochs. It was impossible to take a 10 year old to meet a Norman stonemason who had worked on the White Tower – but he could be encouraged to imagine what it would have been like to have worked on its building, using only hand tools and such power as animals could provide. The eight-year old who has struggled with pen and ink and pencil to draw a portrait can be helped to identify with the artists of the Tudor Court who had the same problems to solve.

These two examples, selected from the hundreds I could have chosen, illustrate the fact that grown-ups are also involved in the Arts and that without the Arts, life would be bleak indeed.

To emphasise this point still further, people who professionally involved in the world of the Arts were invited to meet class groups to explain the tools of their trade and outline how they spent their days. Peter Hall (then of The National Theatre), Peter Copley (Actor, RSC), Kate Castle (Dancer, Royal Opera House), Austin Taylor (Artist), D.S. Johnson and Oliver Pritchett (Authors), Y. Neaman (Musician), Timothy Rose (Master of the choristers, St. Paul's Cathedral) were among many parents and friends of the school who gave freely of their time to supplement and extend the programme.

If I seem to be dwelling on school rather than on Canada, the reason will soon become apparent. The emphasis on the Arts brought many visitors to the school – on average around 4,000 per year (1968–1984). Among these visitors, in 1975 was Robin Smith.

Robin was seeking to introduce an integrated Arts programme into the Elementary Schools in the area he administered. He decided to begin this process by inviting 16 of his most promising classroom teachers to a week-long practical course and by asking me to design it. I accepted his invitation to lead the course and chose as its central theme 'Travel'. This explains the telephone conversation overheard by Mrs. Abercrombie. I needed reassurance that there was evidence of rail transport in Edmonton.

Robin was also a prominent member of the Canadian branch of the Herbert Read Society. Read was a leading philosopher in the 1950s and 60s. 'Education through Art', first published in 1958 by Faber and Faber, attracted much academic interest and acclaim. His key belief, that 'Art should be at the centre of the education process' (page 1, 3rd edition) provoked reaction – of admiration and acceptance from those who wanted to free schools from Gradgrind traditionalism and fierce opposition from those who wanted Gradgrind preserved.

Between 1959 and 1961 I had been able to apply Read's ideas. Watched over and guided by my University of London tutor, Lou Holland, I made Arts the centre point of my work with a small class of socially maladroit 7–11 year olds who had already in their young lives dismissed as irrelevant everything associated with education (e.g. school, reading, number, teachers…). I kept a diary of my battles with this class – a requirement of the advanced course I was taking at the University.

With the blessings of the headteacher of the school, Frank Peacock, I put aside the conventional curriculum and worked broadly within the framework suggested by Read (Page 10, 3rd edition):
"Human beings learn through the following 'instincts',
1)   Communicative – the desire to talk and listen.
2)   Dramatic – the desire to act.

116

3) *Artistic* – the desire to paint, draw, model.
4) *Musical* – the desire to dance and sing.
5) *Inquisitive* – the desire to know the 'why' of things.
6) *Constructive* – the desire to make."

It follows that if Read's 'instincts' facilitate learning then teaching should utilise them too. (In passing, the results with my class at John Ruskin School, Walworth, SE5 were positive). By the end of the 2nd year all the children had learned to read and write and were a pleasure to take out on school visits.

This lengthy explanation of a particular writer's educational philosophy sits somewhat uneasily in this book. But its inclusion is essential. Herbert Read's various writings carried such authority that 'Societies' and discussion groups were established across the world to further his ideas. Robin, who was a committee member of the Herbert Read Society in Alberta, decided that my visit to his school district should coincide with a colloquium organised by The Pan-American Herbert Read Society. The colloquium was to be held in Calgary.

So my visit to Canada had two parallel threads – a workshop for teachers which would focus on Read's 'instincts' and a talk to people who probably understood the significance of Read's work far better than I.

The Air Canada flight to Edmonton lasted about ten and a half hours. It was comfortably tedious. In 1973 long haul tourist travel had yet to be developed on any scale so the space between the seats on the aircraft were sufficiently roomy for individual passengers to fidget continuously and to allow many undisturbed 'cat-naps'. I think I am typical of many air travellers – the first time I flew was exhilarating, seeing earth, sky and water from quite a new angle… a mix of ever-changing cloud, mountains, rippling distant water and patterned landscape. Watching this kaleidoscope is so beguiling that time passes relatively quickly. Sadly, too much flying makes one rather blasé, even if the ticket is Apex and tourist class (with a seat between the tail plane and the toilets!)

So to Edmonton where I was met by Robin. It was the first time I had travelled on a long haul flight where the aircraft parked so far from the airport buildings. On coming to a halt the plane was approached by 3 vehicles, each looking like a conventional coach. One stopped close to my cabin window. To my surprise, I saw the whole coach unit, but not its wheels, rise from the ground. The driver sat stoically in his seat as though it was quite commonplace to drive a vehicle 20 feet (6.5 m) above the roadway. The bus body and its driver stopped level with and close to the exit door on the aircraft's fuselage. The door opened and the two vehicles, bus and plane, went into a mechanical embrace, a covered bridge effecting this strange union. Passengers then passed from plane to bus, accompanied by the repeated demand to "Have a nice day" spoken with that light lilt that distinguishes Canadians from their American cousins. When the bus was full it gently disengaged itself from the plane, the four Meccano-like legs which united cabin and wheels folded gently away until both locked comfortably together. Now, quite bus-like, it made its way to immigration, customs and Robin.

Robin suggested that I spent a few hours resting in the very pleasant hotel room he had booked for me. He arranged to collect me in the early evening and take me for supper at his home. The evening was a happy one, except that too many of Robin's other guests were in the 'education industry'. Instead of the easy introduction into Canadian Society for which I had hoped, I ended the evening feeling rather like Galileo Galilei, post-Inquisition. The sheer enthusiasm of my newly-discovered Canadian friends left me exhausted. I was certain that my little contribution to their coming education week would never meet their high expectations.

It was over supper that I met Isabel. She immediately told me that she was a course member and that "I would be seeing a lot of her over the next few days." This was to prove true – for a lot of her there certainly was.

Isabel was a dark-haired, handsome, though not beautiful, woman. She stood over 6 ft tall (in low heels) and was generously full bodied. She weighed, at a guess, over 18 stone (252 lb or 114 kg). Yet she looked trim rather than fat. Perhaps this was an illusion, created by a good sense of colour and a wise choice of dress pattern.

Smilingly – and without seeking to challenge – she said to me, almost at our moment of meeting. "Meet your problem student. I see the course includes music and movement... dance? There's no dancing in me, never has been, never could be, never will be able to, don't want to... I move when I have to! I'm the child that every teacher has in her class. The emotional non-complier." She smiled again, disarmingly. "Never mind. I'm sure we'll enjoy being together."

I think this salvo was meant to serve as a gentle warning. I could appreciate her problems. Did she really think I could be so

118

insensitive? No one was going to be forced to become a dying swan, a Titania or a frail Ophelia... and certainly not Isabel.

Next day Robin took me to visit two schools. He spent much time explaining the organisation of the public (i.e. state) schools in his district. Late in the afternoon I met a class of 14 and 15 year olds for a 'Question and Answer' session. The questions ranged across every aspect of British life – from enquiring as to whether I would take time to watch the Queen open a Shopping Mall to questions about the similarities and differences of British and Canadian adolescents.

Similarities and differences – two words we use to explore the cultural patterns in a country not our own – are traps for the unwary. Approaches to 'Teaching' and 'Learning' are different in every country – and in every part of every country – that one visits. Some are quite impossible to understand within a British context. How short-sighted and foolhardy to argue that the 'British way' is best! It is impossible and inappropriate to try to take the minutiae of a national policy which has taken generations to evolve and plug them into the cultural heritage of another nation. It is in the noting and acceptance of difference and by respecting the validity of such differences as there are, that makes professional exchange in every academic discipline and at every level so worth while. So I was not in Edmonton to inflict my ideas on 'creativity with young children' on Canadian teachers. Rather I was there to explore some processes which some of the course members could make their own, hopefully having them take root to flourish within a Canadian context.

Over the weekend Robin helped me prepare the large room in which I would work. At one end there were tables on each of which were placed the materials each individual would need at the beginning of the course – paper, pencils, ruler, crayons, pastels, scissors, a plain-leafed scrap book, felt-tipped pens...

Around the edge of this 'formal' area other tables held materials which would be shared – card, craft knives, coloured papers, glue, PVA paints, polymer adhesives, fabric scraps, brushes of all shapes and sizes... The far end of the room was empty apart from a trolley which held a record player and speakers and some percussion instruments.

Monday. The course assembled. We talked about the 'Travel' theme I had chosen. I pointed out, as I introduced the idea, that in a classroom the students could sometimes be given the opportunity to choose the theme themselves. We explored the many avenues we could use to introduce and develop the project, bearing in mind the emphasis which Read placed on harnessing curiosity, the importance of drawing upon all the senses and the value of making and doing.

We also considered ways in which children's work could be presented: in individual folders, group books, classroom displays, prose and poetry, photographs, graphs, maps, tape recordings, dance, drama and song. Note. The computer, the lap top, the video recorder, the digital camera were things of the future and yet to be developed.

I won't attempt to explore in any detail the activities which were undertaken. The following indicates something of their range: individual and group visits to local transport hubs (airport, bus terminal etc.), passenger surveys, the use of timetables and routes for work in mathematics (comparisons, ticket prices, travel costs per mile), poster designs (e.g. "Travel by…"), historical and geographic research, painting and sketching.

Each course member also followed an individual interest e.g. travelling in snow and ice; the sledge; The Canadian Pacific Railroad; folk songs of travel. We also attempted, with some difficulty but with much laughter, Choral Speaking.

An aside. If this group were typical of most Canadians, then Canadians find it difficult to speak with one voice. When we attempted Choral Speaking almost everything went awry. Stress and emphasis on particular words and phrases was agreed upon and marked on the copy of the poem we were reading… or rather agreed upon until the line was spoken together. Rhythm, pitch, volume, speed were unknown areas, entered at my peril. "But, say, my voice is quiet to her quiet" said Rod, pointing at Jean. "How do we know what quiet and loud are when we've all got different voices?" To which Jean replied "But my loud isn't as loud as his loud…!" Impasse.

Against all reason, for Auden's 'Night Mail' tells of the steam train travelling from London to Edinburgh, they enjoyed the struggle of sufficiently mastering the words and rhythms to present it, after five days of rehearsal, as a corporate effort. Even then I had to conduct the final presentation – had I not done so, some of the carriages would have arrived in Edinburgh inordinately early (and probably without the locomotive!)

Every day I led a class in music and movement. Each session lasted ¾ an hour. The method I followed was pioneered by a famous London County Council drama inspector, Maisey Cobby, whose courses I had attended in the mid 1950s. To link with 'Night Mail' I decided to try to help the group create a train through body movement.

To reach this point – when adults are prepared to put aside the embarrassment which often accompanies activities involving moving to music, I presented the idea with enthusiastic caution: enthusiasm because *children* love to move, caution because most *adults* prefer not to!

Each session began with moving to the pattern of the drum beat. Each participant made a body pattern which reflected it, filling all the space around him/her – high, low, to the left, to the right, stretching and curling, all the while adapting these movements to reflect the strength of the drum. This activity was developed/extended by changing the instrument, replacing the drum with the cymbal, castanet, tambourine and chime bar. I suggested working in twos and threes, making movements on the spot and then around the room. This was followed with movement to short excerpts of recorded music. For example I used the opening bars of Stravinsky's 'Petrouchka' to try to create the atmosphere of a busy city terminus at rush hour. Each member contributed as an individual – running to catch a train and avoiding other travellers in the process, arguing with a porter, struggling with luggage, meeting a friend…

In each session I included an excerpt of Honegger's strident tone poem 'Pacific 3-2-1', an evocative sound picture of a steam locomotive. I contrasted this with the much gentler musical journey of 'The Little Train on the Prairie' by Villa-Lobos. The pattern of sounds used to express movement were analysed. What movement can we make to represent rolling wheels, the track, the steam, the pistons, increasing/decreasing speed? Do we need different styles of movement for the two trains? I played the music, the participants responded – individually, making appropriate sounds (if they so wished) for the part of the train they had 'become'.

Over the week the train came together. By the final session we had 'built' by linking individual movements, contrasting engines… the explosively aggressive 'Pacific 321' and the friendly 'Prairie Express'. PE benches and tables were used to give additional height to the 'engines', formed from the combined body shapes/movements of the course members.

For the first couple of sessions, Isabel sat and watched her colleagues move… just like a sensitive, apprehensive child. On the third day she came dressed in a black trouser suit. Again, all smiles, she approached me. "Could I just join in the train bit?" she asked. "I'd make a good smoke stack." She joined in the Pacific group with zest and enthusiasm and even participated, somewhat perspiringly, to a final 'free dance' to the music of 'Zorba the Greek.'

"I've learned something about myself", she told me before she left that evening. "You don't have to be able to dance to teach movement. I'm looking forward to taking a movement lesson on Monday."

The music, the collective pooling of ideas and the manner in which participants sank themselves into the theme triggered all manner of activities – self portraits 'on the move', designs built around wheels, pistons, boilers, signals, rail track. Then there was an outpouring of prose and poetry created individually and collectively around the sounds associated with trains (onomatopoeia) and the smell and 'taste' of diesel, steam and smoke. We also attempted to incorporate rhythm into some of the writing using R.L. Stevenson's 'From a Railway Carriage' as a model:

'Faster than fairies, faster than witches.
Bridges and houses, hedges and ditches:
And charging along like troops in a battle
All through the meadows the horses and cattle:
All of the sights of the hill and plain
Fly as thick as the driving rain;
And ever again, in the wink of an eye
Painted stations whistle by.'

The weekend saw me in Calgary where the colloquium was to be held. I was to open the proceedings with a 45 minute paper on 'The Creative Process'. I remained at the colloquium all day and was impressed at the enthusiasm the delegates showed for the Arts – and the importance of the Arts in school and in society.

My hotel was large, expensive and over-luxurious. Situated in the very centre of Calgary, life seemed to swirl around it, night and day. Only one thing worried me. The sheer quantity of food served but not eaten. Does anyone really need to be offered steaks which cover most of the dinner plate?

Calgary is in the very heart of Canada. In my mind I see one enormous wheat field stretching in an unbroken sweep from the suburbs of Edmonton to Calgary and beyond. How could one possibly harvest such an enormous crop, store it, grind it? Here and there in these unimaginable horizon-to-horizon corn lands were small settlements and in these small settlements, schools.

122

I treasure a conversation I had with an eight-year old lad called Billy.

"Where you from, Mister?"

"London, England."

"How did you come to Canada?"

"By Air Canada, from London to Edmonton."

"Could you have come by boat?"

I took an atlas and together we found a map of the World. London's here, and you live here, Billy."

We fingered our way between the two cities – across the Atlantic, down the St. Lawrence River, across Lakes Ontario, Erie and Huron to Thunder Bay on Lake Superior.

"And I guess, Billy, we'd need to change ship several times to do that!"

"How long would it take, the boat bit?"

"I've no idea, but over two weeks." (I guessed – a poor estimate I think now, 'Times World Atlas' open on my desk.)

There was a long pause.

"All that water! 14 days of water… I've never seen the sea… Water for fourteen days."

"Mister. There must be more water in the sea than in our village pond!"

Puzzled, he went his way. "All that sea. I've never seen the sea…" And looking out of his classroom window I could have been excused for saying, equally truthfully and with just as much wonder. "All that wheat and not a hedge, house or highway in sight…" It's salutary to remember that our understandings are largely shaped and fashioned by our own experiences.

I always brought back from my visits a small memento as a keepsake. (and for my two daughters, local dolls) From Canada I have a small soapstone carving worked by an Inuit (Eskimo) craftsman. Handling it I am reminded of policemen in red coats, of wheat fields, of Isabel, but most of all of Billy.

My return to London did not sever my links with Canada and things Canadian. Some nine months after my visit to Edmonton and Calgary I received another phone call. It was from an office of the Canadian Government Department which was responsible for the education of the children of Canadian Nationals who were employed in Europe (Diplomatic, Military.) There was to be a course for Elementary grade teachers employed by the 'Authority' (similar to our own British Forces Education Service). It was to be held in France in the foothills of the Voges Mountains. The request was simple. "The picture making bits of the course you took in Edmonton."

I accepted the invitation and, having ordered all the materials I required to occupy 15 teachers for 3 days, I found myself, one late spring evening in 1974, in Basel (Basle) Airport en route for the course centre which was near the town of Haricourt (France). At the airport I met my fellow tutors. Avril Dankworth was a respected music lecturer and rightly vexed when she found herself presented as Johnny Dankworth's sister or Cleo Laine's sister-in-law! Vic Roberts, a language consultant, the second tutor, I had never met before – nor have I heard of him since. There were also three French-speaking tutors. They greeted us in French then ignored us altogether.

We all climbed into a small bus and were driven through the late evening to the course centre. The countryside was unspoilt by man and very beautiful. As we moved upwards in the hills, the air became sharp, clean and chill.

The courses were to be centred on six huts. I was given my hut, and like the other tutors, allowed a free day to prepare it. When the course participants arrived they immediately divided into two groups – English-speaking Canadians and those from Quebec, who seemed only to speak French. When the course lists were distributed the same pattern emerged. Avril, Vic and I shared the 45 English teachers, the three French speaking lecturers took the 'Quebecois'.

Throughout the course, the Quebecois quietly but obviously avoided teachers from the English-speaking provinces. On the final evening a party was arranged for all participants, tutors and administrative staff. The 'one party' quickly became two. Each Quebecois, drink and food in hand retreated to a distant hut to sing French folk songs. Accompanied by a guitar, the music drifted pleasantly through the evening air. I realised that music can be employed as a political tool... but I had never before seen it used in so low a key so effectively.

I had an inkling of the reason for the antagonism. France first laid claim to Quebec in 1534. The province became a French Overseas Possession in 1608. It remained in French hands until ceded to Britain in 1763. Quebec is still French speaking and rich in French culture. Over the years the Quebecois grew to resent English (i.e. English-Canadian) cultural and economic imperialism. In the late 1950s and early 1960s the 'Parti Quebecois' was formed and began a campaign for an independent Quebec, a Quebec which was an autonomous nation. The campaign was to dominate Canadian politics until 1980 when the 'Quebec question' was finally ended by referendum. Quebec decided to remain within Canada. What I had experienced was an expression of a fierce divide which could have split Canada in two.

My links with Canada remain – but tenuously. I still exchange Christmas letters with a Prior Weston family, the Endicotts, who live in Toronto. When the children attended the school they were amused by the smart brassed plaque I had brought back with me from Calgary. It read:

"This is one of the best schools in Canada

Help us keep it that way."

As Lorna Endicott observed "You've even put notices on the wall to make me feel at home."

7. Paris, France 1989

I had been to Paris before. In August 1947 I remember causing a passing gendarme, all blue uniform, ribboned hat, cape and drooping moustache, to risk his life by crossing the Champs-Élysées to warn me of the consequences of my bad behaviour. I should explain that my crime was to sit on a patch of grass near the Arc de Triomphe. Pointing at me – or was it the grass – and noticing the small Union Flag I wore on my sleeve, he said, in as fluent English as he could muster:

"We do not have sitters here."

I imagine I replied in my best south London schoolboy French "excusez-moi" or pardonez-moi" I got to my feet slowly. With his hand lightly on my shoulder, he escorted me across the road to the pavement. Then he "tut-tutted" several times, shook his head sadly at the behaviour of British youth and walked slowly away. His departure was very measured, for he turned periodically to make sure I was not in the process of committing another sitting offence.

Fifty years later, in the first week of December 1989 I was once again in Paris. I was not apprehensive about the possibility of my having to confront the gendarme again. Without doubt he now walks some celestial street leading to an Arc of Pearly gates with lawns of everlasting grass, grass which welcomes the occasional sitting spirit.

There was a touch of magic in the air in Paris in those early days of December 1989. The weather was dry and crisp. The shops sparkled with their displays of Christmas goods. Strings of coloured lights emphasised the coming celebrations. Although restaurants and cafes had not yet introduced their Christmas menus, there was a general feeling of the 'unwinding of the year' and with it 'goodwill to all men.'

The skyline of Paris was special too. To commemorate the bi-centenary of the Great Revolution, annually marked on July 14th, by 'Bastille Day', the many historically significant buildings of Paris had been cleaned, the scars of war and climatic erosion removed and the external gilding restored and polished so that it sparkled day and night – in sun, moon and floodlight.

It was not just the exterior of the buildings which had been renovated. Many had been completely refurbished, the civil servants

126

who had slummed in them with their files, cabinets and desks were ejected. They were replaced with period wallpaper, gildings, velvet tasselled curtains, fittings and furniture. In their restored state they were now available for public functions, exhibitions and international meetings.

This commemoration of Revolution deserves respect. The last 30 years of the 18th century were indeed Revolutionary – in 1783 the Americans won their freedom; in 1787 the Netherlands rose up against their Austrian rulers; in France the Jacobins rejected royal authority, the 'reign of terror' ending with the execution of King Louis XVI in 1793. Revolutionary ideas spread across Europe with uprisings in Hungary (1790), Poland (1791), Ireland (1798), Serbia (1804) and Spain (1805). These outbreaks of nationalism with their demands for autonomy – and the revolutionary movements which swept across the continent in 1836 and 1848 – drew much of their inspiration from the cry "Liberty, Equality, Fraternity," three words that will always be associated with revolution in France.

Little wonder, then, that the French viewed their revolution with pride – and Paris, December 1989, proclaimed it.

The minister in the French Government who was responsible for this massive cleaning and refurbishment to commemorate the revolution was Jack Lang.

Jack Lang was also a key figure in the colloquium on the exploration and preservation of sites of cultural significance which I was to attend. Lasting a week, the colloquium attracted delegates from all over the world (900+). Lectures, seminars and discussion groups examined such questions as:

What are the qualities which give a site significance – in a national and international context?

How can such sites be preserved for future generations?

How can cultural tourism be regulated?

How can new discoveries and relevant information best be disseminated?

What methods are being employed to make young people aware of their cultural heritage and what elements of this heritage have come from other parts of their continent/world e.g. the arts and political philosophy of the pre-Christian Greek city states?

The colloquium met from 9–11 a.m. in full session. Academics presented papers which stressed the need for an international approach to heritage and cultural issues. For the rest of the morning, 11.20 a.m.–12.30 p.m., the delegates divided to form small discussion groups. These groups listened to 15 minute papers presented by members of their group. The group of which I was a member was concerned with ways of extending young peoples' understanding of the built environment in which they lived.

Some afternoons were spent in group discussions followed by a formal presentation in the main hall. Two afternoons were given to visits and one evening to role play in costume in a small 'palace' built on the site of the infamous Bastille prison.

The 'palace' in which the role play took place had been recently refurbished. The whole building, interior, exterior and gardens were as they might have been in 1800. They were brought to life by a group of 20 seven to twelve year olds, their parents and teachers, all appropriately costumed. The children sang, accompanied at the fortepiano by a girl of nine – who was more concerned with making sure that her high white wig stayed secure than she was by the complexity of the music.

The presentation ended with dancing. The children now moved to the garden at the back of the house. The adults remained on the first floor and watched through open windows the group present a short series of traditional 'dances of the Court.'

The dancers moved to music we could not hear on a lawn surrounded by low shrubs. The scene was gently lit, a pool of grey-green light illuminated the grass 'stage.' Around and beyond it was total darkness.

Time was suspended. The past contrived to drive out the present. For a brief moment the shades of Parisians past entered and touched the 20th century. As the pool of light faded, they faded too.

One afternoon was set aside for educational visits. I chose to go to a school/college for apprentice masons. In order for there to be a sufficient supply of stone masons in France an effective training programme has been developed. Young people from 16 years of age who attend the school receive the same payment as they would were they already employed in the building industry. The money is raised through a combination of direct taxation and a compulsory payment from every construction company in France. The course lasts between 5 and 7 years.

At the school the students are taught technical drawing – how, for example, to record an arch in a 13th century abbey to show plan and elevations, structural damage and appropriate drawings to indicate areas requiring restoration and the processes recommended for doing so. The technical skills required by a master mason are also taught, as are the architectural styles of different historic epochs and the techniques and fashions which were followed by provincial craftsmen.

The students are based in a barn-like workshop. There were a number of smaller rooms around its perimeter which were used for technical drawing, discussion groups and lectures.

I watched a group of 17-year-old boys working on a copy of a 14th century stairway, the original being in Notre-Dame Cathedral. They had begun their project in the Cathedral, making all drawings they would require to reproduce an exact replica in stone. When I visited, the circular stairway had almost been completed. It was about 4 metres high, in Gothic style and intricately decorated.

There are a number of these schools, spread across the regions of France. This enables schools for masons to exchange students so that they gain awareness of how different stone is worked and finished. For example recently quarried limestone can be cut with a saw. Not so granite.

This programme, far better than we have in the UK more than compensates for retirement and natural wastage. It means that an adequate supply of labour is available to give skilled care to the historic buildings and monuments of France – a reflection of the corporate concern for the built environment in town and country.

Another aspect of the colloquium was an exhibition set up by delegates. Its purpose was to illustrate how specific heritage projects had developed. For example it included a detailed outline of the educational programmes developed at the Acropolis, Athens, employing on-site distant learning techniques to deepen understanding for school children, tourists and the academic researcher. The work of young people was prominent. A set of batik hangings worked in a project promoted by a Catholic Foundation near Toulouse was particularly striking.

What impressed me most was a set of drawings produced by Black American teenagers in the Bronx. These showed streets of once prosperous houses in slow decay. Having been to New York and been made aware of the poverty of the area, these drawings were possessed of an immediacy and a poignancy rarely found in the work of 13 and 14 year olds.

The Bronx drawings were the brainchild of a white, middle-aged lady artist. Appalled at the lack of facilities for youth in the area, particularly during the summer holidays, she decided to establish a drawing class.

So, on impulse and initially fearful of what might happen, she took drawing boards, paper and pencils to a street corner in the Bronx, settled down and began to draw a street scene. As happened in the opening chapter of 'Tom Sawyer' a nascent desire to make and do, allied to their natural curiosity, drew young people to her. They too wanted to draw. They grouped around her – and so began a free, August, street-art-class which had, in 1989, already been running for five years. The drawings on display were a tribute to the perception of a gifted artist, teacher and mother and to the enthusiastic response of youngsters who had discovered that walls and the sides of trains are not the only surfaces on which to 'make marks'.

At the time of the colloquium the Governments of the United States and the United Kingdom had withdrawn financial support from UNESCO (United Nations Educational, Cultural and Scientific Organisation) in protest against its profligacy. This meant that although British and American citizens could attend meetings and conferences organised by UNESCO, their role was restricted. Decisions made by the committees of UNESCO did not require British or United States support to be ratified and acted upon. Thus during the colloquium it was decided to construct an index of world heritage sites together with background material about each. The idea of the index was put forward by French delegates and quickly supported by the French Government with offers of logistical and financial support. The siting of the index in Paris was announced at the conclusion of the colloquium, a beneficial consequence of carefully-planned political opportunism.

It was probably wise to decide to base the index in Paris – for it is in Paris that the headquarters' staff of UNESCO are based. The headquarters building occupies a very small site close to Place de Fontenoy. To maximise the use of the site, the HQ has 4 levels of office accommodation below ground – including the large and well-equipped conference hall in which the delegates to the colloquium met for plenary sessions.

The 'Hotel Bristol' where I had booked a room was close to Place de Fontenoy; near by was Pont des Invalides which crosses the River Seine, Le Tour Eiffel, L'Ecole Militaire, L'Hotel des Invalides (a home built by Louis XIV for wounded soldiers) and the church of St Louis des Invalides in which Napoleon is buried.

From an architectural viewpoint the 'Hotel Bristol' had little to commend it. It was elderly and showed its years. The staff, the furniture, the fittings, the whole ambience were elderly too. Only in

130

the mornings when the dining room opened for the only time of the day did anything new or fresh appear – delicious rolls and steaming coffee.

I could hardly place John Hodgson, at this time the Education Officer of the National Trust, in my collection of 'hotel elderlies'. Young in years he was not, but never lacking in fresh thoughts and new ideas. John was attending the colloquium and staying in the hotel. I was fortunate to discover a kindred spirit that I knew well.

I first met John in the late 1960s when our paths crossed at the Geffrye Museum in Shoreditch where he was a member of the education staff. He was very supportive in encouraging the teaching staff of Prior Weston School to use the facilities of the Museum in an unconventional way... unconventional in 1969 and unconventional today. It was decided to 'immerse' children into a museum setting rather than use the traditional 2 hour "talk and walk, be quiet, don't touch, be interested because I've brought you here" approach – which supported by worksheets is guaranteed to put children off museum visiting for life.

So on some projects – and the Geffrye was one such – class group, teacher and support staff worked within the museum and its grounds for 4 or 5 consecutive days. The programme included painting, writing, map, plan and model making and simple book research. Some of the senior staff at the Geffrye were somewhat sceptical at this approach. John was much more perceptive, appreciated the possibilities and gave us unqualified support. The children (aged between 6–8) were even allowed to use the practical resources room in the museum as a temporary classroom.

I next met John when I went to see an exhibition on 'childhood'. It was displayed at Sudbury Hall, a National Trust property 9 km (6 miles) east of Uttoxeter (Derbyshire). John was employed by the Trust (and also by the local authority) to focus attention upon the built landscape to increase young peoples' understanding of the past, and through this to introduce a much neglected thread into the broadcloth of education – aesthetics.

I think the senior staff at the National Trust were a little surprised when they really began to understand John's educational beliefs. When I next met him in London, he had left Sudbury Hall and been appointed full-time education officer to the Trust. At this time, the 1970s and early 1980s, the National Trust as a body were far more interested in preserving ancient artefacts and protecting their properties than in giving thought to ways in which young people could be encouraged to visit and *enjoy* its properties. "Today's young people are tomorrow's parents. Reject the children now and you reject a considerable proportion of tomorrow's adult customers," was the core of John's message which must have come as a shock to his senior colleagues.

In the late 70s and early 80s I met John regularly. He enticed me onto the National Trust Education Committee, which I was happy to join since the principal reason for its existence was to further John's idea – to promote education as a key feature of National Trust policy. Critical questions were raised. What if activities were offered within NT properties which brought together curators, house managers, volunteers, teachers, children, parents…? How could best current practice be identified and shared?

At this time I was employed as a freelance writer within the Education Department of the Royal Opera House. Since the two departments had similar aims it became apparent that we could combine our distinctive areas of specialism and work on some joint projects. For example at Claydon House in Buckinghamshire a music drama, created by 6 First and Middle schools, told the story of the house and those who had lived in it. The production involved members of the Royal Ballet, the Orchestra of the Royal Opera House and actors from the National Trust Young Peoples' Theatre Group working alongside the children. A similar project was based in Llanhydrock House, Bodmin, where an 'Edwardian Christmas in the Great House' was presented. In this presentation Ben Luxon, who has appeared in all the world's great opera houses, led the singing. Viviane Durante, a prima ballerina, danced in 'the entertainment' (a 'thank you' to the Master and Lady of the House).

So when John walked into the breakfast room we were both delighted by the thought of being able to share some time together.

We spent one evening at the Paris Opera. It is one of the world's largest opera houses, classical in design and dates from 1861. The rich gilded decorations in the entrance lobby are most impressive. We had booked seats which in an English theatre would be called the Dress Circle. On reaching this level we looked for a door whose letter matched our ticket. We found it and discovered that it opened onto a little cubicle overlooking the stage. There were four seats in Box H. We had H1 and H2. Seat H1 was in the front next to H3. Behind H1 and H3 on a raised platform were seats H2 and H4. So John and I watched the ballet 'Giselle' sitting one behind the other like co-travellers in an aeroplane of the 1930s.

132

A young French couple shared our box. They seemed very much in love. We enquired whether they would like to change seats so that they might sit next to each other. They diffidently declined. I understood why. As soon as the house lights dimmed the young man leaned forward and gently caressed his companion's neck, twisting her hair around his fingers. He did this for the whole of the performance, ceasing only when the house lights were alight and when he was eating ice cream. Even then he had that look in his eyes that proclaims the vulnerability of love. John who sat next to the object of such gentle passion, was I am sure, too polite to notice and certainly would never have recorded the episode, as I have, on paper.

We also enjoyed supper together, often in a little café whose speciality was fresh mussels. Before one such meal we hurried to Musée des Monnaies to see the famous series of paintings of the water lilies. Incidentally this was John's first visit to Paris. I had stayed in the city several times since 1947 and the visit I am describing. That said, John would be forgiven for feeling that our explorations were very basic – a consequence of the largely ignorant advising the very trusting!

The perceptive reader may have already noticed that I have avoided attempting to describe John. Possibly this is because I do not want to ruin a long established relationship. Suffice it to say that he is not over-tall, of comfortable girth, neatly dressed in a country manner, sports a beard and wears wise-looking spectacles. I have a photograph of him at Llanhydrock dressed as Father Christmas. The twinkling eyes behind the white beard encapsulate the John I came to know.

I think that both John and I were impressed with Jack Lang who was present throughout the colloquium. He possessed all the qualities needed to become and to remain a politician… he continues to play a role in government after the events I describe. Jack Lang was charismatic and charming whether he was thanking an Italian academic for his presentation or chatting to a seven-year old engaged in role play.

Jack was of medium height and build. His face topped with a generous quantity of thick black hair, was interestingly angular. He dressed smartly but soberly. Overall the impression he gave was of a person rich in experience but young in years. His every intervention in the main conference hall and in group discussion was measured and thoughtful, often accompanied by a light self-deprecating aside.

He spoke English fluently. When I gently remarked after the paper I had presented "that I thought the French were a romantic nation, but that they were far from romantic in the way they presented architectural sites to children – all words and worksheets" Jack Lang sighed, smiled and replied. "Oh dear! What do the English know of romance? Now if you were Italian, Mr. Pluckrose, I might take your comment seriously."

The conclusion of the colloquium smacked of pantomime, though it did contain jarring echoes of the behaviour of the Quebecois (see Canada, p.124)

It was decided to make a presentation to the 'Secretary to the Colloquium' a French civil servant who had been responsible for its organisation and day-to-day running. This remarkably efficient lady I will call Madame la Bec.

To make the presentation reflect the international nature of the colloquium delegates from each continent would, in a short pageant, thank her and present her with gifts of flowers and chocolate. The presentation party, robed according to the continent they represented laid their offerings at the feet of Mme la Bec – she standing on the platform, they in the well of the hall below.

Mme la Bec received the gifts as politely as she was able, bearing in mind that she (suited, short, generously bodied, middle aged and not given to smiling) stood high above those making the presentation.

Mme la Bec received each continent in turn, and stepped to the microphone, the gifts before her on the stage. The applause subsided. She thanked Jack Lang for his support and interest, this in French. She turned to the delegates, all 900 of us, and addressed us in delightful English with strong French overtones. Her speech went something like this:

"M. Jack Lang, Delegates. Thank you for your kindness. I am happy to have helped make the Colloquium a success. I am pleased that my staff and I were able to be of service to you all.

"But I must say this."

There followed a long pause.

"I stand in the headquarters of UNESCO. I did not organise the colloquium for UNESCO.

"I stand on the same stage as M. Jack Lang.

"M. Lang I did not organise this colloquium for you.

"Delegates of the World, I did not organise this colloquium for you.

"Children from every continent, though you may benefit from our discussions, I did not organise this colloquium for you."

An even longer pause followed this Churchillian pronouncement.

134

We held our collective breaths. Then Mme la Bec seemed to grow taller, she swelled with pride and said,

"I ran this colloquium for France."

I'm prepared to swear that on hearing this our collective breaths were exhaled with such force that the Tour de Eiffel trembled!

8. Years of Change
Bulgaria (1981– 1995)

My six visits to Bulgaria, each of which lasted between a week and ten days, took place between 1981 and 1995. During this time I had very regular contact with Dr. Levcho Zdravchev and his colleague Dr. George Kalushev. Both periodically came to the UK and, when they did I usually met them.

Levcho was the moving force behind my first visit, a co-operative venture supported by the British Council and the Bulgarian Ministry of Education.

What made my successive visits interesting was that I watched, in an episodic manner, the slow decline of the Communist regime.

My first visit to Bulgaria, in the late spring of 1981, was in response to an invitation by Dr. Zdravchev to speak at an international conference on giftedness which was to be held in Plovdiv, a town 150 km to the east of Sofia. Plovdiv is steeped in history, being on the old trade route to Constantinople (Istanbul) and Asia. It is a pleasant town, the oldest areas dating from Greco-Roman times. There is an impressive town gateway, its arch shaped in red Roman tiles. Close by the gate is a well-preserved 2nd century theatre. The tiered semi-circular seating faces the stage behind which are walled colonnades.

Many of the houses in Plovdiv are timber-framed and jettied (c.f. Tudor period architecture in England), some are three-storied, all have pantiled roofs. The house fronts face each other across narrow, twisting stone-paved roads, their closeness obscuring the summer sun to give welcome shade.

Levcho invited me to Plovdiv some months after visiting Prior Weston School. He was given a tour of the building by a six year old girl whose task it was to explain classroom layouts and the way the school was organised. This was common practice, the purpose being to encourage children to develop verbal fluency, to give them the opportunity to give visitors a consumer's view of the school and allow them to see the school in action without a senior member of the teaching staff influencing their impressions. This policy was employed throughout my headship – even if the visitor was a prominent MP, a foreign ambassador, a university lecturer, Queen Margareta of Denmark or a prospective parent.

Levcho was so impressed with the poise of his guide, that he always used the experience as the basis of his introduction of me to an audience.

Levcho was an avowed communist, a belief born of family background rather than idealised conversion. The son of a former ambassador to the UK, he had travelled widely in both Europe and the Americas. His father's work meant that during Levcho's formative years he was never for long in any one place. For example he enrolled for courses in at least three different universities (including one in Yugoslavia) but failed to complete any of them.

One of these house moves (in early childhood) was to have a profound long term effect upon Levcho. He became friendly with Ljudmila, a young girl who lived in the house next door. The friendship lasted into adulthood, a friendship of great significance. For Ljudmila's father, Tordor Zjivkov would become the President of Bulgaria and his daughter, Levcho's childhood playmate, a powerful and influential Minister of Culture in his cabinet.

So Levcho began life with advantages denied the ordinary Bulgarian citizen. He had been born into a privileged strata of society and was happy to benefit from the benefits this brought.

In the mid 1970s, Levcho was appointed 'advisor' to the state council, a body which had no power but which provided a salary. He occupied a similar position in The Ministry for Science and Technology. These posts had no job description nor a specific role to play in the education system (in effect they were sinecures, gifts to 'friends' from the ruling elite.) Levcho used them as a springboard for the seminars he organised and the study trips to investigate giftedness he took overseas. The finance for these ventures was provided by the Ministry of Culture and its minister and politburo member, Ljudmila Zjivkova.

Levcho has the sharp mind of an effective politician, even when tired or suffering the after effects of an over bucolic meal. In all the years I knew him, he seemed to be walking a dangerous political tightrope. In a quest to find a model school system (which, he argued, could transform Bulgaria) I think he had as many critics as he had supporters.

Levcho was married and had two sons, one of whom had 'escaped' to a better life in the USA, much to Levcho's regret. He was a slick and persuasive operator, a dissimulator of the type to be found in most parties in government, east or west. He dressed smartly but not ostentatiously preferring the anonymity of blue blazer and slacks to suits or expensive informal clothes. Travelling as he did so extensively outside Bulgaria at Government expense, he was able to acquire consumer goods which were unobtainable by the mass of the population.

When I first met Levcho (in 1980) he was approaching middle age. He was well preserved. Not a hint of grey in his thick, well-cut hair or his neatly trimmed moustache. Of average height and sturdily built, Levcho had presence. I judged him a man who might prove a loyal friend but certainly a man best not to cross.

It was around this time in 1980 Levcho began to organise week-long seminars on educational topics, inviting speakers from many countries to present 'lead' papers. Using – what seemed to me – his 'undefined' position in the Ministry – Levcho was able to advance radical educational ideas through his speakers. At the same time he could deny that he was being subversive. Should Dr. Dorothy Sisk of Tampa University, USA or Dr. Joan Freeman from the UK criticise the policy being followed by the Bulgarian Government, Levcho could stand back and observe "These are the views of academics from a different culture, following a different model. We may not agree with their views, but we may learn a little from them."

In the early years, Levcho's position seemed secure. But in all totalitarian states there lie hidden dangers. Madam Zjivkova's outspoken views on culture, education and science were not appreciated by traditionally-minded communist zealots. At the height of her powers she was stricken with a strange illness and died. Even Levcho found it difficult to explain her death, though rumour suggested it was neither natural nor accidental.

At the beginning of the 1980s the party was very much in control. I remember a lunch towards the end of my first visit in a delightful open-air restaurant in Plovdiv. There were twelve in the group, five visitors from the West, the rest were Bulgarians. In the Bulgarian party were George and Levcho, four university delegates and a suited stranger to whom we were briefly introduced.

The meal had been pre-ordered so apart from the drinks there was no discussion over the menu. Since we all spoke English there was no need for an interpreter. 'All' did not include the suited stranger. He sat next to me and spoke not a word. He was equally taciturn when we moved to the lounge for coffee. He drank in silence, watched, and when we left to go, smiled and shook hands (so he *was* human!) But he did not speak. He turned on his heels and departed.

I enquired of George (who was employed by Levcho to help him with administrative chores) in a whisper who the silent suited-one was. In some telepathic way he managed to convey the message that such questions are best not asked in public. I gathered later that behind the silent face was the enquiring mind of the KGB.

State control was overt. The first time I walked through central Sofia I was surprised at the number of uniformed men – some were soldiers but there were many more police than one sees, for example, in Paris or Berlin. There were police checkpoints along all main roads. Each of these checkpoints had a small hut and many had wooden watch towers which gave the police the facility to watch over the surrounding landscape. Invariably there was a car by the checkpoint and the disconsolate figure of a Bulgarian being questioned about his ID papers, the purpose of his journey or the goods he carried in the boot. There were also control points on all the principal road junctions in central Sofia. Traffic flow could be easily stopped allowing party officials rapid transit across the city.

Two small episodes on my first visit serve to illustrate that the country was in the hands of a ruling clique.

On the day after my arrival I was met by George. He told me that it would be politic for us to attend the May Day parade in Plovdiv town centre. It being a provincial celebration there was little military involvement. Workers groups, young communist units, farmers, factory operatives and trades unionists were brought into town from the surrounding countryside. In columns of eight abreast, and carrying banners they followed their accompanying bands past a temporary podium on which stood numerous party worthies.

George said that the parade would take about an hour to pass and knowingly remarked that there were far more rewarding ways of passing the time than watching poor-quality street theatre. He asked if I felt well, because an illness would provide an appropriate excuse for early departure. So after watching a band march by, I feigned stomach pains. George's whispered explanation of my sickness was accepted by a severe looking party executive… and we departed. Strange to relate, but as soon as we returned to George's car the pain vanished. I felt very well indeed.

The second episode also took place in Plovdiv. The seminar had some 300 delegates, many of whom were staying in the town's principal hotel. On Tuesday evening it was announced, without warning, that all rooms must be vacated on Wednesday morning by 9.00 a.m. A 1 km deep cordon sanitaire would be thrown around the hotel by the army until 4.00 p.m. when the rooms could be re-occupied.

The reason? President Zjivkov was to make a speech in the conference centre we were using. Every centimetre had to be security checked and electronically swept before his arrival. Delegates to Levcho's seminar were firmly but gently informed of the problems which would result from entering the 'no-go' area.

I enquired of Levcho whether Zjivkov had been democratically elected and, if so, how great was his support. The degree of security in such a controlled political environment seemed to me to be excessive. Levcho, who always accepted my questions gracefully but usually answered them as though he wished I'd never asked, explained that the Government was a coalition of two parties – the Democratic Socialists (i.e. communists) and the Agrarian Party. The Democratic Socialists at the last election had won 80% of the vote, the Agrarians 18%. "So about 2% of the electorate do not like Zjovkov?" I asked. "Is there any likelihood that this tiny minority will organise a coup tomorrow?"

My questions were greeted with silence. Levcho busied himself in re-sorting paper that was already sorted. George raised his eyes to heaven and heaved his shoulders. The body language of both was clear. No words were necessary. It was a testimony of how unbridled state power in the hands of the few can cause anxiety in the minds of even the most rational.

Nine years later the political climate was changing rapidly. Zjivkov had been President since 1951. In September 1989 the week before Hilary Devonshire, a fellow lecturer and I arrived in Bulgaria, he had been deposed – as had Ceausecu in Romania, General Jaruzelski in Poland and Honecker in East Germany.

The radicals proclaimed a National Holiday to celebrate the 'liberation' for Sunday, 10th September. This would be marked by a demonstration in Alexander Battenburg Square in central Sofia. Radio announcements inferred that the crowd would be large but peaceful. This latter sentiment was given greater emphasis by linking a second news flash to the first about the rally. The police would also be on the streets and have certain powers of crowd control. This was significant since an immediate effect of the revolution had been the suspension of many police powers.

Levcho and George decided that as we wanted "to drink in the atmosphere", they would accompany us to make sure we came to no harm. We left our hotel which was close to the Cathedral and made our way towards the sounds of shouting and patriotic music. We soon reached the fringe of the crowd – a crowd of over 10,000 men, women and children and some babes-in-arms. Speakers standing on the steps of the National Picture Gallery (once the Palace of the Third Bulgarian Kingdom 1878–1944) addressed the crowd. There was no sign of violence or disorder. Perhaps the demonstrators had satisfied the need for dramatic action during the previous week with the firing of the Government Record Office. This name conceals the building's real function. In practice it was the Office and Headquarters of the Communist Party. That the words 'Government' and 'Party' are interchangeable is characteristic of all one-party states. Here records of all citizens were stored, making the offices the most feared and hated establishment in Sofia. The blackened stonework of the third and fourth floors bore testimony to a determination to exorcise the past.

Watching the crowd from the side streets were detachments of tired, disconsolate-looking police. Three weeks earlier they had been feared (but not respected). Now it was their turn to wonder what the future might hold. Uncertain of their role, they chatted quietly, lounging against walls or sitting on the pavement to while away the time. They looked stressed, tension showing in each weary face... altogether a sad, unloved body of men who realised that should the crowd become restive they were ill-equipped to control it. Their standard black Lada saloons were useful for making a speedy escape, not for confronting ten-thousand determined protesters. From time to time the whispers of the police would cease as the crowd, as if with one voice, shouted a political slogan – a slogan which proclaimed everything the police had been taught to act *against* when Zjivkov was in power.

Fortunately it was cool and the spirit of the crowd was festive rather than riotous. A slight breeze ruffled the long red banners and the streamers bearing the national colours which hung from every lamp post... a photograph I took captures this moment.

Our wanderings brought us to a stone podium on a wide boulevard. George told us that this was the balcony of the mausoleum in which the body of the first communist leader, Georgi Dimitrov, was preserved. It was also the podium used by the ruling politicians and the chiefs of the armed forces to take the salute on the annual May

141

Day march. The procession in Sofia, he added, was much more impressive than the one from which we had escaped on my first visit. In Sofia the marching groups represented every aspect of Bulgarian society.

But at this moment the mausoleum did not reflect power. George grew quiet. I sensed that for him this place represented the distasteful face of communism. Here, before us, were the stone steps which led to the reviewing platform. These were steps which George would never have sought to climb, a privilege he would never have wanted, a position of influence and political patronage to which he would never have aspired.

Yet the mausoleum cum podium had not been destroyed by the crowd. Instead it had been covered with slogans painted in red, black and white. The paint had run downwards from the letters, giving the impression of oozing blood or streaky tears, as if this inanimate thing was in mourning for the dead and despised regime it once represented.

We climbed the steps, George still quiet and obviously sunk in personal memories, said little – apart from the fact that this was like a living dream.

Though it is many years since we stood side-by-side on the podium I still wonder what George was thinking as he gazed across the street at the little knots of protesters making their way home.

Perhaps he was thinking of his family. George wrote me these notes about his father (a person he had spoken about reluctantly during my several visits) to include in this chapter. He wrote:

"My father's year of birth is 1903. The son of an uneducated Black Sea longshoreman, he had finished at commercial secondary school and started working in the shipping agency. He joined the communist party in 1923, but had grown as a business person. The communist regime in 1944 found him director-general and co-founder of the biggest shipping agency in the country (still existing by the same name – Despred). He was conversant in German, French, English, Russian and spoke also some Greek – all self taught. One of my images of him is reading one of his small handwritten dictionaries late at night in bed.

"I have come to this world with the advent of communism in the country (1944). I have very few memories of my father during the first five years of my life, as he would either come home late from work or would be on a business trip abroad. Our family must have been considered as rather well-to-do. We had a family servant to help in the house, whom I remember calling 'mother' for some time, as she was the person responsible for my well-being most of the time. My parents, two sisters and I lived in a nice apartment in the centre of Sofia. Then my father disappeared on one of his business trips to Vienna. During the following three months my mother did not know whether he was alive or dead. The year, 1949, when following instructions from the Stalinist regime in the USSR and duplicating its purges, the Bulgarian puppet government decided to silence all intellectuals and people of some importance who would question its policies. My father was tried in a group with 11 other people, including several ministers in what came to be known as 'the trial of the ministers', accused of "spying for the Americans, British and Yugoslavs" and sentenced to 12½ years 'rigorous regime'. Incidentally the three months prior to the trial, during which it was not known where he was, had been used to torture the prisoners in order to make them 'confess' stories against each other in order to put together the fabricated trial. I learned much later one of the 12 in his particular trial ended his life during this period by cutting his veins in the cell. Following the arrest, our house was searched several times and most of the valuable furniture and items were taken away by the secret police, never to be seen to this day.

"I was sent to be taken care of by an aunt (mother's sister) and uncle to the Black Sea coast. I spent two years there until 1951, when I had to start school and my aunt and uncle moved to Sofia to help our family. For the next 2 years following my father's arrest the family survived thanks largely to the help of relatives. Upon insistence of my father, my mother never held a job or learned a profession. He had not allowed her to study, for she was to take care of him and the three children. She had a gift for painting, for we still keep several oil paintings copied from postcards. Left penniless and without a job, I remember her, my two sisters and aunt sitting for days and late into the night hand knitting pullovers to sell to a local co-operative. These were hard years indeed which left a lasting imprint on everybody. The family was an outcast. I still remember vividly some of my schoolmates calling after me 'traitor, son of a traitor'. Other than several close relatives, most family friends disappeared out of fear or lack of interest.

"My father was released in 1956 (when Nikita Kruschev formally denounced Stalin) and rehabilitated together with other political prisoners in a very low profile way (the same people who put him in jail were still in power). By the way his rehabilitation appeared officially in print (in the State Gazette) 43 years later, in 1999. He came out of prison a bitter person, closed in on himself and not keen to talk about his confinement. Some horror stories reached us through the families of other political prisoners who were set free at the same time. He had a big deep scar on his head whose origin I never learned. Interestingly enough, for all I could tell, his idealist beliefs in the ideas of communism did not appear shattered at all. I believe he believed, possibly until his death, that there was nothing wrong with the theory, only it was misused by the wrong people. No doubt my mother, who had never read his books and who would shiver at the very mention of the word communism, considered him in her heart a naïve idiot, but her personal opinion was of no importance.

"I never managed to come close to my father. The period following his release coincided with my teenage years and I interpreted the various expressions of his concern that I do not 'go astray' as severe restrictions on my personal freedom. At times I even hated him for that. I do not remember a single really friendly conversation with him. A short discourse I do remember and one of some ideological flavour took place while we were in Egypt, maybe in 1963. I asked him "how come under communism (according to Marx), everybody will be receiving according to his/her needs, when human nature is such, that some needs appear never to be satisfied?" All I remember was his laugh. Maybe I was still too young to understand. Lastly, on the theme of communist ideology. During my studies in Cairo I came to like the philosopher Eric Fromm. One of his books, 'The Marxist View of Man' really impressed me. If this was what my father believed in, I had no objections at all. Of course, what it said could not be further away from my life experiences.

"During the years following his release from prison, my father and many of his cell-mates apparently kept asking uneasy questions nobody was willing to answer. They were declared innocent, the trial was called a 'mistake', yet not a word about lost opportunities and income, confiscated property, etc. Upon their release, former communist party members like my father were admitted again to the party, then at one point were again kicked out, then admitted again. Eventually, many were sent to jobs out of the country. Thus my father found himself in a small office in Port Said, responsible for Bulgarian ships passing through the Suez Canal. The year was 1962 and I had just finished high school. It was decided that I should follow my parents to Egypt, where I was admitted to the American University in Cairo. Four years passed, during which I used vacations to see my parents who lived some 300 km away. As fate would have it, later during the day on 6th June 1966, the day I took my very last university exam, a telegram came from Sofia, informing of my father's sudden death during a short business trip to Bulgaria. Mother and I collected quickly our belongings and returned home.

"A few years before his death, following the advice of some friends and for the sake of his three children, my father applied for the title 'Honoured fighter against capitalism and fascism', bestowed on people with long history of allegiance to the communist party. He received the title posthumously around 1968 and it did serve as some protection for me and my two sisters Aneta and Lili, for children of 'honoured fighters' were more difficult to blackmail and manipulate at the whim of different stooges of the regime. What my sisters had suffered as children of a traitor before that, only they know."

George told me a little of this story on my first visit hinting at his personal questioning of Communism in practice, I took it as a signal that he trusted me. I think it was from this moment that we became firm friends.

To return to the demonstration. George was not a triumphalist, but one could feel his heart was with the crowd rather than with those who had lost power.

Levcho, on the other hand, was uneasy. His recent past as a senior civil servant was a job with low profile. His seminars were popular, did not follow the party line and were well supported. He could also draw on the good will of many teachers and educationalists because he supported limited changes in the school system. For example, the support he gave to the Primary School at Illentzy (School 98, see below) almost elevated him to sainthood by the teachers and the parents whose children attended it. Typical of this support was that given by a 90-year-old former nursery school teacher whose school had been closed in 1951 because "it smacked too much of the bourgeoisie." She told me that "Levcho was a good man who had simply been deceived by the communists." (A feeling which George echoes.)

To me it did not ring true: rather our elderly lady had been deceived by Levcho's charm and clever words. He could not tear up his party card as George had done and confine it to the dustbin of history. Levcho had been economically, socially and politically secure for as long as the podium stood pristine and untouched. All through his childhood, May Day processions had passed this spot. Every year they confirmed the faith which Levcho had in a command economy, a strong central government and in time the inevitable Marxist triumph.

For Levcho the desecration of the podium was a shock and a warning. Unless he manoeuvred himself carefully he might find himself caught up in a democratic 'purge' and asked to justify his past. He was well aware that he had aroused antagonism and that some people were prepared to wait years before settling old scores. As early as 1981 Levcho assured me that he would never employ George on a full-time basis. "George is straightforward and hardworking. Should I fall, there is no reason for him to go down with me."

As I stood on the vandalised podium I reflected on the emotions such architectural trifles can stir up. I remembered that the poet Shelley had pointed to the ephemeral nature of political power in his sonnet 'Ozymandias'.

Ozymandias, a Persian King, regarded himself as all powerful. He created an enormous statue of himself. The plinth bore the words "LOOK ON MY WORKS, YE MIGHTY AND DESPAIR." Apart from some scraps of stone that were once his ears, his mouth, his nose, the inscription is all that is left. Shelley sees these fragments as representing the temporary nature of power. He ends the sonnet with the following lines:

"Nothing beside remains. Round the decay
Of that colossal wreck, boundless and bare,
The lone and level sands stretch far away"

I didn't realise it then, but I think that moment on the podium was a turning point in three lives. Levcho continued to work in education for a while and then drifted out of my life. For George new opportunities arose and he deservedly prospered. I am in contact with him still.

Let me interrupt my narrative. Before me I have a letter sent me by George in mid-December 2003… He was about to undertake a 6 month lecture tour in Belize. He writes:

"As I am writing and talking to you in my mind, an image surfaces from memory some time last century. We are about to go in a bus for one of Levcho's seminars. You casually ask me "How can you live in such a country?" I do not recall my response. Possibly with a shrug of the shoulders. As a matter of fact I have always felt a prisoner in what was and still is to me a cave society… Yet I feel strange and this is behind some of these lines – things I must have told you at different times. I had to remind them to myself, taking the

146

excuse of sharing them with you. I am sure you understand as very few of the people I know would."

This gives me the opportunity to describe George. Physically he has not changed over the years. He is now at 60 (2007) contemplating retirement but his boyish, engaging good looks remain. He is a little more rounded now than he was in 1981 but my photographs taken over the years do not reveal many extra worry lines.

When I first met George he was Assistant Professor in Management Studies in the Higher Institute of Economics, Sofia. In the late 80s and 90s he led management courses for Bulgarian students. Some of these courses were validated in the UK, entailing George making regular visits to South Thames University and the University of Hull.

His comments on life, relationships, religion, politics (or whatever) are invariably thought provoking, astute. And often humorous. When one takes into account that our communications are in English, his facility with words is impressive. The notes I have before me, written in 1981, have stood the test of time.

George has long believed it essential that changes had to be made in the social, political and economic policies adopted by the Bulgarian Government and those followed by the other countries in the Eastern block. But, (and I quote from my notes) "he foresees the problems which changes will bring, particularly as they will inevitably result in greater personal autonomy in decision making in adult life." My notes conclude, "George is a person of great charm, willing to share ideas and to intellectually challenge traditionally accepted views." My admiration of George has grown over the years. He has faced and overcome crises in his personal and professional life with courage, integrity and great internal strength.

I don't recall how our demonstration day ended. The crowd dispersed, the police were passive onlookers. Television news carried snippets of the day's events. The considered response of the newspapers next day were that life in Bulgaria would never be quite the same again. This forecast contained more than a grain of truth. I can best describe my subsequent visits by highlighting the changes I noticed.

It is fortunate that the Bulgarians are a stoical people particularly as survival in the 1990s became something of an art. At no time was I short of food, for foreign visitors like me stayed in hotels where food was available. The menu was always more ambitious than the kitchen could manage. (The Bulgarian hotel menu was a feast for the eye and the mind. Not the body). The majority of the dishes listed were "not being served today." Invariably meals in the hotel restaurants were almost identical. For those – the great majority – who could not afford to eat in hotels and cafes, enormous amounts of time were given to queuing for food. Because the command economy was so ineffective, particularly when Russia collapsed and reneged on the trade agreements with her satellite states, foodstuffs seemed to be delivered haphazardly and in bulk. Much was season and weather dependent. There would be a surfeit of beetroot, for example, so every meal was beetroot based. There followed a season of no beetroots and the roadside stalls were piled high with watermelons instead.

A rumour that a shop would be selling eggs reached my interpreters (1990). Both wanted to queue, but knew I could not be left alone. One undertook to translate without breaks, (usually they worked in 15-minute blocks) while the other went to hunt for eggs. Julian remained with me and translated continuously for two hours. Janne eventually returned with 18 eggs, which she shared with her colleague. This 'you queue, I'll remain' was a policy also adopted by course members. One stayed to take notes or complete an assignment whilst the partner spent time in a queue somewhere in Sofia.

I must admit to being fazed by the lack of fresh bread. Bread did reach the shops where it was sold stale. The explanation I was given goes as follows:

Bread was baked by co-operative units. Batches were then sent to predetermined outlets. Each batch had to be sold before subsequent batches were made available for sale. Somewhere in the distant past production had grossly exceeded demand, so the bread which had been baked by the co-operative to meet its target was stored until the retail outlets had cleared their own shelves. By the time the 'fresh' bread reached the shop it was already hard. Repeat this pattern over weeks and the difference between making bread (meeting the production target) and consumption/selling increased. Thus the bread for sale was even harder.

When I enquired why it was impossible to stop production for a few days to allow supply and demand to adjust or convert the stale bread into animal food and sell new bread to the population, I was told that such action would disrupt the economic cycle.

The story of bread making may be apocryphal, but I'm certain it contains a grain of truth, an ordinary Bulgarian's perception of how things were done – and the consequence of doing them that way. The explanation also illustrates how difficulties could be delightfully explained away… as in the next example.

The supply of electricity was rarely disrupted during my early visits (1981–83) but in the late 80s and early 90s supply was very irregular. Certain hotels (like those that were chosen for me) had 'restricted electricity' even when Sofia was virtually blacked out. 'Restricted' meant the electricity was only available on one floor of the hotel – the floor that was given over to guests of significance. I remember watching a fellow lecturer despair when the slide projector, so essential to his presentation, 'died'. He struggled to complete his paper, but finally defeated by the power cut, retired gracefully to his hotel room. I enquired of my neighbour, a Bulgarian, why the electricity had failed. He smiled.

"The two little men
Who peddle the bike
That drives the generator
Have got tired legs."
Don't you have that happen in Britain?"

Sometimes petrol was difficult to obtain. In December 1991 George parked outside the hotel in which I was staying. He wisely removed his windscreen wipers – but had to trust in the security provided by the locking petrol cap to protect his fuel. Returning to his car he found his tank empty. To have petrol stolen, petrol which had been obtained by joining a queue 700 metres long at 4.30 a.m. in a temperature of -8°C, is hard to bear!

Rather like Londoners in the Blitz, Bulgarians were helped to cope by employing, to good effect, their droll sense of humour. As in wartime London, queues in Sofia were a way of life. It is said that two Bulgarians were waiting for a delivery of bread. One turned to the other:

"I'm fed up with all this queuing, I'm going straight to the palace to shoot the President."

He departed, gun in pocket. After only half an hour, to his friend's surprise, he returned.

"Do it?" he asked.

"No", came the reply. "I couldn't get near him. The queue was too long…"

Shortages were compounded by an inefficient service industry. Even some small business units (like hotels) were not always efficiently run.

It's at this point that I should introduce Tom Marjoram, a member (in 1988) of Her Majesty's Inspectorate for Schools. Tom was a very experienced inspector, the editor of educational anthologies, had worked abroad, was pleasant and unassuming, could speak in public effectively. But he had never before been to Bulgaria. Had he done so he would surely have tried to overcome his one weakness. He was naïve.

I had a feeling that Tom believed what he read. If somebody took the trouble, for example, to translate notices into English to display in a hotel then the notices contained information of weight and substance.

Tom and I had agreed to undertake a question and answer session as part of the seminar held in Blagogod in October 1988. Before we began (at 4.30) I told Tom to insist that we had an agreed ending time and that we kept to it. We had eaten very little all day and I warned him that unless we were in the hotel restaurant by 6.30 the kitchen would be closed… as would all the other eating places in town.

But Tom knew better. Adopting the role of an apostle, one who brings news from afar, he was unrestrainable. The session ended at 7.15.

We returned to our hotel. Apart from reception everything was closed. "No worries," said Tom, "we'll use room service." We studied the tiny brochure which had been left on his bedside table. After a short discussion Tom dialled room service and ordered beer and sandwiches for two. We sat in his room and waited. 7.45 came. There had been no response to Tom's order. "Probably my mistake," said Tom. "Perhaps I forgot to give the room number." At 8.00 he phoned again, repeating the order in louder, slower and more distinct English. At 9.00, after a further phone call (during which I asked him if he was sure he was talking to room service and not the local railway station) we decided to dine on chocolate – provided by me – and wine – which Tom had secreted in some abundance in his room. The menu looked like this:

Hors d'oevres
Chocolate   Glass of Chardonnay 1987
Dark, two squares   and a toast to Bulgarian cooking

Plat du jour
Chocolate, white   Glass of Cabernet Sauvignon 1983
4 squares (milk)   and a toast to King Simeon 11

Dessert
Chocolate   Glass of Vouvray 1980
2 dark squares   and a toast to Levcho
1 white square

There being no chocolate left we did not have a cheese course.

The mention of Tom and wine reminds me of his particular idiosyncrasy. He wrote a short note to describe every wine he tasted. There was a ritual. First a little book was produced from an inside pocket in his jacket. Then he examined the bottle carefully noting the information given on the label… name, grape-type, vintage, country of origin. This ceremony, performed in silence but with a spiritual intensity was precursor to the mystery of the cork. Delicately held between finger and thumb it was squeezed, smelt and angled towards the light before being placed reverently on the table. The wine could then, and only then, be sniffed and sipped. Notes were written into the little book which was immediately returned to the deep, inside pocket.

Levcho, who was fond of wine, once tried to distract Tom to enable a Bulgarian friend capture the book but Tom, who must have foiled many similar attempts, thwarted the would-be thief.

Tom took the notebook with him everywhere. Returning to England, I arranged to take him to a Schools' Matinee at Covent Garden Opera House. Before the performance I bought Tom lunch – and with lunch, a bottle of wine. Out came the notebook and the wine cycle began.

Back to Bulgaria. The shortage of food was embarrassing. The children and staff of School 98 (Illientsi) took lunch in a nearby textile factory. The fabric it produced was sold on the Russian market. However the co-operative found it difficult to compete with cheap and better quality woollen fabric from the Far East. When Hilary and I went to the factory it had ceased production and was being 'mothballed'. A small working party remained, including two tiny blackrobed ladies who were the kitchen staff.

We were given a triangular plastic bag containing goat's yoghurt, and a crust of hard uneatable bread. The food was accompanied by the tableware needed i.e. an army-type mess-tin for water, a pair of scissors to open the yoghurt bag, a heavy battered pewter bowl in which to pour the yoghurt and a tablespoon.

It seemed as though the factory had closed some months earlier – when the eating area had last been cleaned. The tables and the plastic

151

table cloths spoke and smelt of meals of yesteryear. We looked for the least food-spattered space. I felt guilty when I thought of the quantity and range of food we consume in the West and the amount we throw away each day.

One element behind Levcho's invitation to people like Tom and me was to help him find ways of changing schools so that they better met children's and society's needs. Change involved an examination of many aspects of school life, the curriculum, the pupil, the nature of life, the school day, teacher skills, class organisation, the place of school in the community.

Levcho sought to achieve his aim by exposing selected Bulgarian educators to the ideas put forward in his seminars. Above all else Levcho was seeking a model – a working example of an approach to learning and teaching – which would be modified to meet the specific restraints of the system traditionally followed by Bulgarian teachers. This is why School 98, Illentsi, Nadeja, features so prominently in this section.

School 98 – which I first visited in 1988, was a school for children aged between 7 and 11+. It stood close to a main road in a field of rough grass. On the far side of this field were the decaying buildings of an earlier school which occupied the site.

The building was a breeze block, brick and concrete construction – factory-like rather than child-friendly. It was a small building of two floors. On the ground floor there was one classroom (unused and unusable), the bank of toilets (holes in the floor, ramshackle doors giving a modicum of privacy), and a wide flight of stone stairs which led to the first floor.

The first floor consisted of a large open space, three generously sized classrooms, a small headteacher's staff room cum general office and a part-carpeted but unfurnished family/activity/general meeting room. The ceilings throughout were high, the walls hard, the breeze block unplastered and decorated in institutional yellow. In the centre of the open area was a wall which jutted out to form a narrow bay. Close to this was a cold water tap fixed above a stone trough. This was the only source of water on the first floor – and was used for cleaning, washing and drinking, (as well as for rinsing paint pots and brushes).

The materials used and the style of construction meant that the teaching staff had to solve two problems before they could begin to re-structure their work with the children. There were two other concerns which were building related. It was very cold in winter... I worked in

152

the school with children who wore outdoor clothing throughout the day and only took their gloves off when they needed to write. The building had exciting acoustics but only if you were a drummer in a pop group! Sounds seemed to double in volume and then reverberate. The sound of a chair tipping over in one classroom would bounce from wall to wall. In consequence, tranquillity and quiet application were very difficult to obtain and sustain.

There were six teachers in the school working a shift system, three in the morning and three in the afternoon. They had 90+ children in their care.

I was invited to make regular yearly visits to the school and to answer by letter any questions which arose in staff discussions. In the event, I visited School 98 four times over a period of four years and spent a week in the school on each occasion. I also answered about a dozen letters.

My first impression of the school was that each of the teachers had potential... but that their individual qualities were haphazardly utilised because they lacked leadership. The practice in this school was for each teacher to take a 6 month term of headship. This was to prevent the development of the 'cult of the individual'. The concept of revolving leadership was quite common to institutions in a number of eastern bloc countries.

One of the first suggestions I made to the staff of School 98 was to determine some form of long-term leadership. Who as a staff would they choose from the teachers already employed there? The person selected needed to possess certain qualities: staying power; the ability to cope with disappointment and frustration; flexibility; the willingness to experiment; the strength to value children as individuals rather than seek the personal comfort and security which comes from making bureaucracy the key feature of school life; to be able to communicate with parents and the local community; to be a leader, i.e. someone the teaching staff were prepared to respect and to follow. And one further dimension – to realise that the problems and issues faced by a Bulgarian school required Bulgarian solutions, not solutions which might be appropriate to a school in Cleveland, Ohio or Tunbridge Wells in the English county of Kent.

The teachers chose Daniella, a caring, thoughtful and respected lady in her mid thirties. It was an intelligent choice.

On my first visit to the school the potential was self evident. The building, though rather unkempt and untidy, could easily be made attractive. The walls were suitable for expansive displays and there

153

was ample space for interest-tables (mini-museums). I suggested softening the institutional-like feeling of the building through the use of carpets, rugs, soft furnishings, fabric drapes, curtains and informal furniture. An area was earmarked for books and a 'home base' planned for a corner of each classroom where children and teachers could come together informally to listen to poetry, music and stories and take part in discussions about future projects or the work in hand.

By 1990 the school had made an impression on its immediate community. The press had given Daniella some coverage and this had encouraged local support. For example two pensioners who lived nearby presented themselves "as volunteers". They were established folk musicians who wanted to pass on the "culture of their childhood" before "we die and then it will be too late". The contribution these elderly folk made was impressive. The children learned and performed the region's folk songs and dances, listened to its stories and made folk costumes to wear.

When the two pensioners came to work with a class, 'Grandpa Serge' appropriately dressed in "the village costume of my youth", played on a battered but well-loved violin the music he wished the children to learn. His wife, Viktoria, taught the words and led rehearsals of songs and organised the complex ritual movements of the dances.

The cascade of notes which flowed from Serge was electrifying. We were all entranced by the sound of the music. It was easy to see why music was given many magical powers in Eastern European folk stories (e.g. 'Schwanda the Bagpiper' which is used as the basis of an opera by the Czech composer Jaromere Weinberger).

Serge swayed as he played, eyes slightly closed, seemingly oblivious to everything except his music. He reminded me of Stephane Grapelli. Viktoria stood close by him, tapping her foot as she 'called' the dance and led the singing, her face alive with enthusiasm, her eyes twinkling.

Joseph, another regular visitor, was also in his seventies. He had lived and worked in the woods and forests since his early teens. He loved trees. He regularly accompanied children and teachers on country walks to collect what he called "nature's shapes". These were pieces of wood which had fallen from trees and been weathered by wind, rain, sun and snow. Together with the school group, he collected twigs and small branches which had grown into unusual shapes and forms. He taught the children how to take a natural form and "look at it". This form was then developed by whittling, cutting away or smoothing part of the surface.

He gave me a number of his creations. I have them still. One I particularly treasure measures 7 cm in length and 5 cm in height. Formed from a knot of hard wood, the golden brown sculpture clearly portrays a naked female figure riding on the back of a sea creature. The children's creations were not so exotic but there were ducks, prehistoric monsters, boats and witches aplenty – all finished to a fine, smooth polish.

School 98 had also established a link with (what was for me a surprise) the local Orthodox Church. On my first visit to Bulgaria I had noticed that most towns boasted both mosque and church. The mosque sat somewhat uneasily in street and square for its presence recalled five centuries when Bulgaria was part of the Ottoman Empire. It was a period of cruel domination searing a bitter 'race memory' into the psyche of every Bulgarian citizen. The Ottoman/Turkish annexation was marked by a harsh military regime. Conditions grew so desperate that an uprising in 1876 was given Russian support. It won for the Bulgarians a measure of local autonomy, eventually leading to the establishment of a monarchy and a Bulgarian state. Throughout the long period of foreign oppression and civil unrest the culture of Bulgaria was preserved by the Orthodox church, which having survived 50 years of State Communism, continues to enjoy a place in the hearts of Bulgarian people.

It was against this background that Genadi, the teacher responsible for the 10 and 11 year olds, gathered his class around him. It was December 6th. Quietly, almost with reverence, Genadi explained why the day was so special. It was the day, he said, when Orthodox Christians remembered and celebrated the life and times of Nikolai Chudovorets (Nicholas the Wonderworker) whose festival marked the beginning of the Christmas season. Long ago on this date the country folk drank specially brewed beer and ate beef, ending their celebrations with singing and dancing. In Western Europe Nicholas was represented as Santa Claus or Father Christmas.

The introduction over, we left school and made our way to the parish church. It was a grey day of continuous drizzle. The walk to church was neither supervised or organised, just little knots of children and adults making their way along muddy paths, avoiding puddles as they went.

Finally we arrived at the battered door of a large stone built hut. The building had seen better days. The paint was peeling, water

155

flowed from the roof of corrugated iron forming little streams on the earth below.

We went inside. Adjusting to the dim light I tried to relate the interior to the Anglican parish churches I knew so well in England. The children clustered round Genadi. Genadi was Moscow-born and had come to Sofia on marriage to his Bulgarian bride. He possessed that rare quality of being able to listen to children as well as to talk to them. He was anxious to acquire as much help as he could in his class management. He told me of his burning ambition, "to be a really good teacher". In my opinion he had achieved this goal already. He was the most sympathetic, observant and thoughtful teacher I met in all of my visits to Bulgaria.

Genadi attempted to introduce me to the Orthodox priest, Father Alexander. Dressed in a splendid cope, bejewelled and sparkling in the flickering candlelight, he looked magisterial and imposing. He was tall (over 2 m), his eyes barely visible, surrounded as they were by an unkempt mass of black hair, bushy eyebrows and a thick beard which concealed the rest of his facial features. The thumb of his left hand was looped through the chain which hung round his neck. It held, at waist level, a crucifix. He fingered it gently, as if preparing himself to meet this sudden and unexpected influx of people.

Priest and people were still. There was no sound except the gentle 'pit-pit' of rain on the makeshift roof. Genadi attempted introduction faded on his now silent lips. The children sensed a tension, not born of conflict, fear or anxiety but of a state of unknowing. They had come to school and ended up in church…

Relief and relaxation came unexpectedly in the shape of an old, bent figure in black… a lady parishioner. She carried a tray on which were some cubes of bread and a bowl of salt. Something was expected of me. But what? She approached me smiling.

Genadi quickly intervened, taking a cube of bread, sprinkling it with salt before swallowing it. He motioned me to copy him, which I did. The little black figure moved away, dispensing bread and salt to adult and child alike. Before attempting to complete the introduction to Father Alex, Genadi explained the symbolism of the salt and the bread. Christ is the bread of life, the salt gives savour and meaning.

Father Alex smiled and we shook hands. He whispered a blessing as he did so. Thinking of that handshake makes me feel an uncomfortable, archetypical Briton. Perhaps as a priest he would rather have greeted me with a touch of his cheeks on mine, or a hug… His English was restricted and it was with some difficulty that he showed me round the church. He indicated a wooden ikon of particular significance, one which all the adults kissed with great reverence. We remained in the church for about half an hour before retracing our steps to school through muddy fields and the grey, cold rain.

I found the church visit emotionally satisfying and did not question its appropriateness. I did wonder how it would be viewed by Levcho, by an agnostic or atheist parent or by the secretary of the village communist party. On the Feastday of Nikolai Chudovorets Genadi seemed to be able to read my mind. "You do realise, Henry, that School 98 was named 'The School of Cyril and Methodious' that's why their portraits have been painted by a local artist on the wall above the stairwell".

Cyril and Methodious, I should explain, were two brothers who, in the ninth century, brought the Christian Gospel to the Slav peoples. (St. Cyril 827–869), St. Methodius 826–885). St. Cyril is credited with the invention of the Slav Alphabet which he developed from 9th Century Greek. The adoption of this *Cyrillic* Alphabet by the ethnic groups who lived in the Balkans and the Russias meant that it became possible to translate the Gospels into the vernacular. Originally the Cyrillic Alphabet had 45 letters. In its modern form about 30 are used.

I appreciated the opportunity to work within a school which had such a range of problems – the curriculum, the inexperience of the teaching staff, the poverty of the equipment, the lack of basic facilities and of quiet spaces to which children could retire to read, talk and reflect. Problems of this magnitude in an equivalent British or Swedish school would have led the teaching staff to a state of angry despair. In contrast the teachers of School 98 were delighted to have challenges to meet and overcome.

I was also privileged to be invited to talk at two parents meetings. At the conclusion of both I remarked that parents across the world share identical dreams for their sons and daughters, the hope that they will grow into well-balanced, successful, contented men and women, at peace with their neighbours near and far. At the second meeting a spokesperson for the parent body was generous in thanks to everybody involved in the project. He wisely and aptly ended his thanks with a sentence of cautionary wisdom.

"Bulgarian schools have problems. You have generously given of your time and expertise to seek ways of making our school more effective. We must not forget that in the end Bulgarian problems must have Bulgarian answers."

I contrast this little state-funded school with the private school in Plovdiv in which we were invited to work. It was 1995. The relaxation of regulations by the post-Zjivkov governments meant that private schools could be established. For the emerging entrepreneurial class they were socially and politically attractive and economically viable. In my English mode, I disapprove of private education. I accepted it in Plovdiv as it provided a cost-free opportunity to continue my association with School 98.

The private school was based in a former office complex. It catered for children between 6 and 12 years of age. Its students followed a unique programme. Apart from lessons to deepen and extend the mother tongue (i.e. reading and writing in Bulgarian), the whole school day was centred upon the mastery of English. I had heard of this practice called 'total immersion in a second language' but had never seen it in action.

The concentration upon English was a ploy which helped 'sell' the school to wealthy parents willing to pay the high fees on which its future depended. English was regarded as the language of fashionable capitalism; Russian, so recently the language of political power, was no longer needed in the world of business. It was the language of a collapsed Empire, a language of a nation unlikely to be able to compete with 'English' speaking USA and the international dominance won by its English language computer technology.

The second curriculum innovation was philosophical rather than pragmatic. The owners of the school (I hesitate to use the word 'educators') believed that self-control was essential for success in adult life. Therefore self-control should be taught – and taught young.

How was this done? The answer lay in the Plovdiv School curriculum. Teach English-American Ballroom Dancing and Karate to every child every day.

English-American Ballroom Dancing was taught by a professional dancer. The pupils aged 6 and above were paired so that they worked with the same partner throughout the school year. When performing each girl dressed for the dance she was presenting, a long gown for the waltz, something more brief for the paso doble. The boys wore dinner jackets and dark trousers. The whole gamut of dances were taught – waltz, quickstep, tango, foxtrot, Latin-American and jive.

Dance was the vehicle which taught body control. Karate taught control of the angry psyche which is in us all. As with dance each child had a daily lesson under the guidance of an accredited instructor.

In addition to the subjects listed – Mother Tongue, English through immersion, Dance and Karate, all the pupils followed a curriculum similar to that found in most primary schools... Mathematics, History, Geography, Science and Art.

The inspiration underpinning and promoting the curriculum was the headmistress, Mdm. Loveska (a pseudonym.) In her mid-forties, she was always immaculately dressed, her hair coiffured rather than combed, her make up essential but invisible. She wore jewellery which was noticeable because each piece was chosen to enhance her wear for the day and she carried an expensive handbag of generous proportions. Indeed she was a commanding lady, whose voice demanded immediate attention. She ran the school from a large, three-telephoned office. In the centre was a desk around which were grouped easy chairs and sofas.

She embraced the "I order" style of headship. Organisation was by diktat. The staff responded to the last command (demand) until the next one was issued. Demands were issued to her husband (school chauffeur and controller of the budget), her daughter (part-time secretary), the housekeeper, the dance and karate instructors and to anyone who chanced to catch her eye or cross her path.

I watched this leadership, amused, for several days. As a guest I did not expect that 'look of cold command' from the eyes of a contemporary, Bulgarian female model of Ozymandias to affect me or to direct me to complete some unexpected task.

Mdm. L was not a respecter of persons. If, 'it moves, tell it!' was not the school motto, it could well have been! On the Wednesday of our visit, I was told, on passing Mdm. L in a corridor that "the parents were looking forward to my talk tomorrow."

"What talk?" I asked.

"Well... the things you have done with the children have impressed the parents. I've decided that you will speak about your beliefs and methods at the meeting tomorrow night. I can give you 25 minutes. The parents are really wanting to watch the children dance".

"I don't give talks without time for preparation. I must have a free afternoon tomorrow to select the children's work I would wish to present."

"That is almost impossible, I'm afraid. Who will teach class 3? You were going to look after it. Ludmilla, the teacher is coming to town with me."

159

I'm afraid I became stubborn. Maintaining self-control (though never exposed in my youth to dance or karate), I said firmly, but quietly.

"No time to prepare
No talk to give."

Mdm. L had the grace to give way – ungracefully.

"I'll tell Ludmilla I'm off to town without her."

Imagine how tedious it must be to confront this style of leadership every day! A bigger problem that faced the school was one of 'ownership'. The grounds and the buildings belonged to the consortium which had made the capital available for its purchase. At the time of my visit the pupils regarded the school as a place to spend their days; the teachers as a place of learning; the parents as a place where, for a fee, they could insulate their children from the harsh shadows which haunted the corridors of state schools. The intention of the financial backers was for 'Plovdiv Private' to grow in two directions and offer both pre-school and pre-university provision. To succeed in this high-risk venture a rigorous academic programme would need to be carefully developed and teachers employed who were capable of effectively delivering it. I remain unconvinced of the merits of either Ballroom Dancing or Karate as mainstream subjects!

Throughout our week in 'Plovdiv Private' Hilary, my fellow English teacher and I were guests of a Bulgarian family in a flat owned by Plovdiv Commune. It consisted of an open-plan living-cum-cooking area, three bedrooms and a bathroom and toilet. The flat was on the ground floor reached via a scruffy porch and stairway. There were two front doors, one closed against the other. The inner door of wood was reinforced with an overcoat of strip steel. The outer door was of metal and resembled a prison gate. Security for the Family Kaptebilev, our hosts, was obviously of some concern. Bulgarians took many precautions to frustrate thieves, including the removal of windscreen wipers when parking their cars.

The Kaptebilevs were a middle aged couple with two daughters, Ina aged nine and Sevdalina, eighteen. It was a well-furnished and comfortable home. We were given the girls' rooms, Sevdalina going to stay with friends and Ina moving into her parents' room during our visit.

Todor, the father, was a musician in a long established pop group which played nightly in a local club. His wife (whose name escapes me) was a secretary. The centre of the family was not Ina, though she was greatly loved, but Lucky Kaptebilev, a miniature French Poodle. He was a bouncy, extrovert creature with an inordinate love of food.

The flat was within walking distance of the school, a short but far from easy journey. Pavements and roads were scarred with deep potholes. These were pedestrian traps after sunset, invisible, filled to the brim with stagnant, evil-smelling oil-covered water.

Around the 12 storey tower blocks which made up the complex, the architects had planned lawns, flower beds and pathways. Sadly these architectural ideals had been superseded by the living style of the local population. The flower beds and lawns had become the final resting place for rusting car bodies, tyres, dead petrol engines, beds, soiled mattresses, chairs with three legs, cushion-less sofas, battered packing boxes and drums partially filled with water, petrol, oil or paint. The resulting industrial 'parkland' was further enhanced by drifts of filthy paper, discarded household refuse and unwanted clothing (everything from shoes and socks to knickers and trousers). Around, through, in, over and under this memorial to civic pride roamed packs of unkempt dogs who chased and barked and generally waylaid every intrepid pedestrian. Their contempt of all things human was the additional hazard they posed to those foolish enough to walk: excreta encrusted every space that was pothole free. Slogans were painted on every bare wall and even on the larger pieces of rubbish further confirming the feeling of neglect.

Despite these symptoms of inner city decay, common to most of Europe, Bulgarians take pride in their personal appearance. I have never been to any other country where women wear so much expensive jewellery to adorn their working clothes.

I have dealt at length with examples of the changes I noticed over the time covered by my visits. I have already expressed my surprise at the impact of Father Alexander and his little church on the pupils of School 98.

In 1983 George and Levcho took a number of visiting speakers to the Rila Monastery, some 65 km south of Sofia in the Rila Mountains. The monastery was unlike any I had seen in the British Isles (I had written a children's book about Monasteries in 1975). In England as with most of Western Europe, Catholicism under Rome enjoyed pre-eminence until the reformation. The Orthodox Church looked to Constantinople for inspiration. The Patriarchs of the Orthodox Church identified more closely with the early Christian churches of the Eastern Mediterranean than with the 'Bishop of Rome'. This explains the differences in liturgical practice of the two churches and their inability through the centuries to agree on the dates of the major church festivals e.g. Christmas and Easter.

The monastic buildings at Rila occupy an extensive enclosed site in a valley between high mountains. The whole complex was dominated by a church in Byzantine style capped by a dome. Next to the church was a tall, square tower, its crenellations more appropriate to the world of knights than of monks. The tower had one unusual feature, a balcony-like construction jutted from one side, reaching from the ground to the third floor.

The church looked over a large paved courtyard along the sides of which were the claustral buildings.

They were four-storied and housed the individual cells of the monastery. The design of the complex was unusual. On one side of the courtyard stood the church. The three remaining sides were defined by the four storey buildings.

On the side facing the courtyard, each building was decorated with rows of open arcading, the base of each arch resting on round, Moorish-style pillars. The arcading provided support for the wooden galleries which lay behind them. The galleries gave access to the cells and rooms which were situated along the inner wall. Entrance to all the upper galleries was gained from the courtyard by a wide wooden staircase.

Put another way it appeared as if the traditional open-arched cloister of a Benedictine Abbey – a roofed walkway round a quadrangle – had been taken apart to give four separate lengths of arches. These lengths, placed one above the other, roofed, give an adequate mental image of the architectural style of Rila.

The arches at Rila were rounded, Normanesque in shape but much more elegant and graceful than the imposing, heavy Norman-period arcading to be seen at Durham Cathedral or St. Bartholomew's Church in Smithfield, London. The columns supporting the arches were finely worked but undecorated. The overall effect was of sophistication born of simplicity.

The external walls were plainly worked, mostly in pretty white stone, enhanced here and there with a patch of brown and white chequer boarding and with regular insertions of brown stripes and blocks.

Each monk had his own plainly furnished room or cell, confirming the contrasting roots of monasticism, East and West. In the 2nd and 3rd centuries the Christian hermits of Asia Minor lived the life of anchorites. The solitary cells of Rila were a comfortable contemporary equivalent. In the Western tradition the monks lived communally and their claustral buildings were designed to reflect this: shared dormitory, refectory, hospital, toilets…

The sober browns and pinky white of the buildings with their tiled red roofs merged subtly with the colour-rich woodlands of the autumn countryside, the golds, yellows, reds and browns fading into the white snow capped peaks of the distant mountains.

George and I climbed to the top of a high tower, giving us a bird's eye view of monastic roofs and the courtyard far below. We watched a monk hurrying from church to gatehouse, blissfully unaware that he was the subject of conversation high above him.

"Do you think that God looks down like this?" I asked.

George was silent for a while. His apparently serious reply was delivered with a wicked smile.

"*If* God has any interest in Bulgaria at all, I'm sure he would discover that the monks do far more good than do our politicians in Sofia."

All of my journeys to Sofia have included a visit to the impressive Cathedral of Alexander Nevski. Situated in the heart of the city it towers above the buildings that surround it. Built in Byzantine style, its golden dome pushes heavenwards from the solid mass of church below.

Whenever I went to the Cathedral during the years of Zjivkov there were few visitors and even fewer worshippers. On one occasion I saw three youthful priests in deep conversation. Remarking on their lack of years encouraged a cynical response from Levcho. "There are times when the church is of use politically. I don't think it would help the Government if the church were to die."

In 1999 I ventured once more into the Cathedral. The day was not a Sunday nor one on which a religious festival was celebrated. The brooding darkness which I had expected to encounter was replaced by a mystery of a different kind. Instead of darkness there was light – an uneven light produced by the flickering flames of hundreds of votive candles. Instead of a solitary visitor there was a milling crowd… so many people were there that they formed queues before sacred relics, queues which shuffled slowly forward as each person bent low to kiss the shrine.

The effect was dramatic, for each face would have graced a Renaissance painting, so gentle did they look in the suffuse, uneven light. A priest appeared, black cassocked, a large crucifix hanging from a chain round his neck. Tall, bearded and dark eyed he strode

163

imperiously across the chair-free church. The curious, the ikon queuers, the casual visitor, moved aside as he approached; some bent a knee or bowed their head in an unspoken token of respect. One woman insisted on kissing a ring on the priest's hand. He acknowledged her but contact was brief: he neither paused or slowed as he moved towards the vestry and disappeared from view.

Before leaving the Cathedral I leant against a pillar to better study the people who were there. I noticed that there were equal numbers of men and women, that young folk were well represented. A cursory glance at the clothes of the visitors suggested that the comfortably secure were not outnumbered by the poor. There were many children, too, clutching the hands of their parents, their solemn faces conveying a mixture of wonder and puzzlement.

At this moment I recalled the tape I have of the famous Bulgarian operatic artist, Boris Christoff. His voice, echoing round this great building would have made my day complete. Sadly that could not be. The only sounds in the Cathedral were scuff of shoe on stone, the whispered aside of a friend to friend, a baby's cry.

As I moved towards the porch and the street beyond I was approached by an old lady, sombrely dressed with her head covered with a black scarf. She carried a tray of bread and salt. Remembering Genadi's advice, I took her offering and thanked her (in English!) for her blessings. She smiled. Although I am sure she did not understand my words I feel she grasped their meaning.

I invariably visited the Cathedral's crypt. It is currently used as an art gallery displaying ikons and religious paintings, many very old, some very modern and challenging to eye and mind.

On the morning I have described, Hilary and I left the Cathedral to return to our hotel. Something was about to happen close by. A small crowd had gathered and there were gaggles of police. The main road was closed to traffic, which was being diverted into side roads. We decided to join the watchers. Our wait was short. Soon we heard the faint beat of martial music.

The sound grew steadily louder and, turning a corner into the main street, the source of the music appeared – a military band. It was impressive, if only for the number of musicians and the range of their instruments: piccolo, clarinet, bassoon, trumpet, horn, tuba, trombone, percussion and three serpents. The musicians looked hot as they marched past, their red tunics and quaint hats providing a stark contrast to the combat dress of the unit which followed. It was a commando section, helmeted and dressed in green-brown camouflage denim, their rapid fire rifles to hand. The clockwork rhythm of their high goose step made them look particularly menacing. The 'high kickers' were followed by an honour party carrying flags. It was escorted by an infantry platoon dressed in blue jackets and trousers and red flat caps. The final group were representatives of the Bulgarian navy, who were easy to identify by the narrow blue and white horizontal lines on their collar-less shirts.

It's odd, I think, that in the space of a few minutes we experienced two such contrasting scenes… the quiet, rediscovered devotion of the shuffling churchgoers and the evocative martial crunch of jackboot on stone. I wonder why these two images remain in my memory while others, equally significant, have vanished? I am certain that those with whom I have shared some of the moments I have described (Levcho, George) recall quite different incidents of the days we spent together.

Dipping into my pot-pourri of Bulgarian memories let me conclude with episodes which give a snap shot of the country and some of the people I came to know.

A drive with Aneta

Aneta Atanosova is George's sister. She is a doctor of medicine who spent much of her professional career working in Libya. Returning to Sofia she was shocked at the shortage of medical provision. To have sufficient income on which to live in her small flat she augmented her pension by becoming a part-time taxi driver. Her little Lada car had a moveable taxi sign which fixed onto the roof with suction pads and was removed for personal journeys.

It was Aneta who drove Hilary, George and me to the café near the summit of Mount Musala (2925 m) the mountain which dominates Sofia. After a short ramble we had lunch before returning to the city. It was a day of oppressive heat, when people seem to droop and a parched landscape cries out for rain. It had been hot and dry for days.

At about 2.00 p.m. and just before our descent, flashes of lightning and loud thunderclaps were followed by a cloudburst. Footpaths became streams and roads resembled rivers. We drove slowly down the twisting mountain road, the rain falling so heavily that the windscreen wipers struggled to cope.

Aneta and her car triumphed over the elements and we reached the centre of Sofia without mishap. Still it rained; lightning flashed across the ever-darkening sky, thunder rolled. Pedestrians, lightly

165

dressed, who like us had hoped for rain 'to clear the air', now wished that it would go away. Clothing clung to their bodies as they huddled together in shop fronts and doorways waiting for the storm to pass. They looked more like survivors from the *Titanic* than citizens of a European capital city.

Then Hilary saw them. They were standing by the side of the road in front of an ancient lorry. Behind the driver's cab was a large tank and from the tank stretched a heavy length of hose.

Still it rained. The gutters were full of water, car tyres left a small wave behind them as they navigated roads that had become shallow rivers.

The centre of Hilary's attention were the men who were in charge of the lorry. Two overalled workmen were struggling with the hose, directing a fierce jet of water along already overflowing gutters. A third man supervised the activity, a fourth leaned against the lorry, the driver in the cab, dry and warm, read a paper.

A few hardy pedestrians passed by, taking the scene for granted, workmen watering the road in a downpour.

Hilary, usually so restrained, could contain herself no longer.

"What ever are those men doing, hosing down a wet road. Don't they know it's raining?"

The response from George was disarmingly honest.

"If the road cleaners are working in the centre of Sofia… (long pause) it must be Thursday."

The Environmental Conference

Sometime in the mid 1980s a week-long international conference on environment and pollution was being hosted by the Bulgarian Government. Much TV and newspaper space was devoted to the event – and strange as it may seem, Sofia was less smog-bound than usual.

As we drove to our morning meeting I noticed that there were enormous queues at every bus stop and hardly any buses on the road. I should explain that there were two types of bus in Sofia; the relatively new and the positively elderly. These older buses were the ones which experienced road users tried to avoid following – for every gear change was signalled by a cloud of black fumes which shot from their exhaust.

On the Monday I am describing there were no old buses to be seen.

I pressed Levcho for an explanation. "For the buses or the queues?" he asked. "The buses? The older buses have been withdrawn for the duration of the conference. They polute. We must make a good impression on our visitors. The queues? Nobody bothered to tell the commuters."

Then an afterthought. "By Friday those who travel by bus will have discovered what's happening. By then the environmental delegates will have gone home."

Interpreters

Until the fall of the Zjivkov Government I met the same interpreters on each visit. The one I remember with affection was Julian, a slim, informally but elegantly dressed man in his mid-30s. He carried a small black handbag under his arm, was expansive in his gestures and quite unlike any interpreter I have ever met. He was a 'touchy-feely' sort of man.

There was much consternation from his colleagues who were to translate my talks to conference. "How can we translate when you tell us he speaks from a series of short notes and not from a formally prepared paper that we have been able to study 24 hours in advance?" they demanded of Julian. A dozen or so interpreters gathered round him, two for each language of the conference – Bulgarian, English, French, German and Russian. The interpreters had a real anxiety. The papers were presented in the mother tongue of the speaker. Their task was to sit in a soundproof glass fronted cubicle situated at balcony level at the back of the hall and translate via a radio link to the headphones worn by each delegate. The interpreters feared that they would easily find themselves lost in my style of presentation.

Julian held up his hand for silence. With a voice at the level used to console a fretting baby he calmed them.

"Please do not worry about Henry", he said. "I will tell him of your problem and ensure that he speaks clearly and slowly. Should his words run ahead of you wave a handkerchief to slow him down."

He left the group and came over to me. He explained the problem I posed his colleagues, adding, "Don't worry about us either. Just remember that you require about 33% more words to translate a sentence from English into German. While you speak keep an eye on the German interpreter. If a handkerchief is waved it means there is danger of breakdown!"

I followed Julian's advice. By the end of the conference the German duo had become my friends.

When visiting the Education Ministry to talk with the Minister, Professor Alexander Fol, I was accompanied by Levcho and the second English interpreter, Janne. This visit was inspired by Levcho. He wanted me to explain recent developments in the English primary school. He also hoped that I would feel able to answer Dr. Fol's questions about the Bulgarian schools I had visited during the preceding week. Knowing of Dr. Fol's interest in History and Archeology I took the opportunity to present him with a beautifully bound and illustrated copy of Pepys's Diary... this at the request of my publisher.

At the meeting Levcho was silent. All my discussions were translated by Janne – English to Bulgarian, Bulgarian to English. I found this puzzling as Levcho and Alexander Fol were both fluent English speakers. I asked Levcho why the minister had kept to his mother tongue and insisted on Janne translating my English – which he could understand.

"Protocol," explain Levcho. "Just protocol. If you reported to the British Council that Dr. Fol said 'this'... and really all that he was giving was a personal rather than a Governmental view... Dr. Fol could deny that your observation was correct. In this event a simple explanation is available to you both. The interpreter was guilty of lazy and inaccurate translation."

The Press

I always felt that good relations with the press ranked high on Levcho's list of conference priorities. It was as though each positive column of newspaper comment secured his position for another month. The press appeared at each conference to report on key speeches, to meet individual delegates and to ask a whole range of questions varying in quality from the mundane and the superficial to the probing and perceptive. I have by me an issue of 'The Sofia Times' dated November 2nd– 8th 1989. A tabloid, printed in English, it illustrates how provocative the reporters could be. Under the headline 'Schools are like factories – producing models' I am quoted as responding critically at a Press Conference to the concept of a National Curriculum. I suggested that however good the model, its designers and controllers would determine what is taught, how it is taught, to whom it is taught and when it is taught. It would be the designers who would construct the methods used to evaluate individual success or failure. I pointed to the similarity between schools and factories. At a factory producing sausages, pigs went in at one end of the industrial process as singularly different animals. They emerged as identical production units. As with sausages in factories, so with children in schools.

Challenged to justify so outrageous a comment (and I quote from the newspaper) I said.

"However sound the model being followed, something of the human being will be destroyed in the process. Can you give a mark, a score, a grade, an average to things in life, the things which make life worth living? Can you give a mark, a score, a grade to the state of being in love or of loving? Can you score or mark the impact on a parent on hearing their newborn's first cry? Can you mark or score or grade a friendship which moves across time and space? I say you can't – yet it is human qualities like these which may, even at this late hour, save the world."

The reporters did a real service when they printed or broadcast such opinions. They provided material for debate and openly challenged long held attitudes.

<u>An economic conundrum.</u>

I must confess that I felt more secure when I wandered alone around Sofia and Plovdiv in the days of communist rule than I did in the days which followed. The Post-Zjivkov period saw inflation rip, and factories, which had been so dependent on Russian orders, collapse and close. The resulting unemployment brought insecurity in its wake and the tensions between the 'haves' and the 'have-nots' . The workings of the free-market which replaced the command economy and the drastic changes which such a revolution brought, were not foreseen, appreciated or understood by the ordinary citizen. The atmosphere was more febrile and the cynic in me observed that capitalism ill-applied was every bit as dangerous as unfettered Marxist-Leninism.

In the time of Zjivkov, a peculiar feature of the Bulgarian economy were the 'dollar' or hard currency shops which were to be found in most town centres. In them Bulgarian citizens who possessed hard currency (i.e. not currency of countries in the Eastern bloc) could buy the consumer products not available on the home market – TV sets, video recorders, transistors, cameras, film, alcohol, clothing, coffee, tea, chocolate and other foodstuffs, watches and fragrances for men and women.

When these shops were open and the window display illuminated, little groups of men, women and children would congregate and stare at the display. They must all at some time have asked the question "How can those Westerners afford to buy these things in their shops, while all we can do is stand and stare?"

The purpose of the exercise, to suck Western currency (legally or illegally obtained) into the National Bank may have succeeded. Paradoxically such success as it enjoyed was an outward and visible sign of sublime failure and a precursor of the economic and political collapse to come.

Strange Meeting

I was staying in a hotel some kilometre from Sofia. Levcho and I had breakfast together. Just before he left to go to attend to some personal matters he said. "As we have some free time this afternoon, I hope you'll be able to come running with me." When I replied, I'm sure he sensed the surprise in my voice at the request. I thought I knew Levcho well and never before had running been an aspect of our relationship!

"Jogging may extend the length of your life but does little to enhance its quality," I replied, quoting a broadcast by Alistair Cook. "Why do we need to go running?"

"Because we need to chat in confidence."

"Can't we talk in my room?"

"I'm afraid not. The woods are more peaceful!"

There was no further explanation. I believe this *was* how Levcho dealt with awkward moments. He paused and then continued:

"Your kit will be in your bedroom by lunchtime. We'll meet in the foyer at 2.00 p.m."

Two o'clock came. There I stood, feeling rather exposed, in the hotel foyer, dressed in perfectly fitting shorts, vest and trainers.

There stood Levcho, similarly clad, but rather fuller of figure than me. We must have looked like runners representing the British Legion in a charity 800 metres.

We left the hotel at a slow trot, and at ever decreasing speed reached the woods which covered a gentle hill on one side of our

170

hotel. I sat down exhausted on the first tree stump I reached. Levcho stopped. He told me, almost conspiratorially that he wanted to share a family problem with me. It concerned his sons and particularly his confrontational relationship with the younger boy, a teenager.

His humility and humanity were breathtaking. He was so humble, far from the man of authority I knew him to be.

We chatted for about an hour, took deep breaths and cantered back down the narrow path to our hotel. Levcho never spoke of his 'problem' again, neither did he offer any explanation for the running kits. I have been silent too – the passage of time allows me only now to comment on the episode.

Why running was an integral part of the afternoon, I do not know. I continue to marvel that my kit fitted so well and at how shoes, vest and shorts appeared in my room and disappeared so miraculously.

Levcho was intelligent and astute. He had seen the world. He wanted to help his family as much as he wanted to help his country.

But he was trapped in his past. And he knew it.

A new generation

Many of the younger teachers and university students I met looked forward to radical changes being made to the education system – from pre school to university.

I have chosen Sanislava Zaprianova for my example. A trainee child-psychologist, she taught at School 98. She was petite, slim and light of movement, having the ideal body shape for a dancer in classical ballet. In her early 20s, she threw herself with total determination into her work with children. She realised that she had much to learn to gain the respect of the school community. Over the four years that I observed her teach, her class management and the ability to foresee a problem before it threatens (the mark of a good teacher) had steadily improved. On a brief stop-over in London in 1996 she confided that teaching had become a job which she found deeply satisfying.

My most recent contact with Sanislava was in April 1997 when she wrote telling me of the non-government agency (NGA) she had helped establish with the teachers of School 98.

I quote from the Mission Statement:

"[One of our aims is] to popularise new teaching approaches and methods based on the experience [of schools and teachers] of Western

171

countries which could make the school environment more friendly, accessible and enjoyable to pupils."

A bold challenge to those who cling to the past.

A bold challenge which could never have been proclaimed by a young Bulgarian woman in the Sofia of my first visit.

9. The Far East, 1970s

When I think about my visits to Hong Kong (twice) and Singapore I invariably begin by reflecting on my first long-haul flight from Brize Norton, the Royal Air Force Base in Oxfordshire. The efficiency of the departure process developed by Transport Command was impressive.

Arriving the evening before my departure, my documents were examined and my flight details confirmed. Before supper was served I was allocated a room "which I could use for a brief rest". Brief indeed! At 4.00 a.m. an alarm sounded in my bedroom. An ethereal disembodied voice coming from somewhere between floor and ceiling told me it was time to shower, dress and go to breakfast. There was no point in ignoring the voice. It was insistent, seeming to get louder and angrier the longer it was neglected. To stop the voice necessitated leaving the warmth of the bed, crossing the room (in that no-man's-land between sleeping and waking) and pushing a button.

After breakfast (at 5.00 a.m.) the embarkation process continued. Because the flight was military we were informed that all passengers would be "under the command" of the senior officer who was travelling with us. This was a reasonable arrangement since the majority of the 90+ passengers were military (Royal Navy, Army, Royal Air Force). A few individuals (like me) were civilians with a specific assignment in Hong Kong or were wives and relatives of military personnel already serving there.

We boarded the plane, not from an apron but by a flight of steps – the sort on which Presidents pause to wave to waiting press photographers when arriving in a foreign country. The aircraft was a VC10, originally developed for long-haul civilian airlines, but which was being superseded by the early Jumbos. The VC10 could carry people, or, stripped down, supplies and equipment. It enjoyed a reputation for safety, had a reasonable maximum speed of 370 mph and, allowing adequate leg room, could accommodate 90 passengers.

What felt odd was that RAF passengers flew backwards, the seats faced the tail not the pilot's cabin.

We took off. The flight path followed the English Channel, then the coast of Europe to Gibraltar, across the Mediterranean to Cyprus where the plane landed for refuelling. Two hours later, we resumed our journey. Soon I was asleep.

For a second time that day my dreams were disturbed by a disembodied voice. Calm, flat, Southern English and seemingly unconcerned, the voice observed that the engine on the port side was "proving a little troublesome." In consequence we would need to land, and the nearest landing place was the sovereign base of Gan, in the Indian Ocean. Nobody seemed to panic. There was general agreement that there was nothing to do but accept what fate would bring and drink to the future in lemonade or orange juice (the strongest alcohol on board).

The landing on Gan proved uneventful. It was midnight, local time. We were gently shepherded from the plane and taken to a reception area. It was incredibly hot... descending from the air conditioned plane to oppressive, breezeless air was like suddenly coming face to face with an invisible, impassable wall.

In reception the problem was made clear. The plane could not continue its flight. The engine could be repaired at Gan but the necessary parts would need to be dispatched from Cyprus... 4 or 5 hours flying time away. On Gan we would therefore remain until repairs had been effected.

There was a small hotel/hostel on the base, but it could only accommodate a limited number of visitors. So while the women and children were dispatched to the comfort of air conditioned bedrooms, the bulk of the passengers, being male, were driven in trucks to a large gymnasium.

The gymnasium had been prepared against our arrival. The floor was laid out like a large dormitory with 80 mattresses neatly dressed with pillows and sheets. Wearily I found a mattress, undressed, slipped between the sheets and fell into a deep sleep.

I've no idea how long I slept. Something (a disembodied inner voice?) caused me to suddenly wake. I sat up naked and confused.

All around me – on the floor of an enormous hall, now bathed in sunlight – were still, white figures laid out in straight lines.

"Good heavens, I'm dead." For seconds (which seemed like minutes) I could not believe the scene around me. It was only when

174

one of the 'corpses' moved and expressed a desire for a cup of tea that I remembered where I was.

Eventually, engine repaired, we departed for Hong Kong, a journey which took over 33 hours to complete.

I had been invited to Hong Kong to organise art courses and to visit primary schools run by the Service Children's School Education Authority (SCSEA). The invitation followed upon a film made at Prior Weston by the Government film unit, the Central Office of Information. The film was one of a series under the umbrella title of 'The Pacemakers'. Each film in the series featured an aspect of life in Britain in the early 1970s – medical discoveries, exploration of the North Sea for gas, developments in manufacturing. Prior Weston School was chosen to represent 'early years' education. The 'Pacemaker' series of films were not shown in the UK. They were distributed to interested overseas TV companies to be used to fill spaces between main programmes. The film of Prior Weston had been shown so many times on public television before I arrived in Hong Kong that many of the teachers I met felt that they already knew me!

'Pacemaker' was showing at a time when I was also chairing a weekly discussion programme on the World Service of the BBC. These were also broadcast in Hong Kong... so one might say my visits smacked a little of 'overkill'.

It was with some apprehension and much tiredness that I found myself descending into Kai Tek airport. Until the mid-1990s when a new international terminal was built on Lantau Island, Kai Tek was the colony's principal airport.

The flight path into Kai Tek ran parallel and very close to an area of picturesque Chinese housing, one street of which continued to the airport perimeter almost touching the runway as it did so.

Before my visit I knew very little about Hong Kong. Such research as I had managed to do was very superficial. I knew that the great majority of the population were Cantonese. I discovered that the island of Hong Kong had been ceded to Britain by treaty in 1841, that the peninsula of Kowloon had been added to the colony in 1860 and the New Territories in 1896. This final expansion pushed the colony's frontier northwards to the Chinese district of Shenzhen. When I visited the treaty which ceded these lands to Britain still had some 25 years to run. On July 1st 1997 British rule ended and China resumed sovereignty. Before the invention of aircraft the British colonies and the Dominions (Canada, Australia, S. Africa, New Zealand) were linked by passenger and cargo ships. These sea routes and the ports

175

and harbours on them were protected by the ships of the Royal Navy. In addition each colony became a military base with regiments sent out from Britain to train alongside colonial soldiers. These combined army units protected the colony from attack and ensured the safety of cargo and passenger ships that visited their harbours.

Hong Kong and Singapore were important colonies and played a part in this linking together of Empire. Both had excellent natural harbours. In them, ships could be repaired, replenish their supplies and refuel (with coal before the development of the diesel engine).

On landing at Kai Tek, I was met by John, a second-lieutenant in the Royal Artillery who was the officer responsible for watching over service schools in the colony. He was a fresh-faced young man in his mid 20s who wore his uniform as though he had been born to military service. He helped with my luggage which was rather extensive. I had to bring a range of craft materials with me. Jacobean embroidery canvas and water soluble stains were unobtainable locally.

After depositing me in my hotel on Kowloon (i.e. the mainland) he told me that he would return in 4 hours (at 7.00 p.m.) and take me to his home for dinner. This he duly did.

His flat, which we reached after a 20 minute drive, overlooked Repulse Bay. I was introduced to his wife, Jane, and baby daughter Milly. Their flat was on the fourth floor of a low-rise development and was generously proportioned. A large sitting room with picture-windows faced seawards. There was an even larger dining room, three bedrooms and an expensively equipped kitchen. After a joint session of Milly-admiring, she was deposited in the arms of a Chinese maid servant (the Amah) and whisked away to her nursery.

Over the evening meal John proposed to explain what he called "the set up". i.e. what I would do where and with whom, discuss the lecture I was to give to students at the University and outline the days he would like me to spend with the local (Chinese) education authority.

"But first", he said, "after such an eventful flight, let's have a drink to celebrate your safe arrival". Whereupon his wife produced a very large bottle of vintage port, observing as she poured it into three glasses that "it's our favourite drink". I took care to drink very little, knowing that tiredness and alcohol are dangerous bedfellows. John, however, was happy with the bottle and drank three glasses before the Amah came into the room to announce that dinner was ready. The meal, of Chinese style prepared and served by the Amah, was generously supported with red wine. Coffee followed, "supported",

176

said John "with a little port." John noticed I had only a drain in my glass so he refilled mine and, with sophistication born of long experience, his wife's glass and then his own. "We must get round to talk about tomorrow", he said, "but why spoil a lovely evening? Let's have the last of the port. I find it loses flavour when opened in this climate." There was enough port in the bottle for one more glass. Jane and I declined John's offer "to kill the bottle". Hating waste, he did so, remarking how smooth it was to the palate.

There was a pause. "We'd better not open another. It's time to take you back to your hotel." It was then that Jane became forceful. "I've ordered a taxi for Henry. You are not in a fit state to drive into town and get back. I'd worry all the time you were away".

The taxi arrived and, clutching the briefing papers which Jane had thrust into my hands, I got into the cab. Soon I reached the hotel – and quickly fell asleep.

In the morning before breakfast, I read my briefing which informed me that John would meet me with his army driver and accompany me on visits to four Chinese schools. At 9.00 a.m. a driver arrived, but without John who, I was told, was "indisposed". The driver, an army corporal, said that he would make sure "that I kept my appointments."

I visited two 'morning' schools and two 'afternoon' schools. As the names imply these were schools which children attended for the required number of hours (8.00 a.m.–1.00 p.m. or 1.30 p.m.– 6.30 p.m.). Two schools, two teaching faculties used each building, each classroom, each specialist facility. Even the classroom walls and the notice boards were shared. The classes I observed were very well behaved and motivated and showed great respect for their teachers.

The following day I was entertained by Chinese teachers and education staff to an informal lunch. We sat at a large round table which had revolving central shelves on which the food was arranged. So it was a 'help yourself' buffet with a difference. I quickly discovered that I was inept in handling chopsticks – and that there was much in Chinese food which was never served in London take-aways. This 'new' food I tried to avoid. I needed to be able to live with my stomach!

It was not until the third day that I was reunited with John. I was in a staff room of a services' school. Here I had chanced to meet a teacher from Kennington, London, where I had spent much of my childhood. He told me he had seen the 'Pacemaker' film several times. Though he was impressed with the film he told me he was even more admiring of my ability to 'outdrink' John! Apparently John had the reputation of being able to weather heavy drinking sessions. In order to explain his absence from duty he whispered, to any who might listen, that he had tried to match *my* evening's consumption of port, presenting himself as a good host who had failed (and fallen?) I did not confront John over his untruths. I simply avoided accepting alcohol for the rest of my stay, becoming a teetotaller for its duration. My new found abstinence puzzled John and those to whom he had whispered my invented shortcomings. My little act caused me but one moment of embarrassment. I found myself in an Officers' Mess toasting 'The Queen' in Coca-Cola.

In reflecting on meals and 'eating out', I will always remember visiting 'Wu's'. I was taken to 'Wu's' close on midnight by Jack, a Primary headteacher, and his wife, Alice. We parked the car on a well-lit and busy main street on Kowloon and walked down a dark, dirty, smelly alley. At the end of the alley was a neon sign proclaiming 'Wu'. A garish orange/red light illuminated a grubby staircase. The 'restaurant' was on the first floor and consisted of about ten rough wooden tables. Their tops were covered with cracked and worn sheets of American cloth on which stood candles, most of them reduced to congealed wax in the beer bottles in which they were fixed. All the tables were occupied by Chinese – except one half-hidden in a dark corner.

Mr Wu (I suppose it was he) led us to this table at which sat, slumped and somewhat drugged or drunk, a friend of Jack. Edward was dressed in a checked shirt, dirty jeans and sockless sandals. He sported a mop of unwashed grey hair – hair which looked as if it had avoided a comb, brush, shampoo or cut for over a year. His beard was equally well kept, containing the odd bit of food which missed his mouth during his last meal. His eyes were bright blue and they lit up when we appeared. He stumbled to his feet to welcome us, ordering drinks as he shook our hands. "Good to see you Jack! How's things?"

'Eddie', storyteller, comedian and journalist was something of a legend. Born in New York he had come to Hong Kong to revitalise a breaking marriage. He had stayed for 25 years, his erstwhile wife had returned home within a week. He lived by sending 'news snips' and stories about South East Asia to a variety of American and Canadian news agencies and journals.

Two hours and numerous glasses of a white liquid later Eddie regaled us with a selection of the news stories he had dispatched to the States – he told of hair raising meetings with Triads, of confrontations with the police, of drugs, vice and prostitution and of the lighter side of his work (like following up a story of a Chinese lady of 80 who kept a small flock of ducks in her flat to save her the bother of going out to buy eggs).

He was most incensed that his most recent copy to the States had somehow found its way back 'with additions' into a Hong Kong tabloid. Its publication had resulted in a confrontation with the British military. The story was bizarre.

A lady teacher employed by SCSEA decided to augment her salary by serving drinks on Saturday and Sunday evenings in a topless bar in downtown Kowloon. Whilst at 'work' she was 'recognised' (an odd verb to use) by the parent of a child in her class, a parent who 'chanced to be passing by'. The parent was a major in the Royal Artillery. 'Disgusted' at seeing her at the bar he reported her misdemeanour to school management. Her 'case' was heard within a week. She was summarily dismissed and sent back to England, disgraced.

Eddie explained that his story was about the inequalities suffered by women. Without naming the two people involved his article suggested that, in the interests of justice and even-handedness the major should also suffer public rebuke.

A Hong Kong reporter in Washington read the story and suggested to his editor (in Kowloon) that if the names were included and the happening sensationalised, it would amuse his Chinese readership. The article duly appeared, complete with names and photographs. The major was furious, particularly as the lady involved was, on the day of publication, out of harm's way in West Yorkshire.

Eddie was better known in Kowloon by his nickname, 'The Fireman'. He was always willing (for a free drink or a publishable story) to swallow fire and spit it, in a controlled jet, from his mouth. He performed his act for us while we were with him at Wu's; responding to a Chinese gentleman who challenged Eddie to light a single candle which had been placed on a high shelf for the purpose. Eddie did so – and as an encore, reduced the Chinaman's expensive cigar to ashes.

Thinking back, I suppose Eddie was a poor man's Hemmingway. He spent many hours at that half hidden table, meeting the many friends he had made over 25 years, a survivor in an alien culture.

Another happening had repercussions for me on a personal level. Towards the end of my second visit I gave a short interview on Force's Radio and was invited by the studio staff to join them at a party where I would meet 'another Henry'. The party was held in the flat of a teacher who lived in a high-rise block overlooking Victoria Harbour. And in the flat I met 'Henry'.

Henry was the headteacher of a school which was built within the army headquarters. So he was rich in local gossip. He is best described as a 'twinkle', for everything about him was animated and enthusiastic. When he smiled his whole being seemed to radiate happiness. He was, like Eddie, rich in stories. Army padres, irritated colonels, majors' wives, Chinese laundries and Government inspectors provided material of wit, common sense and wisdom. Each episode was delivered with impeccable timing and delightful humour. The strain of continual talk encouraged Henry to drink rather more of the local, chemical-based beer than was good for him. Notwithstanding his condition and despite his wife pleading with him to stay, Henry determined to "take me to the taxi". We reached the roadway – high kerbed to control the fall of typhoon rains. Confessing that his legs were a "touch tired" he proclaimed in a loud Yorkshire voice, "Henry says goodbye to Henry. Henry hopes to meet Henry in England." His voice was ragged, his demeanour far from headlike. Sitting on a high kerb meant he could shake his legs and wave his arms in farewell. I stopped a taxi, climbed in and left Henry kerb bound, waving uncontrollably.

Imagine the shock Henry Bird must have suffered when I went with my young daughter, Hilary, to her school (St. John's, Danbury, Essex) to meet the recently appointed headteacher.

There sitting in an imposing chair, leaning on an imposing desk, admiring his imposing room was the imposingly twinkly Henry Bird. St. John's was a very large school and he was a very new head so he had had no time to link my daughter with a kerb in Kowloon.

I smiled at Henry's discomfiture when I said "Hello, do you remember our last goodbye?" I shook my left leg to help him recall my departure. "You said you would meet me in England. Here I am!"

His comments, later and out of my daughters hearing are unprintable. "Did you tell Hilary about the goodbye?" he asked. "Of course", I replied "what sort of father is it that conceals things from his youngest daughter?"

While in Hong Kong I made two visits to the New Territory, an area of land leased to Britain until 1997. The road from Kowloon ran through some wild landscape as well as through areas which were cultivated. I saw peasants working in paddy-fields using techniques generations old to cultivate and harvest rice. Teams of buffalo, ankle-deep in water pulled wooden ploughs: indeed the buffalo was the farmer's principal source of power, dragging heavy loads which were attached to the animal's harness with chains and pulling wooden carts piled with containers of chicken, duck or pig to the local market.

Respect for the traditions and the religious beliefs which underpin them was a characteristic of the people who live here. For example I was asked not to take photographs of Chinese folk without first asking their permission – it was believed that something of their eternal souls was stolen in the process. (There was one Chinese family in the New Territory who spent their working lives at a strategic spot on the border which overlooked Shenzhen. For three Hong Kong dollars it was possible to photograph grandparents, children and grandchildren – in a group or individually!)

A diversion here. The sophisticated Hong Kong banker or school teacher was also given to superstitious beliefs. The late 60s saw the retirement of two of the most famous passenger liners that ever served the White Star Cunard Line – 'The Queen Mary' and 'The Queen Elizabeth'. Both were sold as scrap. 'The Queen Elizabeth' was towed to Victoria Harbour to be converted into a floating university.

The liner was moored facing a small river which ran into the harbour. According to legend this river was one along which the souls of the dead travelled on their last journey to the world of spirits. And by the river, high in the hills, was a Chinese graveyard! The liner had been given this anchorage to mock the Gods. And so it proved. The Gods wreaked their revenge.

On Sunday, November 9th, 1972 a fierce fire broke out on the liner, which left it a smoking hulk. I asked a Chinese teacher if he knew how the fire started. "Officially", he said, "a workman was careless with an electrical installation. But really it was the other world working through people."

Returning to my central theme; many of the children attending the primary school in the New Territory were the sons and daughters of soldiers of the Ghurkha Brigade, whose units were at the time patrolling the border. Their Commanding Officer was Lt.Col. 'S' whose own children had attended Prior Weston School in London. His two daughters Amanda and Sarah were amazed to see me out of context but were quick to regale me with all the rich experiences they had enjoyed since leaving England. Both expressed concern that when they reached 11 they would be returning home to a boarding school in Surrey.

Meeting Amanda and Sarah enabled me to resolve something which had puzzled me – why the British children in the Far East looked somehow different from those I taught at home: the answer was hair colour. In London Amanda's hair was a gentle brown. The sun had the effect of turning it into a darkish blonde... in Hong Kong and Singapore the range of children's hair colouring ranged from ultra blonde to almost blonde... with eyebrows to match.

The Primary School was run by a staff of 10 lady teachers working under a headmaster. It was a somewhat inward looking community, for the school was very isolated. There was little for the teachers to do when the school day was over. They lived together in the Officers' Mess which meant that, members of staff rarely had time to escape the gaze of their colleagues. One teacher, Naomi, told me that she had volunteered for the post because "if you can live with yourself here you spend very little and can easily save for exotic trips to Indonesia and Thailand." Not the best reason for following a teaching career!

It was while on my second visit to Hong Kong that I chanced to meet General (or was he by then already a Field Marshall?) Ashley-Bramall, who was visiting bases in the Far East. On being introduced he said, "I expect you've met my brother. Give him my regards if you see him before I do." His brother was a major political force on the Inner London Education Authority – the body that employed me as a teacher.

It is said that, with the exception of the Australians, the Chinese are the most enthusiastic gamblers in the world. The Happy Valley racing track attracted riders, trainers and their horses from the USA, France, UK, Ireland and Australia – and a large number of the local population.

Across a narrow straight in the South China Sea was another popular gambling spot – Macau (at the time I am describing, a Portuguese colony). Every weekend a ferry crossed to Macau (on the mainland) carrying Hong Kong residents, sophisticated Chinese and tourists from all over the world to a town whose livelihood depended on the success of its casinos. I never visited Macau, though I would have liked to have done so. Its beautiful colonial style houses and the ambience of faded Empire (not the gambling!) would surely have drawn me there – had there been time.

It is difficult to describe the vibrancy of life in Hong Kong. A mixture of impressions remain with me... the warm clammy air enhanced and thickened by the aromas from a hundred woks simmering simultaneously, each wok cooking a different food... Cantonese-speaking Chinese bustling with quick short steps along the roadways, their exaggerated vowel sounds blending with the clatter of everyday street noise to produce a never ending 'Symphony of the pavements.' The ground bass to this strange music was provided by the Mahjong players who in the tenements above the shops tapped out a regular 'clack, clack, clack' as they laid their ivory pieces onto the hard playing surface. The sharp, short 'clack-clack' seemed to come from every direction, from every room in every tenement and flat. The nearest I came to seeing a game were sitting silhouettes thrown against a lightly curtained window.

Because of the shortage of land each house or tenement accommodated a number of families. This sometimes resulted in a family living together in one room. Often beds were occupied 24 hours a day. When a bed was vacated by one family member, who worked during the day, it would immediately become the sleeping place of another family member, who worked nights. It was impossible to walk down a street and not find a house crumbling into its foundations. It was equally common to find Hakka women involved in its repair. The Hakka women seemed to be the heavy gang on building sites, mixing mortar, carrying hods of bricks up ladders, replacing and repairing rooms and windows – all this after erecting scaffolding made of bamboo. The Hakka were a Chinese 'clan' – the womenfolk easily recognised by the coolie hats they wore, made distinctive by a black edging of fabric around the brim. Incidentally, I never saw a Hakka man working on a building site!

In contrast to the hardworking Hakka, the young people enjoyed sport. In most areas, between housing complexes and in any temporarily cleared piece of waste ground, basketball was played. The permanent pitches were floodlit so that games could be played until the early hours.

The old tenement blocks particularly interested me. The ground floor was used for shops and workshops – and as a place to store many an elderly bicycle. Cycling was a form of transport popular with all age groups.

The rooms in the floors above the 'shop' provided accommodation. Most of the flats, each of one or two rooms, had a roughly constructed balcony which overlooked the street. Each balcony was filled with oddments – boxes, large woven baskets, lines of washing, drying carpets, discarded pieces of furniture. One feature was common to all, a singing bird in a wickerwork cage.

183

The shops, with their open fronts, were to my western eyes rather mysterious places. What was that lurking deep in shadow at the rear? In the food shops were foodstuffs which I recognised, and many dried and smoked foods which I could not ever imagine eating. Rice was dug from deep baskets, wrapped and weighed on hand-held scales. The final bill was totalled on an abacus (beads on rails). The speed of this operation was amazing. A local shopkeeper competed with a colleague using a hand-held electronic calculator. In a 'race' to add ten items, the abacus proved to be the quicker.

On the pavement by the shop or market stall would be ducks and chickens, large snakes secured with tight netting, containers of live sea creatures – on display and awaiting a buyer. On payment the selected creature would be quickly dispatched prior to cooking in a pot or wok. Such sights made me realise that vegetarians occupy a moral highground.

Each shop had its own atmosphere and smell. The pharmacy, usually glass fronted, was full of bottles containing ingredients employed by the pharmacist-cum-doctor. Strange vegetable roots, powdered rhinoceros horn, extracts from leaves, flowers and trees.

The funeral parlour, sold a wide range of paper goods which were ceremoniously burned at the funeral of even the poorest Hong Kong resident. Tradition demanded that the possessions of the dead person were burnt at the funeral. To burn a house, a car, tools, books and furniture, boats, banknotes and share documents was obviously a waste of family resources. So the tradition is kept alive by burning paper replicas instead.

Many of the shop fronts were used as workshops where craftsmen worked all manner of materials – leather, wood, clay, silver, pewter and cane. There were shoe makers and repairers, cycle mechanics, tailors, dressmakers and clock makers. There were shops selling lengths of silk fabric in traditional designs; there were bakers and laundries; barbers, each customer having a spittoon placed before him so that he could spit out the tobacco wad he was sucking when it had lost its flavour. There were shops and stalls selling fruits, flowers and vegetables, old books, pictures and '45s' and '33s'. (These were record discs which predated today's tapes, CDs and DVDs). Often the stallholders or shopkeepers would eat as they worked, rice bowls and chopsticks were always visible.

I discovered that I could also go to a shop to have a letter or document written for me… in Chinese. In the workshop the letter writer used traditional pen/brush and ink. He was a very old man who provided a service for equally old Chinese men and women who wanted to communicate with their family (perhaps living in mainland China). If a reply to a letter was received it was usually brought back to the letter writer – to be read and explained. All this for a small fee.

Thronging the market places were people, young people carrying satchels and bags full of school books, mothers with babies strapped to their backs, old men smoking the most pungent of tobacco; people wearing a mixture of dress – traditional Cantonese, mingled with traditional western and the occasional costume of a visitor from Africa or the saffron robe of a monk.

Now and then policemen would stroll by, watching over shops and shoppers. Their presence had a quieting effect upon the strident demands of the 'shoe shine boys' (often quite elderly men who would demand to clean the shoes of every European that passed by.) They gesticulated threateningly, pointing at each pair of dusty shoes – or in my case, sandals. One particular 'boy' – in his mid 60s – was notorious and, when met for the first time, frightening. Refusal to employ him caused him to leap from his stand. Clutching a shoe brush in each hand he hopped, his head almost at ground level, alongside the offender's feet. He hopped because he was one-legged. The pathos which this performance induced, caused many a pedestrian to return to his stand to have him minister to his shoes – or to toss coins in the street and encourage him to pick them up (so providing time to escape).

During one of my explorations of Kowloon I chanced upon a Chinese Opera Company. These companies only performed in the streets. A rough stage had been erected at a road junction and all the traffic was diverted for the duration of the performance, which could last several hours. The singers were dressed in the court costumes of Imperial China, rich in silver and gold thread. The makeup and the masks of the magicians and sorcerers who played a central part of the story were strikingly demonic. The plot/libretto was built upon a legend, and like all legends and folk stories there was a maiden who needed to be rescued from a cruel fate by a brave warrior who would even fight dragons to win her love.

The lead singers were supported by a cast of musicians and dancers. The production I came upon, quite by accident, was surely designed to test my intelligence. I could identify the good and evil characters in the story, but I had to invent a narrative of my own to explain their actions. At the end of the performance the audience paid for the entertainment by dropping coins into a collecting dish.

Another way of 'experiencing' Hong Kong was to make the short ferry crossing between the island and Kowloon on a 'Star Ferry'. These boats ran 24 hours a day and always seemed to be full. Every crossing provided a snap shot of life – of ordinary people, of the activity in the harbour, alive with sea going ships, barges, wherries and tugs. Most of all I watched the junks, their spiked sails conveying what romantics call the 'Mystery of the East'. A junk moving seawards into the setting sun invariably caused my spine to tingle.

Between running two 'picture making' courses I seized the opportunity to visit Aberdeen, a village in which inhabitants lived in boats. The village consists of a fleet of sampans and junks roped together on fixed moorings. Between the blocks of boats there were waterways (like streets on land) to allow the movement of people and goods between the blocks of moorings. It is said that some of the boat people of Aberdeen never walk on dry land during their lifetime.

Many of the Aberdeen folk earn their living as fishermen. Fish is an important item in the diet of the Cantonese, so the Aberdeen fishermen make a significant contribution to the local economy. Like all sea going communities life involves a continual battle with nature – wind and wave. And of this battle, legends are born. The most touching tells of the wife of a Kowloon fisherman. Recently married and deeply in love she wishes her husband 'God speed' as he departs on his latest trip. She waits and waits but he never returns. She still stands today looking out to sea, transformed by the Gods into a rock. Every time a fisherman passes that rock, high on a cliff he is reminded of the story of LiWee and of his own family awaiting his return.

When Hong Kong was leased to Britain in 1841 it became an important station for ships of the Royal Navy. When I visited Hong Kong there were many glass and steel high rise office developments along the waterfront, but many buildings remained reminders of an Imperial past. These old buildings projected a solid Victorian, almost Kiplingesque, view of the Empire. Many of the more important thoroughfares in the colony had names redolent of this period in our national history: Argyle Street, Chatham Road, Victoria Park Road, Waterloo Road.

For me 'The Yacht Club' epitomized the time when one sixth of the world owed a degree of allegiance to the British Crown.

Decorated in red and gold, with pictures of HM the Queen in nearly every room and corridor, gentlemen members, sunk deep in leather armchairs, gossiped over their gin and tonics. Uniformed waiters hurried to and fro and in the centre of one large area, impressive tall punka-wallahs pulled the strings that operated the fans which kept the air circulating. Outside, the harbour waters lapped on the stones of a rocky beach. On one large rock sat the Little Mermaid we usually associate with Copenhagen. (Two statues were made. One for Copenhagen, one for Hong Kong.)

My two visits to the club convinced me that it was not the kind of institution I would ever join. Everything about it – from the building itself to the members who patronised it – projected a cosy, privileged, comfortable, self-satisfied society differentiated by class. At the time of my visit Chinese rule was still 25 years away, by which time the members I met would be enjoying the autumn of their lives in a retirement apartment in Bournemouth or a villa in Tuscany.

The trips I made to Hong Kong were some 18 months apart. Between these two trips was a visit to Singapore, again for SCSEA. The programme involved organising an art course for teachers in primary schools and visits to schools to advise on display.

Like Hong Kong, Singapore fell to the Japanese in the Second World War (1939–1945). There was little evidence of the invasion – except the 'memorial to the fallen' which is to be found in every British town and village and in every present and former colony and dominion. Singapore also had a war cemetery, which I discovered quite by accident.

I had been visiting a nursery which grew orchids. The flowers were unlike any I had seen in England. There were enormous blooms in strident blues, reds and yellows, some so large that they deserve to be described as vulgar. These orchids competed for attention with others, so light and ephemeral, so delicate in colour that I could only stand and stare, speechless at their beauty. Each bloom, large and small was secure in its own pot. 'Own' is a well-used word in 'Orchidlean'. Each orchid had its roots around the pot, gripping it lest the pot escape.

I left the nursery and followed a footpath to the allied war cemetery. Sleek green grass. Line upon line of white gravestones. Standing alone, the two images came together – the exquisite beauty of the flowers, the stark bleakness of the stones, each stone carrying its minimalist inscription recording the death of a loved one.

United, the images represent for me the parameters of human existence… the garden which some call Eden and the Fall which some call Hell.

The cemetery was something of a shock but it made me realise that the trappings of Singapore's Imperial past were still strong. On

187

my second day I was taken to tea in the 'Raffles' Hotel'. This hotel features in nearly every book and travelogue about S.E. Asia. I remember 'Raffles' for its expensive menu and the cynical exploitation of its colonial past to attract visitors interested in the island's history.

Sir Stanford Raffles, whose name graces the hotel, was a merchant adventurer. He had links with the East India Company, a company operated under Royal Charter granted in 1600 by Queen Elizabeth 1.

Raffles realised that Singapore had potential. In 1819 he negotiated the lease of the town, derelict and with few inhabitants, from the Sultan of Jahore. Five years later, the East India Company acquired the whole island (42 km wide and 28 km across) preserving its name – Singapore means Lion Town in Sanskrit.

Like Hong Kong, Singapore has a large natural harbour which proved a useful staging post for British cargo ships and the warships of the South China Fleet. In 1867 Singapore became a Crown Colony, eventually achieving independence in June 1989.

For me Singapore was unusual because climate had such a profound effect upon all aspects of life. I realise that this statement *is* simplistic because climate has an impact wherever we find ourselves on the globe. The climate in Singapore was different from any I had previously experienced. Climatologists clarify Singapore as 'hot equatorial', having over 180 days of rain each year and an average daily temperature of 30°C. This means that palm trees line the roads (rather than the common plane beloved of Londoners). The palms added a touch of glamour to the monsoon drains which ran down the centre of many main roads.

Each evening of my short stay brought with it a surprise – the sudden transition from day to night. Darkness fell without a prolonged dusk, morning broke after a very short dawn – at around 6.00 p.m. and 6.00 a.m. every day of the year. This 12 hour spread of darkness and light is easily explained (though never in a school textbook) because Singapore is almost on the equator. This means that the sun is always directly overhead at noon.

Another treasured memory of my stay was breakfast in the air conditioned dining room at the hotel... large slices of fresh local pineapple, 18 cm across and 2 cm thick washed down with dark coffee and glasses of ice-cool water.

Singapore was a popular posting for Service families. English was the lingua franca, uniting the Chinese, Malay, Indian, Eurasian and European who made up the population. The shops were full of quality goods at low prices and life on the streets was safe – the Government's attitude to petty criminals was uncompromisingly strict. Part of Singapore's popularity was owed to its geographic position – its airport being a hub for flights to holiday resorts in Malaysia, Thailand, Sumatra and the islands of the Adaman Sea.

My notes contain very little about people I met in the colony.

I experienced one embarrassing evening. I was invited to join a dinner party in the house of a senior army officer. Pre-dinner drinks were served in the garden. The garden was gently floodlit and chairs were informally spread between the hedges which marked its border.

The Lt. Colonel's wife was presiding in a matronly way over the proceedings – indicating to the servants' guests who required more wine, a serviette or savouries. She was a lady of generous proportions and decided to rest for a moment on one of the metal garden chairs.

Conversation ceased when a sudden loud crack was followed by an involuntary scream from our hostess. There she was, her hips trapped in a broken chair frame, her legs in such a position that the gentlemen who rushed to her aid approached with eyes either averted heavenwards or tightly closed. The rescue was effectively accomplished to grunts of sympathy from the men and enquiries about bruises from the women. Her two terriers, alerted by her cry, entertained us by comforting their mistress by barking at the rescue team and stealing the food from the plates they had left unguarded on the ground.

The meal in a large candlelit dining room was also something of a disaster. During the soup course the room was inexplicably invaded by an army of small, brown lizard-like creatures. Each measuring about 7 cm they ran across the floor, across the ceiling, up and down the walls, over the table, plates, bread and cutlery. Their invasion lasted about 15 minutes. Their interest in humans over, they disappeared as suddenly as they had come. After a short delay and much 'behind the door' discussion between the colonel and his wife, the table was cleared, relaid and the meal proceeded with hot food which, because it was in the kitchen, had not been raced over.

It was at this dinner party that I took part in an age old ceremony I had read about in books, a ceremony that recalls society of a different age. The Colonel said "Ladies"; whereupon half the guests disappeared to the powder-room. The men (and me!) remained to drink brandy and smoke cigars.

189

One other incident is worth retelling. It was arranged that I visit 'X' primary school on Thursday and to remain there all day. Desmond, an army captain insisted that Thursday was set aside for the visit... which he said must not *under any circumstance* be changed. It would he said "solve the little local difficulty that was troubling him." When Bob – the head was informed of the arrangement he advanced every possible reason for the day being unsuitable... nurse was coming to inspect hair and feet, the reception class teacher had a longstanding hospital appointment, Class 8 were on a museum trip, there was a leak in the boys toilets (to be repaired on Thursday) all these and several others were dismissed by Desmond as "quite irrelevant to our visit." Thursday had been selected and Thursday it would be.

And Thursday came. We met Bob, a short sturdy figure with an ashen face and no smile. At this point I should explain that we had arrived at school about half an hour earlier than the appointment time given to Bob. The army driver parked our car – on Desmond's instructions – in the headteacher's parking space. We did not go directly to the school but did what Desmond called "a recci" of the school grounds. I was by now – like you – quite confused. "That must be it," exclaimed Desmond as we rounded a tree lined bend in the path we were following.

The 'it', concealed by a clump of bushes was a very new, very shiny, very expensive red, Fiat sports car.

"Wonder who can afford that and why leave it here?" mused Desmond. A smile played around his lips as we went up the steps and into the school.

I was introduced to Bob. The formalities over, Desmond explained that we would be staying all day. He appreciated Bob's willingness to accompany us on a tour of the classrooms. He ended by saying that the army driver could not return until 4.30 p.m., so when school closed (at 1.30 p.m.) there would be plenty of time to discuss what we had seen. It was obvious to me that Desmond was following a plan of his own. No other teacher or head on any previous school visit had been handled like this!

Bob's ashen complexion turned a shade paler.

The children arrived and went to their classrooms. After Assembly "always taken on Thursdays and Fridays by the Deputy Head" we made a tour of the school. In slow procession, as though to kill time, we visited each classroom. I was impressed by the general 'feeling' of the school, the displays, the condition of the books in the library. Periodically the Deputy joined us to explain in detail any organisational matter which Bob said was outside his province.

Lunch time came. During coffee Desmond disappeared for a few minutes "to make a phone call." Returning he sat next to me and whispered conspiratorially. "The car's still there."

We stayed beyond 4.30 p.m., occupying ourselves with the most trivial points on curriculum matters – all raised by Desmond. Eventually our driver arrived, diplomatically late (I discovered) to take Desmond and me to dinner.

It was during dinner that Desmond explained the little game I had unknowingly played.

Apparently Bob wrote regular motoring columns for the local newspaper. These often included road test reports on new models, based on a popular drive from Singapore to Kuala Lumpur in Malaysia. The test report was delivered to the newspaper on Friday, mid-morning, which involved Bob spending all Thursday 'on the road' and most of the small hours of Friday preparing copy.

The Fiat was the Saturday feature… a feature which could not appear this week. Desmond's visit to the school with me was a gentle attempt to let Bob know that his end of week 'second job' had been noted. He could not be a part-time head and a part-time newspaper reporter.

There is a sequel to this story. Some months after our Thursday visit, Bob resigned and went to teach, part-time, in a private school run by his wife in the centre of Singapore. The pupils were the children of British families living and working in Singapore. I knew of the school because there were details of its programme, fees and curriculum prominently pinned to the parents' notice board in the school Bob ran for SCSEA!

My return flight from Changi Airport, Singapore differed in one respect from my homeward flights from Hong Kong. The VC10 landed in heavy rain at Colombo Airport (Sri Lanka, then called Ceylon) for refuelling. There were no buses to take the passengers to the Terminal building to buy refreshments. So we were conveyed there, two and three passengers a time, in open cars. Each passenger was given a large umbrella as protection against the driving rain. The troop of Morris 1000 coupes with bright umbrellas replacing roofs brought tears of laughter into the eyes of the most jaded travellers!

I bought refreshments in the Terminal and 2lbs of the most delicious, new season Ceylon tea.

191

Ceylon tea. A further reminder of our imperial past – but a more refreshing and wholesome one than most!

10. Around the Mediterranean

In the wonderland world of Lewis Carroll it is possible to begin at the end so as to better end at the beginning. Following Carroll's example I will therefore begin at the end of my visits to schools in and around the Mediterranean for I well remember my feelings when I returned to London on what proved to be my final teaching journey to that part of the world.

Strange though it may seem all of my flights on planes manned by RAF personnel to visit military schools involved travelling backwards... in the RAF version of the VC10 all passenger seats face the tail.

Whether this prompted me to pull my Mediterranean experiences together I'm not certain, but as the pilot prepared to land I remember looking at the countryside below. Sunlight cast blue-grey shadows across a green and almost coiffured landscape; houses nestled in neat, green gardens; hills cloaked with trees of green framed a landscape united by colour – a myriad of greens of every tint, tone and hue.

The subtleness of the colour of the land below me, gently darkening under cloud and lightening when cloud passed, encouraged me to wonder why the very greenness bred in me feelings of nostalgia.

And then the answer came to me. Green was the colour I most missed when working abroad. The Mediterranean lands could be colour-coded too – in my mind by an all pervasive yellowy-brown. Lit by the midday sun the landscape shimmered in a yellowy-white heat... a contrast to the browny-black shadows thrown by rock, tree, church, house or city wall. The heat of the sun singed such vegetation as was brave enough to grow turning the leaves into a dreary shade of blue.

If colour united the places I had visited – Cyprus, Naples, Malta, Gibraltar, Rome – they were also united by the nature of my trips. Apart from a course in Rome, the work that took me to the Mediterranean was to run workshops for English primary school teachers employed by the SCSEA.

The heads and teachers employed directly by the Authority worked on a 3-year contract which was renewable. The majority of these English trained and domiciled teachers were single women

193

although most of the headteachers were men. (This relates to the 1970s and 1980s when equality of opportunity was politically correct but ill-applied). Some local teaching staff were employed, drawn from families of serving soldiers.

One never asked why young teachers should sign away 3 years of their lives to work in schools attached to military bases. The overseas allowance was an attraction as was the improved pension scheme. There was always the opportunity of cheap overseas travel. That said, a proportion of the teaching force must have been made up of people who wanted to escape from their ties in the UK, thereby achieving at little personal cost a space in which to review their lives.

Although the initial posting (note the military touch) was for 3 years, it was often extended to 6. This gave a degree of stability to the school. Most heads were also moved on after two 3-year terms. They could apply for another vacant headship in another command (e.g. SE Asia or Germany) or seek a post in an education authority at home.

The schools were well equipped. Capitation (money given to the head to be spent per child per year) was generous, invariably better than was found in the UK. The curriculum followed by primary age children – books used, topics covered – was very similar to that found in an English classroom, except that environmental projects could draw upon the richness of the local surroundings. There was much talk among teachers of the 'disturbance factor' which affected service schools – the disruption caused by regular changes of school which children faced when their fathers were posted to a new command.

Although each course I organised was prepared against requests sent to me in advance – like practical courses in picture-making, printing, display – the pattern of my days was similar, whether I was in Malta or Naples.

I prepared my course room as if it were a primary classroom. Each table, seating 6 or 8 course members, had a selection of materials which would be used. This was an essential teaching hint. At whatever level we teach – and remember primary school teachers usually work with their class from 9–4 day after day – we cannot hope to be continually inspired. Being inspirational is about 5% of the task of the successful teacher. It is the 95% of effort ploughed into the organisation of minutiae which guarantees success.

When the course members entered my 'child-centred' classroom, I made a 'contract' with them. I would pretend they were nine-year olds. They would respond/behave accordingly. Course members would follow basic processes as I presented them (and I presented them as though I was working with a class of primary age children). The teachers, (my nine-year olds) responded at their own level... which varied from the disastrous and chaotic to the supremely gifted.

The activities ran through the day with short breaks for coffee and tidying up and longer breaks in which I showed transparencies and chaired discussions. Most courses ran for 3 days, some ran through the week, the teachers attending half days. Each course ended with a display of work and a discussion centring on the successes and failures of the whole experience. This often prompted the participants to confess that they had confronted – often for the first time in their lives – the frustrations caused by being unable to complete an activity in the time allowed. Hopefully this led to a greater awareness of how children feel when a rigid timetable is arbitrarily imposed upon creative activities.

In addition to running courses I was also expected to visit the schools from which the teachers were drawn, to comment on the art work as reflected by classroom displays, project presentation and children's folders and exercise books. Oral reports to the headteacher and to the military officer who had general oversight of all the schools on the base followed upon the classroom visits. On returning home I wrote a more detailed and reflective report for use by headquarters staff of SCSEA in Eltham, London.

Another element which united the courses I undertook emerged from the places themselves. I have always been fascinated by history and architecture. On every trip I have made, at home or abroad, as an employee or a tourist, I have made time for historical exploration.

The roots of European civilisation lie in the Mediterranean lands. This part of the world has a certain awe: for these lands are the social, scientific and political seed-bed from which Western society has grown. It is so easy to reduce the lives and work of people of genius – such as Euclid, Euripides, Michelangelo, Leonardo, Gregory the Great, Cicero, Aristotle, Livi, Palladio – to obituary-like biographies written by learned academics. Important as these writings are, significant though they may be to our understanding of the past, the people featured walked, made love, had families, fell sick, suffered failure and enjoyed success.

These are areas which should encourage us to speculate, for the landscapes in which they lived remain – as do artefacts and structures with which these men and women may have been familiar.

I try to allow myself the luxury for brief moments to escape the straightjacket of academic research and examine the past through more imaginative and romantic eyes. What might stone, brick or artefact say – could they but talk!

Sadly they remain silent… but live and speak through interpretation. The stones we interpret may outline the foundation walls of a Roman villa or placed and mortared one against another form the 'envelope' of some great building. The spaces defined by the walls tell us something too, as does the relationship between each building, shell or ruin and its neighbour. The structure we are calling to life might be finely fashioned like the Parthenon in Rome or a lone standing stone from prehistory. Every intrusion on the natural landscape speaks of time past, of people long dead, perhaps of political confrontation, religious belief, of economic success or decline.

Wherever and whenever we teach and wherever or whenever we learn, we do so within a landscape worked and shaped by human beings – and the landscape of the past touches every generation of children and influences their thoughts, attitudes and beliefs.

So the comments I make about my journeys include my personal discoveries about places which many people visit only vicariously through book, magazine or TV programme.

In the pages which follow, location is linked to location by three parallel threads – the colour and tone of the landscape in unique Mediterranean light, the similarity of the courses I led and the historic past which confronted me whenever I gave myself the time to stand, stare, wonder – *and listen.*

Cyprus

I visited Cyprus in the spring of 1976. At that time my knowledge of the island was minimal. My research told me that Cyprus was loaned to Great Britain by Turkey in 1878, that it became a colony in 1925 and that its population was part-Greek Cypriot (81%) and part-Turkish (19%). I remembered from my army service (1950–52) that Cyprus was a posting to avoid. From 1950 onwards a guerrilla movement, led by Archbishop Makarios of the Greek-Orthodox Church, staged a military campaign with the aim of obtaining independence. Fighting under the banner EOKA (Union with Greece), Makarios and his supporters achieved their purpose. A republic was established with the Archbishop as President.

The settlement allowed the United Kingdom to retain two sovereign bases which they could use for military purposes – at Akrotiri in the south of the island and Dhekalia in the east. The settlement satisfied the Greek Cypriots but frustrated those whose links were with Turkey. The situation became volatile and exploded in 1974 when Turkish forces invaded. The Turkish military eventually withdrew, but only after a Turkish enclave had been established in the north of the island.

Driven from their homes in northern Cyprus by the Turkish Cypriots, many Greek Cypriots became refugees in their own country. The division of the island remains to this day. Indeed, unification plans drawn up by UNO were rejected (April 2004) in an all-island plebiscite. The two Cypriot peoples remain antagonistic towards each other, each secure behind the 'Green Line', an artificial frontier manned by troops drawn from United Nations members which runs around the land annexed by Turkey.

On the first day of my visit I was taken, as part of my familiarisation programme, to the 'Green Line'. Being 'dipped' quickly into the local environment helps to acquire a 'local flavour' which can be used in subsequent workshops. The trip, which began in the early morning, took in the foothills of the Troodos Mountains (the base of the EOKA terrorists), numerous archaeological sites and the small bay from whose waters (according to legend) Venus emerged standing on a shell.

As I stood on the foreshore I tried to recall reproductions of Sandro Botticelli's painting. The painting, which years later I was to see in the Uffizi Gallery, Florence, was commissioned by the Medici family in about 1485. It shows Venus, her nakedness covered by her flowing auburn hair, about to step onto the shore, helped by a nymph. The shell on which Venus stands has been blown to land by Zephyrs (wind Gods) who shower her with roses.

The painting, according to E.H. Gombrich in the 'Story of Art' (Phaidon, 1972) carries a message from the classical world of the Greeks and Romans. It portrays a moment when the God(s) intervene on earth. Divinity has come to humankind. But strangely (for this is a time when the Catholic Church was all powerful), the image of Divinity is not Mary and Jesus but of an unclothed female. Could the legend be discussed in an RE lesson I wondered?

Two less profound memories remain of my first day in Cyprus… the sinister black silhouettes of kites circling high against the hazy blue of the sky. In flocks they wheeled in great arcs above their

197

territories; threatening, silent, watchful. I never saw them move earthwards. It was as though they were trapped in the thermal currents on which they drifted so effortlessly.

Then there were the grape notices... of bends in the road which bore dire warnings of driving too fast during the months when the vine was harvested. Notices, written in free hand in black paint on scraps of board advised road users to 'Beware! Grapes on road'. One proclaimed 'Harvesting Grapes'. (Was the motorist really under threat from marauding vines?); another simply read 'Grape juice on bends'.

Appropriately my day ended with wine and refreshments in a bar in Nicosia. My companion, Graham, head of the school I was to visit next day, spent much of the time telling me of the excitement of "running a school away from home". I think his teaching experience was rooted in rural Cornwall. Consequently the level of excitement he described was somewhat minimalistic. "I would *never*, as headteacher, drink wine like this in my village", he explained, "and with a stranger!" He paused for effect. "People would talk." Excitement indeed.

Graham's school was orderly and ran like clockwork. Between the bells, automatically controlled, which defined the beginning and ending of each period there was silent endeavour in every classroom. I think much the same could be said of my courses. Graham's teachers were diligent to distraction, inspired they were not. The principal thrill of each day was that of being disturbed. "Oh I did jump, Mavis" said the deputy-head. "Those bells are such a surprise."

My next course was in Dhekalia, some 85 km from Akrotiri. I travelled by 'Tilly', a small army vehicle of the type on which I learned to drive in 1952 when in the army. The Tilly was a cross between an estate car and an open van. For a short journey the Tilly gave a reasonably comfortable ride. My driver, a corporal in the RASC, was not comfortable at all. "Sunday's for cricket, not school visitors," he said. "No offence, Sir, but when the school teachers have their courses our children have to stay at home. Makes my wife real mad!" What parents say in Bermondsey they also say in Akrotiri.

At the conclusion of my course at Dhekalia School, I spent a pleasant evening in the home of John, the teacher responsible for Art and Craft. Everyone who worked in the school attended, as did some of his Cypriot neighbours. I experienced a range of local dishes, many based on yoghurt... though I had to take great care to avoid the ubiquitous cheeses.

The following afternoon, a Friday, I was en route from Nicosia to Naples. It was an Air-Italia flight. By contemporary standards, security was non-existent. The captain and co-pilot sat chatting with a stewardess through an open cockpit door, quite oblivious to the needs of their passengers. They spoke in loud Italian; gesture-rich, their arms and hands brushed each other with singular regularity. The plane was obviously flying itself. We passed over Vesuvius. It was smoking languidly. I wondered whether Air-Italia's wandering arms were sufficiently alert to take over control of the plane should it begin to inadvertently drift towards the smouldering crater.

Naples

Naples, a stop-over on my way back to London, was a revelation. I was to work with a dozen teachers who were employed in the British Primary School in the Allied Headquarters, Southern Mediterranean. The officer in charge was an RAF Wing-Commander (who was also a qualified teacher, PGCE). He had arranged for me to be met at Naples Airport by a civilian driver, locally employed by the Ministry of Defence, and taken to my hotel (from which I would be collected next day). The driver introduced himself, raced me and my bags to a large black car, hurried me into the back seat and drove like one possessed through the streets.

To Marco, traffic lights were simply street decorations, other cars were moving hazards, Vespa riders he saw as gnats to terrify, and pedestrians as quite unnecessary obstructions to his path. My driver was satisfying the ecstasy and danger which comes from speed and an associated delight – of encouraging his passengers to contemplate mortality and its close companion – eternity.

I arrived at the hotel in Central Naples hoping that Marco was not assigned to me for future journeys. I was lucky. I was met next day by an RAF driver who viewed battling with Naples traffic as a useful way of developing co-ordination of hand, foot and eye! "That was close," he observed dryly as we missed a flower van by inches. "If he goes on like that the flowers will be around him before his funeral."

I was fortunate indeed to be given the opportunity to lead a course in Naples. The teachers could only be released outside normal working hours, so I met them from 3–7 p.m. for four days. The group was small: the activities undertaken were in response to individual requests. The nature of the course meant that I had an unusual amount of free time.

Wing Commander Bob Wilson, a cheerful rubicund man looked more like a Welsh hill farmer than an erstwhile fighter pilot. He used my visit as an excuse to share with me his enthusiasm for ancient Roman civilisation. He was indeed fortunate with his present posting, close to the ruins of Pompeii and its port Herculaneum. Both towns were destroyed by the cataclysmic eruption of Vesuvius in 79AD. The flow of lava was so fast that the two towns were enveloped with burning ash. Over 2000 people died.

The hot ash had one beneficial side-effect. It covered the buildings to a considerable depth – and so preserved them for future archaeologists to excavate and historians to analyse.

Visiting Herculaneum was a rewarding experience... and not for its more bizarre features like the mummified bodies of Roman citizens, their limbs taut as though frozen with fear as well as by choking fumes. Then there were the erotic frescoes. Most of these were covered with curtains lest an unsuspecting visitor came upon them unawares. How I wondered did the Roman house God, still secure in his niche by the villa's entrance, view such censorship?

I was also impressed by the height of the buildings. With few exceptions Roman remains in the UK are little more than 'explained' foundations: i.e. we see lines of neat stones and interpret them via a guidebook. In Herculaneum the ruins 'stand tall'. It is often possible to go upstairs and look down on a courtyard through an upper window – just as senator or slave might have done 2000 years ago.

The streets now followed by groups of school children, tourists and academics speak of centuries long gone... the stepping stones which link pavement to pavement must have felt many a sandaled step of slave and freeman, of shopkeeper and servant girl, of prosperous trader and his lady. In the road the deep ruts cut by the wheels of innumerable carts are clearly visible.

When visiting an historic site rich in atmosphere I invariably remember words spoken by Chorus in the Prologue to Shakespeare's 'Henry V':

"On your imaginary forces work...
...tis your thoughts which now must deck [the scene]".

Adopting this suggestion I stood against a villa near the Forum. In my reverie the long dead townsfolk swirled around me; past the wine shop, its amphora filled with wine; past the bakers with its mouth-watering smell of freshly baked bread; past the weaver's workshop and the click-clack of the looms, past the potter and the slap of clay on board. In the distance I heard the far-off chanting of an angry crowd. I'm reminded of Elspeth's (my daughter) comment when she visited, at the age of 7, Fountains Abbey in Yorkshire.

"Daddy", she said, "you can almost feel the monks".

Next morning John, Bob's son, was given the task of taking me to Vesuvius. John was a lively eight-year old with an amazingly rich and diverse vocabulary. He spoke to me not patronisingly, but as an equal. Before long – as far as volcanoes were concerned – I realised that he was the teacher and I was the child. My first need, he said, was to choose a pair of shoes from a pile by the back door. The reason for this, he explained, was that the ground was "hot, up there," and that heat would ruin good shoes.

Clad in old shoes, Bob drove us to a wide footpath near the base of the volcano and parked. "This is John's contribution. I'll wait here and read." John and I walked slowly up the path, he explaining to me the nature of volcanoes, the event of 79AD, the make up of the soil on which we were walking, the flora and fauna and the all-pervasive sulphur-like smell.

We paused, for the climb was long and tiring. John looked me in the eye. "My mother wants me to tell you of a concern. When I come up here I must promise not to look at the benches. I expect this means that you must promise too." He turned and pointed to a fixed wooden table which stood close by the path. Benches lay along the two long sides, the whole unit being surrounded by a pergola-like construction supporting a light wooden roof.

"Apparently," said John without a trace of a smile, "Italian ladies come up here to take the air. They think the gases from the volcano improve the skin. So they take off nearly all their clothes and lie on the benches and tables… which is why my mother tells me to look elsewhere. Of course, I usually remember."

When I had photographed the volcano (but *not* the ladies) we returned to Bob. Subsequently I remarked to him of John's breadth of knowledge of Vesuvius. "If a child's interested in something he'll learn beyond his years."

Bob gave me many insights into life and living during my brief time with him. Late one evening he took Jane (his wife) and me for dinner. The restaurant was in central Naples. Bob parked the car in a street close by, fixed an anti-theft bar across the steering wheel, locked the driver's door and then felt all 4 doors and the boot to make sure they were secure. He then put his right hand to his mouth and whistled loudly through his fingers.

Within seconds a gang of street urchins emerged from the shadows. In Italian, he asked them to mind his car for a couple of hours. The gang leader agreed to do so – and the 'fee' payable on our return. "Never pay until you come back" said Bob. "I did once, and when I returned there was no gang, no windscreen wipers, no hubcaps, no wing mirrors and no manufacturer's badges." It was while eating my meal that I had my second lesson on surviving in Naples. A gypsy group approached our table, determined to sing. Bob stopped them in their tracks by paying them in advance – to go away.

The manner in which Bob dealt with the car minders and the gypsy quartet are examples of the kind of insights which one gains from spending time in a new place with someone with local knowledge. The car minders also indicated something of the mixture of poverty, squalor and crime which was the negative face of Napoli in the 1970s.

My background – to some extent Puritan – has had the effect of protecting me from any interest in the more bizarre manifestations of human behaviour. Until visiting Naples I had never realised that prostitution could be so visible in any community, particularly one dominated by the Roman Catholic Church. Was it because Naples was a port and a military base that the sex industry flourished?

In my innocence I had not realised until I came to Naples that cars were used as a platform to advertise prostitution. Along a wide road, not far from the military HQ stood lines of parked cars – new, polished, speaking of upper class affluence. Each car was accompanied by a girl – draped provocatively over the bonnet, perched on the boot or nestled demurely in the driver's seat. Expensively, though minimally dressed, each girl waited for custom. These were those who could afford to 'work' during the cool of the morning and early evening.

Close by the street of cars was a depressed area of squalid housing. Here the second act of this dark drama was played out and the pseudonym 'ladies of the night' utterly appropriate. Instead of cars, the kerbsides were lined with burning tyres, each some 10 metres from its neighbour. Red and orange flames flickered skywards, encircled with swirls of dense black smoke. The waiting girls, undefined shapes, seemed to move in and out of sight as the fire flared or dimmed. Their bodies and their shadows became so intermingled that medieval wall paintings came to mind – of souls in torment in some unimaginable hell. I wondered what kind of life people in this sordid business could look forward to – and felt sad that men should prey upon the vulnerable and economically insecure.

To return from this diversion to the restaurant and meals! I had one other meal worthy of mention, but not primarily for the food.

Employed in the HQ in Naples were soldiers, sailors and airmen from the nations of Western Europe. By military tradition officers shared one mess, warrant officers and sergeants a second, and other ranks a third. Whatever the mess, it was customary to leave hat and belt (and presumably the weapons the belt might carry) in the entrance lobby. Entrance to the Naples Officers' Mess would be a veritable delight to a milliner, haberdasher or costume designer. There, in a space 3 m x 2 m, was a garden of hats. On hooks, on chairs, on shelf and on table, even on the floor were hats from many lands. Hats for colonels, wing commanders, commodores, hats for the youngest lieutenant and the oldest admiral, hats decorated in braids of red, yellow, white and gold... a garden of hats in black, khaki, blue and green; small discreet hats, grand flamboyant hats, hats with brims and peaks and buttons, hats with tassels, hats with badges, hats for almost any function – society wedding, battlefield or palace.

How one retrieved one's hat from so many on leaving I never discovered... though there were stories of hats ending up in wrong hands (or on wrong heads).

My departure from Naples is also fixed in my memory. Sitting in the departure lounge for the flight to Heathrow, I saw Robin Ray buying drinks at the bar. I had met Robin several times. He was a popular TV and radio personality and married to Sue Stranks, the anchor person on 'Magpie' the ITV children's programme. At this time (the early 1970s) Sue and I were employed, freelance, by EJ Arnold, a Leeds-based educational supplier... which explains how I knew Robin.

To return to Robin. He was so surprised to see me (out of context) that he turned to call Sue, stumbled and dropped the tray he was holding. Sue was much amused. We chatted for a while before we boarded our planes to go our separate ways, Sue and Robin to Paris, I to London. "Odd people you meet in Naples", said Robin as we parted. To this day I wonder what he meant!

(Robin and Sue moved to Sussex in the 80s. Sue retired from 'Magpie' but Robin continued to broadcast being particularly associated with 'middle brow' quiz shows e.g. 'My Music', 'My Word'. He was also a popular classical disc-jockey. Involvement with the entertainment industry ran in Robin's family. His father, Ted, was a successful comedian in the late 1940s, the 50s, and the 60s.)

Malta

Some months after my trip to Cyprus I visited military schools in Malta. The military link here was with the Officer in Charge of the naval base in Valletta harbour. I recall that the course I prepared sought to provide links between specific art techniques (like print making) and the built environment. For me it was a course that fulfilled its aims and on which nothing unexpected happened.

It took considerable time for me to discover much about Sir William, but his links with Malta were well established. Before returning to England to become Prior of St John's, Sir William had been a senior admiral of 'The Knights Hospitallers of the Order of St. John of Jerusalem.' This religious order dates from about 1070 and dedicated to St. John the Baptist. Its founder Raymond Le Puy, realised that Christian Pilgrims needed hospitality and protection as they followed the traditional Pilgrim routes to the Holy Land. So Hospitaller 'Commanderies' were built along the most used routes. (There is a famous example in Rochester, Kent). The Knights of St. John were recognised by the emblem each wore – a white cross on a black background.

On being driven from the Holy Land, the Knights established themselves on the island of Rhodes. In 1528 the Ottomans drove the Knights from the island; Prior William was in charge of the seaborne evacuation getting the Knights and their servants to Malta. It was following upon this successful operation that William returned to London and the position of Prior of Clerkenwell.

I found Malta a fascinating place, not least because of the tenuous links it had with the school in which I worked situated close to London's Barbican complex. The school was named after Prior Weston, the last prior of St. John's Priory, Clerkenwell. The gate house of the Priory still stands. Close by is a chapel in the crypt of which lies the recumbent effigy of Prior Sir William Weston. The Priory was one of many sequestered by the Commissioners of Henry VIII in 1536/37. Sir William was not treated badly by the king, being given an adequate pension for life. However William was heartbroken by the destruction of the priory "and unconsoled, took to his bed and died." The school, in Whitecross Street EC1 stood on what, in Prior William's day, was a priory orchard.

Evidence of the Knights was to be found everywhere in Malta. Buildings, churches and memorials were signposts to the past. For example Valletta, the capital, was named after Jean Parisot de la Vallette, Grand Master of the Order of the Knights of St. John. Parisot was so honoured because he successfully led the defence of the island during the Turkish siege of 1565.

Malta remained a base for the Hospitallers until Napoleonic times, becoming a British Colony in 1814. The islanders became independent in 1964 and a Republic within the British Commonwealth in 1974.

The importance of the Hospitallers has long since past but the inheritance they left contributed a very significant element to my course.

Malta supported human life in the Stone Age. Like many early cultures, a Mother Earth figure was included in the Pantheon of the Gods. As I have previously observed, my hosts (wherever I was visiting) were always willing to arrange for their guests to be taken to local places of interest.

So it was that I was taken to a Stone Age religious site. Brooding over the entrance to an underground chamber was a huge stone female torso. Although most of her legs were missing, she stood some 4 metres tall. Her power to impress had not diminished over time. She dominated the small courtyard giving a feeling of mature motherhood – not the motherhood of youth and beauty but the motherhood of experienced middle age, that period in a woman's life when the hope or expectation of child bearing has past and the role of advisor, confidant, experience-sharer begins to be respected by her offspring.

Being a God, this figure, through her priests and acolytes, brought wisdom and gave advice to her followers. Standing before her I thought of my own mother and how she tried to possess and manipulate, of my friends' mothers who always seemed more gentle and caring than my own.

The site she watched over was deep below ground and reached by descending flights of stone steps cut into the floor of a narrow sloping passageway. My guide did not come with me. Equipped with a torch (carried lest the electric lights failed) I made my way down the 90 uneven steps to the central chamber.

A single pale spotlight illuminated a horizontal stone slab. Incised along one side was a deep groove which led to a drainage hole. Was this used, I conjectured, to carry away blood when a sacrifice was offered to the Gods?

The chamber was possessed of a rare, almost frightening, characteristic. So far below ground and with no other visitors, it was utterly silent... silence of a kind I have never again experienced.

As I made my way slowly to the surface I noticed that whorls had been scratched into the stone walls. Similar whorls are to be found in Anglesey, Ireland and South America. It's thought provoking to reflect how the open whorl became an accepted symbol of female fertility, of Mother Earth by primitive peoples unable to communicate with each other and separated by thousands of miles. (Incidentally, the Irish Goddess of Fertility was called Macha. Her feast day, Lugnasard, was taken over by the church and her role given to Bridget, the saint to whom women appealed for help to become pregnant and for support during childbirth).

I explored Valletta on foot finding the richly-carved Baroque architecture of particular interest. I travelled by bus to the towns of Bugibba, Rabid and Birzebugga. The fares were low, the seats uncomfortable, the roads pitted and dusty.

I ignored the midday siesta and found cool in the churches and the chapels I explored. The bulk of the population are Roman Catholic. At the time of my visit the great majority of the religious houses (of which there were many) were largely unreformed – by which I mean the 'outward and visible signs' of religious practice (to quote the Anglican prayer book) seemed still locked into seventeenth century Europe. Cassock-wearing priests, their faces protected from the hot sun by wide, soft-brimmed black hats, were a common sight. Occasionally priest walked with monk or nun. The monk's heavy habit, knotted belt, rosary and sandaled feet were in complete harmony with the stone pavements, the narrow streets and the white and yellow houses with their shuttered windows.

This impression of time stopped – a return to the days when the trappings of the religious life were commonplace – was given greater emphasis by the nuns who busied themselves in schools, hospitals and churches. Wearing voluminous black dresses to neuter their femininity and wing-like wimples to conceal their faces, they merged very well into life on a twentieth century island which somehow had managed to preserve an atmosphere more in keeping with the seventeenth.

At almost any time of the day one would see small groups of nuns hurrying along the streets. I rarely heard them talk to each other as they moved silently by, eyes downcast. It was as though they were engaged in some unending treasure hunt, an activity they were forbidden to undertake alone.

On one occasion when the strength of the midday sun made the white walls of the shuttered houses reflect an almost supernatural light, two 'canticles' of nuns (my own collective noun), each canticle 8 in number, approached each other on a narrow sun drenched pavement. The coming together of their black silhouettes on the wall beside them was true street theatre. The 2 canticles met and mingled, passing each other in single file, like dancers in a nineteenth century ball. The dancing silhouettes echoed their movements, though the overlapping and distortion of flowing dress and wimple made the silhouettes look comically irreligious. The wall shadows were there for a few brief moments. Then the wall was white again. But the drama was not quite over. A new silhouette was on stage – again the silhouette of a nun, older, rounder, more slow-moving than her sisters performed a graceful Viennese 'Gallop' as she hastened to join her 'canticle', which by now had disappeared from view.

For me Malta is a fascinating island because the past is continually merging with the present.

The memory I treasure most is my trip around Grand Harbour in the motor cruiser used by the commanding officer. I was able to view the city of Valletta from a completely new angle. As the cruiser purred across the water its captain reminded me that the harbour was the focus of attacks by German and Italian bombers "in the great siege of 1942."

"Did I remember that the heroics of the people of Malta earned them a George Cross?" he asked.

I think he was impressed when I told him that I did!

Gibraltar 1979–81

When making a visit to a 'foreign' country the traveller invariably makes comparisons with life at home. Not so the visitor to Gibraltar which even today, 25 years after my 2 one-week visits, remains a somewhat beleaguered outpost of the United Kingdom. The similarities are all too obvious! English is the lingua franca, Spanish being spoken only by the migrant workers who cross the border daily.

There are the everyday things. The post boxes are identical to those found in any English village; the policemen wear uniforms one would see in Cardiff or Midlothian. I was amused, on both of my visits, to discover a thriving branch of Marks and Spencer selling the things for which it is famous: lingerie, male underwear and lightweight shirts.

The street signs, the advertisements, the hotel names (I stayed for a week in 'The Bristol Hotel'), the presence of so many families with direct links with 'the home country' – the families of service personnel and business executives of UK-based companies, and the daily flying of the Union Flag reinforces this strange feeling of almost being at home!

'Almost' is the significant word, for there are differences. Gibraltar is so small (2.5 sq.miles: 6.5 sq.km). Compared with the inhabitants of the wild open moorland of Yorkshire, or the rugged wilderness found in Wales and Scotland, the Gibraltarians must have a singular mind-set to choose to spend their lives on a rocky outcrop of limestock, 1400 ft (427 m) high where the waters of the Atlantic and the Mediterranean meet and mingle.

It's easy to understand why rival states have since Roman times appreciated the strategic importance of 'The Rock'. Its key position, controlling the narrow passageway into the Mediterranean (8 miles: 13 km), gave considerable advantage to the nation which held it.

Gibraltar has been a British protectorate since 1713 when Spain ceded the Rock under the terms of the Treaty of Utrecht. In earlier centuries Gibraltar was part of the Moorish Empire from 717 until 1482 when it was annexed by the Royal House of Castille. There are 2 other significant dates in Gibraltar's history: 1830, when it became a Crown Colony, and 1969, when the Gibraltarians were granted self-government but without control over issues of defence or foreign affairs.

Even as I write (in May 2004) a radio newscaster is speaking of "growing tension between Britain and Spain," the Spanish prohibiting cruise liners visiting Spanish ports if they had previously spent time (24 hours) taking in Gibraltar.

For the last 50 years successive governments have sought a fair solution to the issue of sovereignty of the Rock.

"Why should the government of the United Kingdom exercise control over a tiny patch of land on the tip of Spain?" asks the Spanish Foreign Secretary. To which the Prime Minister of Gibraltar replies "Why should we be forced to become Spaniards against our will?"

No doubt the two powers would have resolved this problem long ago but for the intransigence of 30,000 Gibraltarians who in a 2002 referendum expressed (with an overwhelming majority) their wish to stay British.

Like all the places 'visited' in this chapter, Gibraltar has its own special legend. The legend explains how the Rock of Gibraltar was formed and why it's matched across the straits by a similar high peak.

The Greek hero Heracles – in Roman legend he is called Hercules – was set 12 labours to perform by King Eurystheus. The tenth labour involved capturing the cattle of Giant Geryon and bringing them to the king.

Geryon lived at the Western end of the 'great middle sea' (our Mediterranean). When Heracles reached its farthest point west, he found his way blocked by an enormous mountain. Throwing his arms around the mountain, he tore it apart. One piece fell on Africa and was called Abyta (near the town of Ceuta in present day Morocco). The other fell on the tip of the land we now call Spain. The half mountain was called Calpe, our modern Gibraltar. As Calpe and Abyta fell to earth, the Mediterranean and the Atlantic Ocean met – so Heracles also formed the Straits of Gibraltar. When today you stand on Calpe and look across to Africa you can see Abyta. In legend these rocky outcrops are called the 'Pillars of Heracles.'

The two visits I made to Gibraltar were quite different from each other, though the adult participants were, in the main, the same.

On the first occasion I went alone to take a course on art and display. On the second I was accompanied by a colleague, Hilary Devonshire. One task was to create a demonstration classroom for 20 8 and 9 year olds of mixed ability: our second was to use the environment to trigger creative work (painting and a range of art processes) as well as conventional subject areas (poetry, prose, mathematics, verbal skills, mapping, geography and history).

The children were with us for one week during normal school hours. For short periods throughout each day we were visited, observed and questioned by small groups of teaching staff. In the late afternoon we received all the teachers in the demonstration classroom for further input and discussion. The walls of the classroom were bare on our arrival. On our departure the room was left as an exhibition to be visited by classes within the school.

The course I ran explains the purpose of my visits. But what of the Rock itself which dominates everything – houses, roads, the 19th century defensive wall, the people and the airport.

A consequence of being in air space controlled by Spain meant that the flight path into Gibraltar Airport was very restricted. Landing was a little nerve-racking. If an aircraft can be described as being mesmerised, my plane certainly was! It moved toward the solid wall of rock with its dull green patches of vegetation like an unwilling moth drawn to a candle flame.

As the aircraft glided towards the peak, the passengers became silent; those sitting on the port side showing distinct signs of tension. To them, the rock seemed far too close! With great care the pilot eased the aircraft downwards – at least the rippling sea offered a softer landing place than the threatening rock. A sudden acceleration, a roar from the jet engines and a soft bump of wheels touching the ground – and we were landed. This plane had personality and it showed it now. With a shake of its wing tips it seemed to say "No matter the Rock, the impossible approach, the smallness of the landing strip. I've made it!"

On Gibraltar the schools were the responsibility of an officer in the RAF. On both visits I met him on arrival and departure, but my principal link was with the headteacher of a school built almost within the old fortifications at Europa Point, the very tip of Europe.

The response of the teachers on my first visit was positive, even though I queried the content of the environmental studies programme which the majority of classes were following. It was based, inappropriately, on expensive source material which centred upon the fishing industry of NE Scotland. I remember pointing out that Gibraltar had a long established fishing industry too, with boats designed specifically for catching the edible Mediterranean octopus.

The discussions I had with the staff resulted in a request for a second visit and a pupil based course (described below). The use of the local environment was no worse than in many schools in England. It just seemed odd in this case that the fishermen of Aberdeen so beautifully presented in project books and classroom walls should feature so prominently in the curriculum of children presently living in Gibraltar whose parents regarded Southampton and Portsmouth as 'home'.

The pupil-based course involved learning through looking and seeing. To quote T.S. Eliot to see so deeply "that we come to know the place for the first time"!

We took the children to the summit. Looking across to Africa, several children observed that they had "been in Gib for 2 years and this was the first visit to its peak." It was here high above the harbour and the houses, that we met the Barbary Apes, Europe's only native monkey. It was here that we stood in complete silence, later trying to describe the sounds we heard – the chatter of the Apes, the rustle of wind through the scrubby vegetation, the call of birds.

210

We explored the narrow, winding streets of Gibraltar, made rubbings from the headstones which mark the graves of sailors who fought and died at Trafalgar (1805), sketched the old defensive wall, its gates and its 19th century naval guns. We looked for evidence of Moorish occupation (717–1482) and Gibraltar under the Spaniards (1482–1713). On each of our visits the children recorded: in words (spoken and written), in poetry and prose, in sketch and painting, in number, map and diagram. This material was the basis for the more traditional work we followed in the classroom.

On both of my visits one day was left free to follow personal interests. I spent both days in Tangier, Morocco.

On my first visit I was advised that the safest way of guaranteeing that one returned on the agreed date at the agreed time was to book through 'Air Gibraltar', a company which had developed into an art form the offer to 'Live Tangier for a day.'

If the chosen travel agent was a form of insurance, further protection was provided by the Ministry of Defence in the shape of a lady member of the armed forces.

I met 'Jane' at the airport. Somewhere in her mid twenties she was dressed in a flowered cotton two-piece. She was quick to inform me that she had "done this job before". For me this was the beginning of a unique experience. Never before (nor have I since) been 'escorted'. Jane (not her real name) seemed to have been selected by a verbal fluency test. She chatted remorselessly about everything – her breakfast, her 'last' boyfriend, her office job at HQ, Marks and Spencer, her prowess at swimming, her mum. She chatted while we waited to take off, she chatted in the air, in Tangier and back again.

The travel company supplied a guide, a car and a driver to meet the flight and take us into Tangier. We drove quickly into town, passing on the outskirts an enormous settlement of home-made huts, bivouacs and lean-tos made from sheets of corrugated iron and wooden planks.

In Tangier we were taken to the Anglican Church, the Arab Market and Bazaar, stopping at places chosen by our rather decadent looking guide. Once inside a 'shop' it was difficult to escape. All manner of goods were produced – elaborate 'Arab' jewellery, clothes (mostly of goat skin), richly patterned 'throws' and handcrafted plates, goblets and trays. The price of everything offered was agreed after lengthy haggling and the drinking of an inordinate amount of black coffee.

211

The guide left Jane and me to find lunch 'where we would.' Tangier was rich in eating places of all types and every price range. Guide and driver would pick us up at 4.00 p.m. for the return journey.

It was hot, the humidity was high and life in Tangier was very slow. We chose a French restaurant and watched camels vie with cars for road space, groups of children playing on the sidewalk... and such a variety of costume, the man and his lady in traditional western dress, oblivious to sun and dust, Arabs dressed like T.E. Lawrence, Moslem ladies covered with all embracing black.

Jane chatted... on... and on... and on. My grunts of agreement or surprise were sufficient to keep her going (I think she used my brief comments as moments in which to take breath). We ate slowly, because the courses came slowly. Nobody else came into the restaurant while we were there. Everything had almost stopped – except Jane.

In a welcome pause I asked Jane gently and with a smile whether she had joined the WRAC to gain experience before returning to civilian life to run an escort agency. Her response was immediate and unequivocal. It gave her a 'day off', a good meal and the opportunity to meet interesting people. No, she wouldn't do it at home – it seemed that mother would disapprove. I enquired whether she thought I needed a chaperone. She became suddenly formal. "The policy is to support male visitors with a lady and lady visitors with a man." Whose policy and with what authority the policy was implemented, I never discovered. Apparently the 'twinning' was to dissuade Moroccan youth to intrude upon innocent visitors – like me – with inappropriate invitations and suggestions.

At the agreed hour we returned to The Square, met our driver and guide and were taken to the airport. A short flight and we were once again in Gibraltar. Jane bade me goodbye and walked out of my life. Or so I thought.

In early November following my visit, my secretary at my publishers, Julia Hagerdorn, was opening my office mail. To her surprise and my astonishment it included a flowery letter from Jane. Its purpose – to invite me to spend the coming Christmas "quietly and discreetly" with her in Gibraltar. Had my grunts and stutters and half finished sentences charmed her – or had she met, for the first time in her life, a man she could talk over, conquered by her endless repartee?

My simple and brief reply to her letter gave her no opportunity to explain. As Julia observed, somewhat acidly "strange creatures, women."

This first visit remains in my memory not because of Jane but because of Gustav – Gustav Mahler.

Most overseas British Forces garrisons enjoy their own radio service whose broadcasts can be heard within the area that the Forces serve. I was invited, as 'guest of the week' to be interviewed on Gibraltar Forces Radio. The programme lasted an hour, during which time I was served some very friendly questions about education, schools and parenting. Just before the programme ended I was given a 'prize', the opportunity to choose a piece of music, have it broadcast and explain why it was special to me.

I chose the opening of the first movement of Gustav Mahler's Second Symphony in C Minor. 'The Resurrection.' The explanation I gave for my choice may appear sentimental, but the story I told runs as follows.

Driving across Suffolk on a misty Saturday afternoon in the middle of December in 1971 I decided to stop at Ely to find a café where my young family could have tea. I parked close to the Cathedral, a great, black, towering mass against the slowly darkening sky. The Cathedral doors were open, the dimmed lights of the nave and the Christmas lights of the town combining to create a sense of mystery. Instead of going straight to find a place to eat, I was drawn to the Cathedral's west door. Followed by my three children – Patrick (11), Elspeth (8) and Hilary (5) I slipped into the porch. We stood in a little group at the end of the nave.

The crossing, where transepts meet nave below the chancel arch was ablaze with light. Facing us was a full symphony orchestra. At right angles to the orchestra were two choirs, one in the South Transept, the second in the North. Facing the orchestra, on a dais, stood Daniel Barenboim, motionless, baton raised. A lady soloist, dressed in white, stood close by him. The television lights (I subsequently discovered that Ely had been chosen as the venue for an ITV presentation for Easter) had created a well of brilliance against the blackness of the cathedral walls.

Then Barenboim moved, drawing his baton imperiously downwards. There followed an explosion of sound from the timpani which reverberated around the building, for the opening bars of the symphony create a sensation of hellfire and doom. It was an electrifying moment. We stood transfixed. The mood slowly changed as orchestra, soloist and choir moved in typical Mahler mode into a rich lyrical theme. I think that each of us was touched by a moment of serenity and wonder. Its impact stays with me – a moment when music shapes and transforms an everyday happening, gracing it with something of the eternal.

I wonder how many service families I encouraged to taste Mahler?

I had listened to British Forces Radio earlier in the week. The programme featured Ted Moult and a quiz team. Ted Moult was a well known broadcaster in the 1960s and 70s, a Midlands farmer with a delightful personality, a rich accent and a sense of humour. It happened that Ted and a colleague travelled back to England on the same flight as me – and we sat in adjacent seats. I gave them a lift back to London, my car having been conveniently left at the airport. I remember gently teasing him about double glazing, for his ITV advertisements for 'Everest' (glass) were legendary.

On my second visit I came to understand why Gibraltarians were so insistent that their ties with Britain be preserved. Whatever alternative system was introduced Gibraltar would remain locked into the time of Empire. "We have been British since 1713. Why change now?"

Rome

I had throughout the late 1960s and early 1970s given lectures and run courses for teachers in Roman Catholic schools. I had even presented a paper at the National Conference of the Roman Catholic Teachers' Federation. My links were invariably through individuals and not with the church bureaucracy.

Notwithstanding my Catholic connections, the invitation from a privately run Roman Catholic primary school in Rome 'to visit and advise' came as a surprise. I had never met the lay headteacher or any of her staff, nor any of the nuns who were associated with the school – though I think they were Ursulines.

The trip – I arrived in Rome on Saturday morning and returned to London on the Sunday of the following week – was organised by the headteacher whom I'll call Mimi. She explained in her letter of invitation that "I was known to some of her fellow headteachers and if I could find time to visit her she would seize the opportunity to have me visit Rome." My brief was to comment on organisation, curriculum, timetable and logistics, teach if appropriate (the children were all English speaking), attend a staff meeting, and meet parents. The school was in a large, decaying house in the centre of Rome. Some of the classrooms were no bigger than a domestic lounge. There were 90+ children on roll. In the moments when I was not involved

214

with the school, I made lightning forays into Rome with Mimi and Mother Francis, the senior nun in the Convent which supported the school.

Each evening was taken up with gentle but exhaustive discussions over supper, the restaurant selected being chosen because one could eat al fresco far from the traffic. I could not attempt to guess the quantity of wine which was consumed over the week at these 'professional suppers' – but I remember keeping to my personal rule, born of parent-teacher socials at Prior Weston School. One glass of white wine topped up with fizzy water must last from eight to midnight.

The visit gave me the opportunity to discard many of the prejudices I had long held about Catholicism and the theology and philosophy from which it had grown. As a humanist I had long regarded them as 'my separated brethren' whenever social issues which impinge upon late childhood and sometimes tempestuous adolescence were discussed. But in all the school meetings I was able to talk rationally across the religious and cultural divide about abortion, contraception, marriage and divorce. There was a tolerance, an acceptance of different viewpoints in this small Catholic community which was refreshingly honest and open.

I think I had become aware that my appreciation of the Catholic faith would be challenged the moment Mother Francis greeted me at Leonardo da Vinci Airport.

She stood in the middle of a group of chauffeurs, each bearing a board with a name printed on it. She had a board too, my name glowed in red wax crayon. Surrounded by tall, suited, capped, olive skinned Italians, she looked utterly out of place. She was fair skinned and blonde, of medium height and on the youthful side of middle age. Thinking back, had the group been photographed for the press the caption writers could have had fun. 'Nun converts Mafia bosses'... or 'Have you seen this nun?'

I approached her and smiled. With a toss of her head and a twinkle in her eye she said, "Welcome to Rome, I'm Mother Francis... my car's this way." Dressed neatly in light blue – a knee length cotton skirt, light seersucker top, sandals and headscarf – she looked from behind far from nun-like.

We reached the parking lot and stopped beside a 2x2 sports car. My luggage was dropped in the back. This really *was* our car! We climbed in. Seat belts fastened, Mother Francis drove rather rapidly towards Rome. Now wearing sunglasses, she seemed to relish the breeze on her face and the quality of the car's handling.

After a few kilometres, when I had time to grasp the unusual situation I was in, Mother Francis, as if reading my thoughts, said, "Henry. Do you always look as if you don't know where you are? Was the flight difficult? Have you forgotten something?"

"I'm sorry if I appear to be gauche," I replied. "I'm just speechless at finding myself hurtling towards Rome in a blue sports car with a nun who just doesn't look like any nun I've ever met before."

Mother Francis was momentarily silent. "Our small house (i.e. religious community) decided to reform last year in order to be better able to meet the challenge of an uncaring God-less society." She paused then continued. "Think of it. How can we religious (i.e. in Holy Orders) be taken seriously by young people we meet and those who may need our help if, when we approach them, we are dressed in black robes and wimples? How can we begin to understand the pressures on the young and the temptations of the contemporary world if we give out signals which say "Don't come near me, I'm holy?" Look at my collar." She pointed to a tiny gold cross, clipped to her blouse. "That's my badge of Faith."

It was clear that Mother Francis had expressed her feelings about the religious life many times before and I was deeply impressed by the conviction with which she spoke. (Later in the week she told of the pain the changes had brought to older members of her community. Two sisters were so upset that they moved to another convent which kept to the old traditions of dress and practice.)

We reached the centre of Rome. The traffic was heavy, but far more orderly than in Naples. The hotel was close to the memorial to King Vittorio Emanuele II off the Via Cimmera. It was a one star and quite spartan; a very basic bedroom with a washbasin. Toilets and bathroom were at the end of a gloomy passage.

When I met the school staff I could appreciate the difficulties they were facing. Like Mother Francis, they needed new ideas to drive them forward. Like Mother Francis they carried with them the burden of established tradition, a tradition that was also embedded in the psyche of the pupils' parents. "We did this in school. It didn't hurt us. Look at us now! The things you want to change enabled us to succeed. We can even afford private education! We could always take Peter or Mary elsewhere."

This mirrored my own experience as head of a London primary school. Most parents cling to the past when the education of their children is threatened by change. When it comes to education everybody is an expert because everybody has suffered that tiny element of education which we call schooling. The meetings I had with parents in Rome were just like those I had in London.

My role in the school debate was very similar to that articulated by Mother Francis and her church. We both sought to challenge, to question and review current practice and to seek intelligent and rational alternatives when traditional approaches were failing.

I hope I helped the teaching staff in their struggle for change. For them I'm sure it was supportive to hear ideas one holds dear proclaimed in other tongues and other voices.

I spent much time in the school and there were few opportunities for me to explore Rome. However Mimi and Mother Francis contrived to find moments when they could slip me away. These one hour 'breaks' became part of my day. I remember 'doing' the Spanish Steps, the Trevi Fountain and the Fountain of Rivers in 45 minutes. Similar brief trips took me to the Vatican and St. Peters. Mother Francis told me I had time for a glance at one treasure – Michelangelo's 'Pieta' was her choice. My trips to the Baths of Caracalla and the Coliseum were similarly planned and equally short.

I saw the Via Appia Antica, the first Imperial Road (built in 312 AD) from another perspective – from a restaurant chair on one of our discussion evenings. To think... divisions of the Roman Army marched this way.

There was one statue that records the legend of the founding of Rome. Romulus and Remus were the twin sons of the God Mars. At the time of their birth King Amulius had seized the Roman throne. On hearing of the babies, Amulius ordered them to be drowned in the River Tiber. The servant charged with the task decided to place them in a basket and allow the river to carry them away. Found and succoured by a she-wolf the boys grew strong. Eventually they were given a home by a shepherd, Faustulus and brought up as his sons. The statue, used as an emblem throughout Rome, shows the boys feeding from the teats of the wolf.

On the final Saturday I went alone to the Capitoline Hill and dreamed my way through the Rome of Caesar, Augustus and Vespasian.

My taste of Rome was too hurried, giving little time to relate one piece of the jigsaw of its history to the next. One incident sticks in my mind. An American tourist, complete with camera and tripod, stood close beside me inside the Parthenon, the Roman temple which honoured all the Gods.

Sweating and breathing heavily he turned to his wife. "Say, Martha," he drawled. "If this place really is for *all* the Gods do we *still* have to go to St. Peters and the Vat-i-can?"

It was at this moment that I realised that Mimi and Mother Francis had taken me on a tour of Rome, American style.

Some weeks after my return to London I found myself in a convent of teaching sisters in Marylebone, NW London. I had agreed to select paintings sent in by Roman Catholic schools across the Archdiocese for an exhibition at Westminster Cathedral.

Quite by chance the nun with whom I was working, Sister Agnes, had been in Rome at the same time as me. She was fascinated by my experience at the school and the changes the sisters had made.

After a period of quiet contemplation Agnes put her hand on mine. "Henry," she said, "had I known you were in Rome I'm sure I could have arranged for you to come with me to the general audience given by the Holy Father. I'm sure it would have helped you gain further insight into Mother Church and its teaching." Then as if to rescue a rebellious soul from damnation, she invited me to Compline, the last service of the day. As an ex-chorister (Anglican Cathedral) how could I refuse!

This was not the first time I had caused a nun to try to re-shape my thoughts and beliefs. Nor was it the last…

By ending this section of my travels with my visit to Rome I have travelled full circle. Rome was the centre of an Empire which touched many of the places I have described.

So it is that I have indeed ended this chapter at the beginning…

…and begun it at the end.

Epilogue

Winter 2006–2007

"When an old person dies
it is as if an irreplaceable
library has been destroyed
by fire"

West African Proverb

In 1955, when I was a very new and inexperienced teacher, I had a nine year old girl in my class whose name was Sarah. She was, like most children, fascinated by dinosaurs.

"Did you meet any dinosaurs when you were my age?" She asked. It was an honest, enquiring question, devoid of irony.

I assured her that I had not – and I think she was a little disappointed at my reply. Her question serves a useful point with which to conclude this collection of traveller's tales. It indicates how young children view stories of life before they were born.

The world of dinosaurs exists in its own time frame, a frame that I can only enter by linking my knowledge of dinosaurs and my imagination. Similarly, although much more recent in historical time, my stories are set in the time frame of my life as a teacher.

The most recent of the happenings described here just break into the last decade of the 20th century. The world has moved on since then and most of the places, happenings and people I have described are now history… not history with a capital letter, but history personal to me.

Some of the events I mention were of national and international significance and will pass into school text books as well as providing plots for future works of fiction, theatre and cinema.

I experienced the 'two Germanys' born of World War II, I went through 'Checkpoint Charlie', the gateway for Westerners who

219

wished to cross into East Berlin. Since my visit two Germanys have become one – the wall and the gate a memory.

I stood in the New Territory of Hong Kong and gazed into China – mile upon mile of paddy fields which stretched into the distant horizon. Were I to stand in the same spot today I would perhaps see a vast industrial complex, office blocks and housing. The economic development area of Shenzhen has replaced paddy field and peasant.

I visited Serbia when Tito ruled over a peaceful Yugoslavia, a country then much visited by British tourists. Tito is long since dead, the nation he governed shattered by war and racked with ethnic tension.

I stood in Sofia in 1989 while the excited victors of the peaceful overthrow of a harsh communist regime swirled around me.

All of the events I have described – newsworthy or personal, all the people who appear in them, are 'ghosts' from my past. Each of these 'ghosts' also had a past like me, they live in and through time. Like me, each life is preserved in a unique personal lifeline.

I have written this account because my father, a brilliant story teller failed to record the many tales with which he enriched my childhood. Consequently, like the old person in the African legend, they are lost for ever.

This account of my experiences when working overseas as a teacher have been specifically prepared for my children and grandchildren – and hopefully for a generation yet to be born. They are also published because I believe that teachers in our primary schools need to appreciate the range of methods employed in different parts of the world and take pride in the impact that British primary schools made before the implementation of the Education Reform Act of 1988, which has destroyed innovative teaching in the British Isles.

A final thought. With the passing of a few more years, I am sure that the many events I have described will seem as quaint and old fashioned as Nelson's navy, the London of Samuel Pepys, the medieval pilgrims en route for Canterbury – or Sarah's dinosaurs!

H.P. London
Christmas 2006